PAST IMPERATIVE

My Life in India 1927-1947

PAST IMPERATIVE

My Life in India 1927-1947

EDWARD WAKEFIELD

GYAN

Published by

GYAN

Gyan Publishing House
5, Ansari Road
Daryaganj, New Delhi-110002
Phone: 011-47034999, 9811692060
E-mail: books@gyanbooks.com

Distribution Network
gyanbooks.com
India, USA, Canada, UK, Australia

ISBN: 978-93-7169-101-7 (PB)

2nd Impression 2025

Printed at: Gyan Press, Delhi.

PAST IMPERATIVE: MY LIFE IN INDIA 1927-1947
Author: EDWARD WAKEFIELD

PAST IMPERATIVE

My Life in India

PAST IMPERATIVE

My Life in India

1927–1947

by

Sir Edward Wakefield

1966

Contents

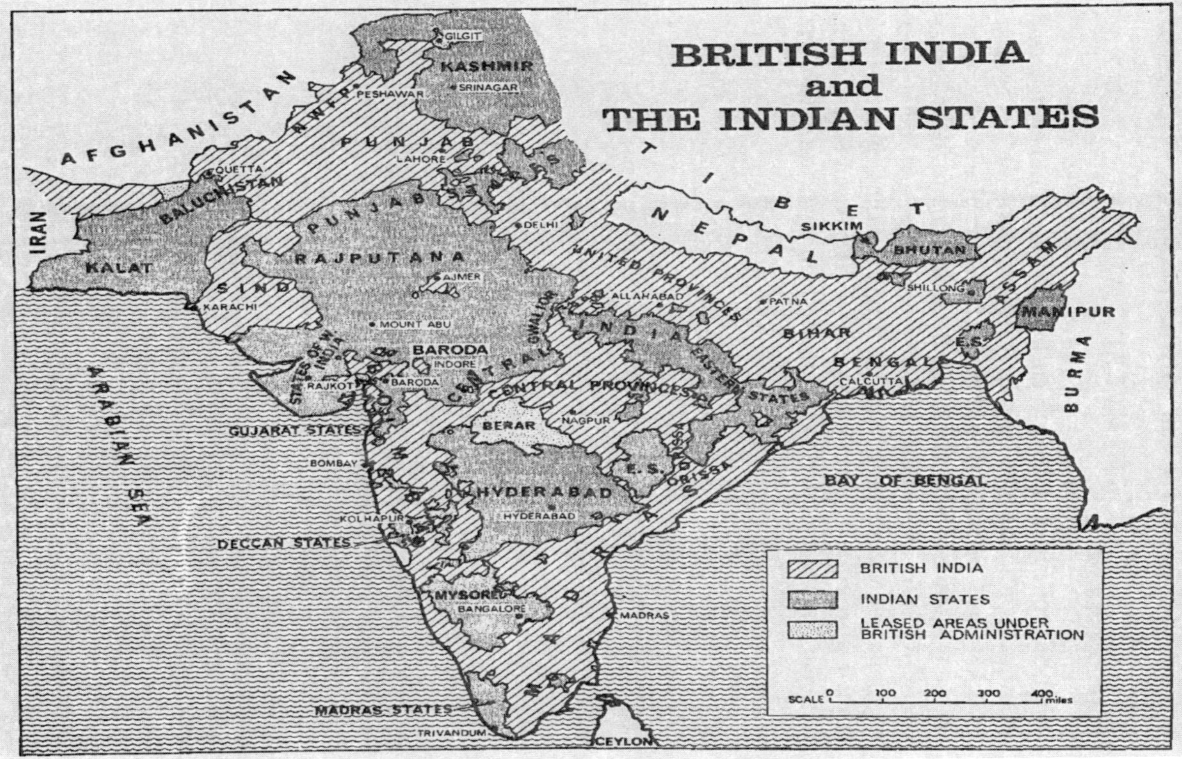

BRITISH INDIA
and
THE INDIAN STATES
AFGHANISTAN
IRAN
KALAT
BALUCHISTAN
QUETTA
N.W.F.P.
PESHAWAR
GILGIT
KASHMIR
SRINAGAR
PUNJAB
LAHORE
PUNJAB STATES
DELHI
SIND
KARACHI
RAJPUTANA
AJMER
MOUNT ABU
BARODA
INDORE
STATES OF W. INDIA
RAJKOT
GUJARAT STATES
BOMBAY
KOLHAPUR
DECCAN STATES
CENTRAL INDIA
GWALIOR
CENTRAL PROVINCES
NAGPUR
BERAR
HYDERABAD
MYSORE
BANGALORE
MADRAS
MADRAS STATES
TRIVANDUM
CEYLON
TIBET
NEPAL
SIKKIM
BHUTAN
SHILLONG
ASSAM
MANIPUR
BURMA
E.S.
UNITED PROVINCES
ALLAHABAD
PATNA
BIHAR
BENGAL
CALCUTTA
EASTERN STATES
ORISSA
BAY OF BENGAL
ARABIAN SEA
BRITISH INDIA
INDIAN STATES
LEASED AREAS UNDER BRITISH ADMINISTRATION
SCALE 0 100 200 300 400 miles

ACKNOWLEDGMENTS

In writing this book I have been helped by a number of friends whose generous assistance I gladly acknowledge.

Sir Conrad Corfield and Mr Achilles Papadopoulos have given me encouragement and wise advice. Sir Penderel Moon and Sir Terence Creagh-Coen suggested amendments to passages that might otherwise have been misleading. And the original manuscript was typed in their spare time by three busy people – by my son Hady, by my daughter Xanthe (she died in 1962) and by Hon. Mrs Ross de Moleyns.

Preface

INDIA, in the years of which I write (1927–47), comprised what are now the two separate Commonwealth countries of India and Pakistan.

Some three-fifths of India was sub-divided into Provinces and was administered by the British through the Government of India. The territory thus administered was known as British India. The other two-fifths of the sub-continent consisted of Native States, comprehensively termed 'The Indian States'. These were administered, not by the British or their agents the Government of India, but by their own hereditary rulers.

The distinction between British India and the Indian States had its origins in the distant past. The British went to India to trade. But traders need security, and security could only be obtained by negotiation or conquest. When negotiation was successful, the British entered into treaties or engagements with the native rulers guaranteeing to them and their successors the maintenance of their sovereign rights and powers. When fighting was necessary the British usually, though not invariably, took over the administration of the territory they had conquered.

In British India democratic forms of government were gradually established. In the Indian States the indigenous form of government – the rule of the hereditary chief or monarch – persisted. Thus the character of government in the Indian States was totally different from that which developed in British India.

The branch of the Government of India responsible for the conduct of the Crown's relations with foreign countries adjacent to India and with the rulers of the Indian States was called the Foreign and Political Department. In India the term 'Political' simply meant 'Diplomatic'. Macaulay, in his essay on Warren Hastings, written in 1841, explained the reason for this. He wrote:

> The English functionaries at Fort William [Calcutta] had as yet [i.e. in 1772] paid little or no attention to the internal government of Bengal. The only branch of Politics about which they much busied themselves was negotiation with the native Princes. The police, the administration of justice, the details of the collection of revenue, were almost entirely neglected. We may remark that the phraseology of the Company's servants still bears the trace of this state of things. To this day they always use the word 'political' as synonymous with 'diplomatic'.

Thus the Foreign and Political Department was essentially India's Diplomatic Service though, for historical reasons, it was additionally responsible for the administration of the North West Frontier Province and the Provinces of Baluchistan and Ajmer-Merwara. It had a cadre of some 120 officers personally selected by the Viceroy, 75 per cent from the Indian Army and 25 per cent from the Indian Civil Service.

Up to 1936 the Government of India conducted its relations with Durbars (the Governments of Indian States) through senior officials of the Foreign and Political Department known as Agents to the Governor-General. In 1936, however, changes in India's constitution led to these senior officials being termed Residents, and the Viceroy, though he remained Governor-General of British India, assumed a new designation for his relations with Durbars and was called the Crown Representative. At the same time the Foreign and Political Department was divided into two separate and distinct Departments, the External Affairs Department under the Governor-General and the Political Department under the Crown Representative. However, the cadre of the old Foreign and Political Department was not divided and became known as the Indian Political Service.

I have said that the Indian States were administered by their own hereditary rulers. That is true; but the rulers were required, by usage if not by treaty, to accept the advice of the British Government in matters which affected the interests of India as a whole.

This advice was tendered to them by the Viceroy, usually through the Residents; but the Viceroy was precluded from intervening in the internal affairs of a State unless misrule had become so gross as to be intolerable.

I hope that this prefatory explanation will help to clarify, for those who did not know India in the years of which I write, some of the terms used in the ensuing chapters which they might otherwise find puzzling.

CHAPTER 1

Arrival in India

ON November 11th, 1927, I set sail for India. Newly appointed to the celebrated Indian Civil Service I was bound for a district with a hybrid name situated somewhere in the middle of the Punjab. The letter containing the first official orders I ever received had been dated October 6th, 1927. It came from the office of the High Commissioner for India and was couched in characteristically cold and formal language. 'Sir,' the letter ran, 'I am directed to inform you that you have been posted to Lyallpur, Punjab, and to instruct you to proceed direct to that station.'

Why, I wondered, did the officials in the High Commissioner's office insist that I was to proceed 'direct' to Lyallpur? At the age of twenty-four, with my life before me and the whole world to choose from, I had decided to accept the challenge of India. They should have known, those officials in the High Commissioner's office, that my most ardent desire was to enter on my new life in India as soon as I possibly could. However, dismissing unimaginative officialdom from my mind, I set about making preparations for the journey.

The voyage out was uneventful. I shared a cabin with an I.C.S. colleague whom I had not met before as he had spent his probationary year at Oxford, I at Cambridge. He was dull, virtuous and kindly. In those distant days of high-spirited and self-centred youthfulness I thought it more blessed – and certainly more clever – to receive than to give; and shamelessly, encountering no protest from my amiable travelling companion, I spread my belongings over at least two-thirds of the cabin.

Travelling by the same ship and returning to India from his first home leave was a friendly young Indian Cavalry Officer named Rushton. To him the I.C.S. recruits, about a dozen in all, turned for enlightenment and guidance. He told us that the solar topees with which we had equipped ourselves were of the wrong pattern. 'Only station-masters and Anglo-Indians wear that kind of topee.' We did not want to signalise our entry on to the Indian stage by committing what we were given to understand would be a major social solecism, so we cast our topees overboard and watched them bobbing away in the ship's wake. And when we reached Port Said we all flocked to Simon Arzt and there bought topees of a socially acceptable pattern.

I said 'We cast our topees overboard.' That statement is not wholly true. I myself, though I was constrained to buy a new topee at Port Said, could not bear to throw away my earlier purchase as though it were so much junk. After all, it had cost me a guinea or more at a tropical outfitter's in Regent Street. . . . And so, not without a slight feeling of guilt, I covertly retained possession of the topee I was told I must not wear – and subsequently wore it, as I shall record, in a country where the Rushton standards were unknown.

The town of Lyallpur, in the centre of a district to which the development of a complex system of canal irrigation had brought great prosperity, was flourishing. The volume of litigation was proof of that. And the Club ('Europeans only') had some seventy or eighty members. I had read, of course, E. M. Forster's *Passage to India*. But it was only when I joined the Lyallpur Club that I realised how cruelly true to life was much of his characterisation. I hated the social life of the Club. But Mr Mitchell, my Deputy Commissioner, wisely made me go there sometimes in the evenings for the sake of my own good name, in order that I should not be accused of being stand-offish.

The English, as a race, are said to be exceptionally class conscious. But never, I am sure, has there existed in England such an elaborate structure of class distinction as British exiles erected for themselves in up-country clubs in India. Those born in Britain looked down on those who were 'country-bred'. The country-bred families scorned those of mixed blood; and those of mixed blood seemed to think that, by disparaging everything Indian, they were somehow purging themselves of an impurity. Service snobberies provided an additional complication. The I.C.S. stood unchallenged at the apex of the social pyramid. Next, I think, came two other all-India Services, the Indian Medical Service and the Indian Police. After that came a number of miscellaneous Services—Public Works Department, Education, Posts and Telegraphs, Railways, and a host of others. And there was always, of course, the Imperial Bank of India.

I must not forget the Imperial Bank of India. One of my first duties after arriving at Lyallpur had been to pay a round of social calls. I was given a list of some thirty or forty names and told to leave my visiting card in the little black tin box that I would find attached to a board at the entrance to each bungalow. Each box had painted on it in white letters (not very hospitably, I thought) the words 'Not at home'. Conscientiously, on a bicycle, I did the tedious round, gradually working through the list. Three weeks had passed, and I had still not ticked off every name on the list, when Mr Mitchell sent for me.

'Have you called on the Johnsons yet?'

'Who are they, sir?'

'The Bank Manager and his wife.'

'No, I don't think I have. Ah – I remember now – I couldn't find their house.'

'Well,' said Mr Mitchell, 'perhaps you'd leave a card this evening. The house is behind the Bank, you can't see it from the road.'

'Of course I will,' I replied, and looked at Mr Mitchell inquiringly. He hesitated a moment and then handed me a letter. 'Dear Mr Mitchell,' the letter ran. 'It was kind of Mrs Mitchell to ask me and my wife to dinner on Thursday. I understand, however, that the new Assistant Commissioner is staying at your house and will be having dinner with you. As he has not had the courtesy to call on us we would prefer not to meet him. In the circumstances we must decline the invitation.' The letter was signed, with an indignant flourish, 'David Johnson.'

I was glad that Indians were not eligible for membership of the Club. I was glad, for their sake, that they were spared the humiliation of feeling that they were regarded by the white (or near-white) clubmen of Lyallpur as being socially inferior. And I was glad, for the sake of my own race, that our failings were not exposed to the critical appraisal of outsiders. In our work, of course, we all had close and continuous contact with Indians of every class and caste and community. But social contacts were less common and had to be artificially contrived. Generally they took the form of garden parties, facetiously called 'Bridge Parties' because they were supposed to 'bridge' the gulf between the races. At such parties the bonhomie never seemed quite natural. On both sides there was, not coldness, certainly, but an element of restraint, of reserve. The better disposed Indians and the better disposed Europeans wanted to be, but were afraid to be, friends. The Indians were afraid that, if the barriers were down, they would be misunderstood and perhaps snubbed. The Europeans were afraid that they would be taken advantage of. In both cases the fears probably had some foundation in actual experience. It was unfortunate, too, that in Lyallpur few Indians would bring their wives to social gatherings. Either the wives were in purdah or, if not, had little acquaintance with Western manners and customs.

From time to time political issues would be discussed at the Club. Some degree of Indianisation of the Services was accepted as a regrettable but unavoidable necessity. The appointment to Lyallpur of an Indian Assistant Commissioner had caused a stir; but the prospect of an Indian Deputy Commissioner was discounted as too remote to cause anxiety. And it was assumed, with a confident certainty that was unquestioning and unquestioned, that the process of Indianising the Indian Medical Service would stop far short of the point at which the posting of an Indian Civil Surgeon to Lyallpur could be contemplated. It was unthinkable that European women should have to receive medical attention from an Indian doctor. Quite unthinkable.

I had been posted to Lyallpur to receive training in the multifarious duties that a District Officer in the Punjab was expected to perform. As a Magistrate, with strictly limited powers, I sat in court three days a week and tried innumerable petty cases. My clerk of court, or Munshi as he was called, was a stout, pale-faced, bespectacled, middle-caste Hindu named Pindi Das. He taught me, amongst other things, how to judge whether a witness was telling the truth or not. One of his tests, I remember, was to watch the witness's toes. If they were wiggling, their owner was telling lies! He would also explain to me how the police prepared their evidence in criminal cases. An honest Police Inspector would rig the evidence to incriminate the person whom he believed to be guilty. A dishonest Inspector would rig the evidence to incriminate an innocent party. There were, at Lyallpur, a number of professional witnesses; and Pindi Das would always warn me when one of these was giving evidence. How far Pindi Das himself was to be relied upon I do not know. But he was certainly most knowledgeable in matters of law and court procedure and had great ambitions for himself and his numerous relations. He would constantly express the hope that when I became Lat Sahib (H.E. the Governor) I would remember and reward his services.

The training of newly-arrived members of the I.C.S. was, at least in the Punjab, both comprehensive and thorough. We had to pass departmental examinations in Punjabi (we had already learnt Urdu), in Criminal and Civil Law, in Revenue and Treasury and Excise matters. In truth, we had to learn about every branch of the administration from the bottom upwards. For the most part we learned each job by doing it under the surveillance of an experienced practitioner. In some cases, however, we had to rely on our own common sense. I myself, for example, at an early stage of my training, was made Chairman of two Local Councils. I was fully prepared, in my capacity as Chairman, to listen to the views of my fellow Councillors on each item of the agenda and to advocate such action as seemed to me to have majority support. But I found, to my consternation, that nobody would express a view until I myself had given a lead. This deference annoyed and embarrassed me. I had come to India to serve, I reflected, but I was not permitted to serve. I was permitted only to lead.

There was an Agricultural College at Lyallpur and here I and a dozen other trainees underwent a three-week course of instruction. At the end of the course we had to submit to our lecturers our written-up notebooks. These were duly marked, and a report on our diligence and proficiency was sent to the Punjab Government. It so happened that the lectures on wheat cultivation vividly recalled to my mind the advice given to farmers by Virgil in his first Georgic. I amused myself by writing up my notes in flowing Virgilian hexameters. I sent in these notes at the end of the course and thought no more about the matter. But the lecturer concerned, a humourless Sikh, sensing that his dignity had been in some way affronted, reported my misdemeanour to the Punjab Government. Mr Boyd, the Chief Secretary, asked to be shown the notes, and they were sent to him. On the occasion of my next visit to Lahore I was told that Mr Boyd wished to see me. Ignorant of what had happened, I duly called on him in his office. He told me, reprovingly, that one of the lecturers at the Agricultural College had found my notes unsatisfactory. 'Oh dear,' I thought to myself, 'I am in for trouble now.' But he went on: 'I have myself studied your notes. I am sorry to say that they contain at least one false quantity. Nevertheless, they are in other respects admirable: and H.E. has agreed that they should be kept on record in the archives of the Punjab Government.'

From November to March the weather at Lyallpur was ideal. The air was invigorating, the days sunny and the nights cold. My leisure hours were happily occupied in playing polo or tennis, and breaks in the routine of court and office work were frequent. In March 1928, when the Simon Commission visited Lyallpur, I had the excitement of driving Sir John Simon in Mr Mitchell's Sunbeam car through crowds of hostile demonstrators. Khaddar-clad and wearing Gandhi caps, they thronged round us waving black flags and chanting, 'Simon, go back; Simon, go back.' Often Mr Mitchell would take me with him on his district tours. Travelling by car along the straight dusty service roads that lined the canal banks, we would generally spend the night at a canal Rest House. But sometimes, in areas where there were no canals, we would spend the night under canvas. The tents would all have been pitched, and the camp furniture arranged, long before we arrived. One always changed for dinner, of course. That was taken for granted. Does it now seem absurd that one should change for dinner when in camp? In India in 1927 it seemed, not absurd, but sensible, and cleanly, and no more out of the ordinary than brushing one's teeth or shaving.

New impressions, novel experiences, crowded in on me. A few weeks after my arrival a pleader who had once or twice argued cases in my court joined me as I left the court precincts and strolled with me for a quarter of a mile chatting pleasantly enough on topics unconnected with his work. I was told by Pindi Das (and Mr Mitchell confirmed this) that the friendliness of this particular pleader had a strictly professional motive. He was merely advertising to potential clients his value to them as a man who, being on friendly terms with the new Assistant Commissioner, would be able to influence him in court. On the other hand, when I was invited to dinner at their club by the local Lawyers' Society, I was encouraged by Mr Mitchell to accept the invitation. I enjoyed the evening. The Lyallpur men of law were like lawyers the world over. They had their own brand of joke, they were intelligent, and cynical, and hospitable, and they certainly played bridge very much better than I did.

Other early impressions can be described briefly: motherly Mrs Mitchell's uncontrollable fit of giggling when, at the end of a tea-party while we were on tour, the bulky, bearded Sikh guests, soldiers turned farmers, expressed their appreciation of the good food by belching, some of them eruptively, others discreetly, but all of them with the utmost determination to prove their good manners; the puzzlement of my bearer – he understood no English – when I despatched him to the bazaar to summon a Dai (midwife) when I meant a Nai (barber); my embarrassment when, invited to a partridge shoot by the Superintendent of Police (Scott, the scourge of cattle-lifters) I turned up in collar and tie and plus-fours when all the others were wearing open-necked khaki shirts and shorts; my wonder at the long hours spent daily in motionless contemplation by a young Indian colleague, a Brahmin. All the time I was eagerly, even greedily, recording impressions and storing them up for future use.

I enjoyed the winter months. But then came the dreaded hot weather. The sun ceased to be genial. First it became oppressive and finally it became tyrannous. Women and children left for hill stations. Courts and offices opened at six o'clock in the morning. In those days there was no electricity in Lyallpur. In the afternoon one lay on a matting bed, bathed in sweat, unable either to sleep or to study, while a punkah-wala intermittently tugged at a fan which scarcely stirred the sluggish heat-laden air. When darkness came there would be some relief from the intense heat. The shade temperature would gradually fall from 115 degrees to 95. And, for an hour or so before dawn, it would even fall below 90. But the problem of illumination at night admitted no solution. One could not sit indoors near a lamp because of the heat; and punkahs could not be used because they made the lamps flare up. Equally one could not sit out of doors anywhere near a lamp because the light attracted flying insects innumerable. One could only sit outside in the dark and talk and smoke and drink, and drink and smoke and talk, until sufficient heat had drained from the air to allow some hope of sleep.

Sometimes, in the weeks before the monsoon arrived, the atmosphere would become intolerably oppressive; and then, quite suddenly, a dust-storm would break. The sky would darken, even at midday, and savage whirlwinds of dust would swirl around, battering at one's body with gusty violence. It was on the occasion of such a dust-storm that I first met Pandit

Lahori Ram Sharma. I had been out riding, had not noticed signs of the impending storm, and found myself suddenly enveloped in darkness, face and hands stinging from the impact of flying dust and sand. When the fury of the storm had somewhat abated I heard a gentle voice saying, 'Can I help you, Sahib?' 'Yes, please,' I replied. 'I want to get back to the Deputy Commissioner Sahib's Kothi.' Lahori Ram took Chineh's bridle and led her and me, in the twilight of the storm, back to Mr Mitchell's bungalow.

Lahori Ram was a lanky, pale-faced, ill-nourished youth a year or two younger than myself. A schoolmaster by profession, he was not the sort of person one could reward with a tip. So I asked him to come to tea with me next day. He accepted the invitation and took his leave of me. But he did not appear the next day. He did, however, turn up a few days later 'to pay his respects', he said. I asked him why he had not come to tea on the day on which I had invited him. 'Oh,' he said, 'I had other things to do.' I thought this reply casual if not positively rude. But he had helped me when I had been in difficulties so I showed no annoyance. And I subsequently learned that, to his way of thinking, he had been sufficiently rewarded for his services to me by being *asked* to tea. To accept my invitation was only courteous: but to have actually arrived and sat down to tea with me would, as he saw it, have been unwarrantably presumptuous.

I visited the school where Lahori Ram taught and I was told about (but not permitted to meet) his wife and children. He often complained of his meagre pay and eventually he succeeded in persuading me to write to the Railway authorities and ask them to provide him with better-paid employment. To my surprise he was given a clerical post at Ferozpore; and thereafter, for nearly twenty years, he regarded me as his own special Patron and Protector from whom he could expect favours and assistance as of right.

As the weeks went by I found the heat of Lyallpur less and less endurable. Beginning as discomfort it developed finally into an obsessive torture dominating thought and talk and action.

Tossing and turning restlessly on my bed, soaked in sweat, I thought longingly of cool rain on mist-shawled fells of home. But there was no consolation in such imaginings.

O! who can hold a fire in his hand
By thinking on the frosty Caucasus?

Shakespeare, of course, was right. Imagined nostalgic contrasts rendered my present plight, not better, but worse.

O, no! the apprehension of the good
Gives but the greater feeling to the worse.

My growing misery attracted Mr Mitchell's sympathetic attention and, with typical kindness, he arranged for me to go to Simla, in the hills, for six weeks' training in Treasury work. My spirits at once revived; and later, as the train climbed steeply and slowly from Kalka to Solan, from Solan to Simla, and as the heat of the plains gradually receded, I rejoiced at my escape as from a prison-house; and I resolved that, with the aid of Providence, never again would I spend a hot weather in the Punjab plains.

In Simla I had been given a room at the United Service Club. And there I settled down to the enjoyment of comfort and good company. In less than a fortnight I had learned all that I needed to know about Treasury work. Thereafter my official duties did not occupy more than an hour of each day and, having nothing to do during the hours when my friends were at work in their offices, I began to feel bored. At the Club the room next to mine was occupied by a small wiry nervous man, with kind eyes and care-creased face. His name was Jenkyns and he was Commissioner of the Lahore Division of the Punjab. Every day, at about 6.30 p.m., he would return from his office accompanied by two peons laden with cloth bundles containing Government files. These files would be taken into his room and there, after dinner, he would labour away at them far into the early hours of the morning. One evening, sitting next to him at dinner, I commiserated with him over his ill-fortune in having so much work to do.

'I suppose I couldn't help you?' I said inquiringly. 'I really haven't any work of my own to do.'

'It's very kind of you,' he replied. 'Do you really mean it?'

'Yes, of course.'

'Well,' he said, 'I have a couple of cases with me now on which I have to pass orders. They are long and complicated. All I want is a précis, with a brief recommendation at the end. Do you think you could manage that for me? There's no hurry. You could deal with them whenever you can spare the time.'

I dealt with both cases next day. Mr Jenkyns was delighted and gave me more work to do. Within a fortnight he found that my help afforded him such relief from the pressure of overwork that he decided he must have a Personal Assistant. The post was created, and I was asked to fill it. I accepted with alacrity, collected my belongings from Lyallpur (a place I was never to see again) and, at the beginning of the cold weather, returned with Mr Jenkyns to Lahore.

CHAPTER 2

Growing Responsibilities

THE three months that I spent at Lahore passed happily and therefore quickly. I stayed at the Aitchison College as the guest of the Principal, Mr Kelly, and his wife. They were as kind to me as they were to the sons of the Punjab Princes and Chiefs who were in their educational charge. I played hockey and tennis with the boys, taught them Rugby football and took them out riding. In the evening we sometimes played chess. When I used to play chess as a schoolboy at Haileybury I would become most indignant if bystanders intervened in any way. But now, at the Chiefs' College, I learned that chess could be played in a different way. A group of interested boys would discuss audibly each situation as it arose, analyse the possibilities, and groan or applaud as the player made his move. Played in this way chess became less competitive but much more interesting.

Daily, from 10 a.m. to 5 p.m., I worked in the Commissioner's office. After a few weeks Mr Jenkyns, who had been suffering from nerve-strain, left for England and was replaced by Mr Kennaway, who had previously been officiating in the higher post of Financial Commissioner. This change of masters placed me, on one particular occasion, in a position of acute embarrassment. Mr Jenkyns had submitted to the Punjab Government a proposal for changing the method of appointing local Magistrates. The proposal had gone to the Financial Commissioner, Mr Kennaway, who, in rejecting it, had given his reasons for doing so at some length. Mr Jenkyns marked the file to me with the written query, 'What do you think?' I had no hesitation in expressing my view. 'The arguments advanced by the Financial Commissioner,' I wrote, 'are not only tedious and repetitive; they are also illogical and largely irrelevant.' And my note continued in this strain for several pages.

A week or so after Mr Kennaway had taken over charge I arrived at the office at 10 a.m. as usual. 'Good morning,' I greeted him. Mr Kennaway looked at me in silence. Then he handed me a slip of paper. I took it and looked at it. 'Is there any reason,' I read, 'why you should not be reported to the Government for gross insolence and insubordination?' I was staggered. I was not conscious of having been insolent or insubordinate to Mr Kennaway or, indeed, to anyone. Mr Kennaway must have seen that I was puzzled. He beckoned me over to his desk and pointed to the note that I had written and that he found so offensive. Short in stature, red-faced and fiery-tempered, Mr Kennaway, when angry, was always a frightening spectacle. But now, when his anger was directed against me, he seemed quite terrifying. He was seething with rage, bubbling with it, and nothing that I could say, no attempt at justification or excuse or apology, seemed to have the slightest effect on him. Eventually he said that, in my interest, though I did not deserve such consideration, he was going to disobey official rules and destroy Government property. Taking a match he lit, first one page of the record, then another, until the whole was in ashes. For the rest of that day, though we worked in the same room, he would not address a word to me. And I was far too awed to speak to him. The next day, however, it seemed that the 'gross insolence and insubordination' had been forgotten. Then and thereafter he was in every way as kind and friendly to me as he had been before the unhappy incident occurred.

The routine of office work was interrupted when the Simon Commission visited Lahore. My services (for what they were worth) were placed at the disposal of the Deputy Commissioner, who shared with the police the responsibility for ensuring that demonstrations against the Simon Commission did not get out of hand. For several days before the Commission arrived I attended conferences of military and police officers at which were discussed plans for controlling the expected hostile crowds. And I made anxious study of what the law required when an assembly was declared unlawful and became liable to dispersal by force.

The members of the Simon Commission were to travel to Lahore by train. On the night before their arrival a substantial sand-bag and barbed-wire barricade, some 4 feet in height, was erected along the City side of the route by which they would travel by car from the Railway Station to Government House. As the time for the arrival of the train drew near, procession after procession of khaddar-clad demonstrators flowed into Station Square, the wide, open space on the City side of the barricade. There were tens of thousands of them and, as at Lyallpur, they were waving black flags and crying 'Simon go back, Simon go back.' They were in a state of high excitement, their feelings having been worked up by a number of Congress Party leaders, chief of whom was Lajpat Rai, popularly known as 'the lion of the Punjab'. Police lined the road alongside the sand-bag barrier. Troops were held in reserve, out of sight. I noticed with interest the behaviour of the two senior police officers present. Both were Europeans, both had been decorated for gallantry. One of them appeared as calm and unconcerned as if he were engaged on a routine exercise. The other was taut with nervous tension and never still for a moment.

As the crowd grew in number, and as the demonstrators at the back tried to force their way forward, so the pressure on the barricade increased and those in front found themselves crushed against it. Lajpat Rai, who had earlier been inciting the crowd to ever greater extremes of enthusiasm, now tried to calm them down. Clad in a white dhoti, wearing a Gandhi cap and carrying a black umbrella, he turned his back on the barricade and, facing the crowd, sought to restrain their forward surge. His words and gestures were of no avail. The forward pressure continued and lifted him off his feet on to the top of the barricade. A police constable, who had been looking in a different direction, turned round, saw a man apparently scaling the barricade, and brought down his 'lathi' smartly on his head and shoulders. Lajpat Rai fell back, injured, and was taken away by his friends. A fortnight later, possibly as an indirect consequence of the injury, he contracted pneumonia and died.

I had witnessed the whole of this incident from a distance of only a few yards and dreaded the prospect of giving evidence at a public inquiry. The Congress Party demanded that a Judicial Commission of Inquiry be set up but the Punjab Government would only concede a Departmental Inquiry. Suspicious of Departmental proceedings the Congress Party refused to co-operate. They would neither put forward witnesses of their own nor cross-examine witnesses called by the Government. To my great relief I was only required to make a brief formal statement.

Towards the end of December 1928 I received the exciting news that I had been appointed Subdivisional Officer, Palwal, and was to take over charge of my new duties after the Christmas holidays. Travelling to Delhi with my two horses, Golden Glory and Chineh, I spent a happy Christmas at the Chief Commissioner's House as the guest of Sir John and Lady Thompson whose son I had known at Cambridge and whose daughter I was destined to marry the following year. I was elated at being given, for the first time, an independent charge. Palwal was a subdivision of the Gurgaon District. Situated thirty miles south of Delhi, with a quarter of a million inhabitants, it had been the centre of Mr Brayne's experiments in Rural Uplift. These experiments, not all of which had proved successful, had cost a good deal of public money, and one of my duties was to restore to solvency the various local bodies whose financial resources had been overstrained. I was, additionally, called upon to organise relief for a fodder famine which had devastated the southern districts of the Punjab. On all sides cattle were dying from starvation—it was a piteous sight—and I spent anxious days and nights procuring consignments of fodder from the United Provinces and arranging for its distribution in the areas worst affected.

These tasks I carried out with a reasonable degree of efficiency. In the performance of another duty, however, I was less proficient. I had inherited from my predecessor a Court case in which some sixty people were charged with rioting. The rioters belonged to two separate and opposed factions, each headed by a wealthy landowner. These landowners employed the ablest advocates in Delhi to protect the interests of their respective adherents. Day after day I found my small Court crowded with the accused while the advocates argued interminably, far above my head, subtle points of interpretation of the Criminal Procedure Code. The case could not proceed against all the accused jointly when any one of them was absent. Was I to adjourn the case on every occasion when any of the accused were absent? I tried this course for a time but was able to make no progress as two or three of the accused were invariably absent and, when they did turn up at a later sitting, came armed with medical certificates (which cost little) and thus escaped forfeiture of their bail. So I tried to make progress with the trial of those accused who were present at any sitting while, at the same time, starting separate proceedings against those who were absent. But the number of separate cases grew alarmingly; and this meant that the police witnesses had to attend Court to give the same evidence, subject to cross-examination and re-examination, over and over again, in each separate case. The flies, the heat, the smell in the overcrowded Court, tried my patience beyond endurance. And the Delhi advocates, as they were fully entitled to do in the interests of their clients, took advantage of my inexperience as a magistrate to frustrate all my efforts to make progress with the trial. By the end of February the case was in a hopeless tangle.

Shortly after I had arrived at Palwal the Deputy Commissioner of the Gurgaon District, Mr Stuart Thomson, asked me to visit him. He told me that in January of the previous year, on the occasion of a Mohammedan festival, there had been serious riots in Palwal. The Muslims had resolved to slaughter a cow and the Hindus had been determined that the cow should not be slaughtered. In the struggle for possession of the beast a number of people had been killed and a great many more injured. The cow had been an exhibit in the court proceedings that ensued and now, just when the time for the festival was coming round again, the High Court had delivered judgment and ordered the release of the animal to its former owners. It was not always a good thing, observed Mr Thomson drily, that the Judiciary should be so independent of the Executive. The release of the cow at this particular moment was bound, he said, to lead to further outbreaks of communal trouble and it was for this reason that he had asked for a European to be sent to Palwal.

Mr Thomson made it quite clear that responsibility for ensuring the maintenance of peace in Palwal during the next critical three weeks rested with me and with me alone. That was in accordance with the I.C.S. tradition – to give a man a job and trust him to carry it out. At the same time he told me that, if I wanted advice or help of any kind, he was available to give it. I said that I certainly wanted advice.

'You know Palwal very much better than I do, Sir. Where is trouble most likely to occur, who are the mischief-makers, and who are the people capable of exercising a restraining influence?'

Mr Thomson took a large-scale map of the Palwal Sub-division, marked on it the places where communal feelings had been inflamed, told me who were the ring-leaders of each communal faction and who were potential peace-makers; and advised me to forestall trouble by making certain arrangements and dispositions. Troops would be available in case of emergency but I was not to call on these except through him.

I took action as Mr Thomson had advised. I arranged that the cow which had been the cause of all the trouble the previous year should, when released from judicial custody, be retained in police custody (illegally) until after the festival was over. I set up in each potential danger-area, under the chairmanship of a local official, joint Hindu-Muslim Conciliation Committees, the function of these Committees being to settle local communal differences, including disputes about procession routes. I arranged that the police, acting under a general power conferred by the Criminal Procedure Code, should take known mischief-mongers into custody on the day before the festival. And I disposed the magistracy and police under my control in such a manner that, if trouble occurred at any of the places where it was expected, they would be at hand to restore order.

The day of the festival arrived. As it was a Muslim holiday the courts were closed for the day and I had nothing to do but sit at home and wait on events. I thought of the police officers whom I had observed outside the Railway Station at Lahore when the Simon Commission were due to arrive. Alas! I found myself not, as I would have wished, calm and relaxed, but restive, nervy, apprehensive. How much more trying to the nervous system is inaction than action! By midday no news of any kind had come in. I was tempted (so compelling was the urge to do something, anything) to walk down to the Palwal bazaar and see how things were going there. But no, I reflected, I must be at my bungalow to receive any messages that came in and give any orders required.

At about 12.30 a telegram arrived. It was from Hindu shopkeepers, at a place where trouble had not been expected, asking for help as they were being attacked by 'Muslim fanatics'. I studied the map and saw that police would have to be despatched from Ballabgarh. I took up the telephone to give the necessary orders but the line I wanted was engaged. At this point another telegram arrived. It was from Ballabgarh, from a Maulvi, to say that the Muslims there were being set upon by a disorderly Hindu mob. The police at Ballabgarh were not strong enough in numbers – even I realised this – to be divided. What was I to do? Again I studied the map. But then, to add to my confusion of mind, other telegrams began to arrive, all of them telling of attacks, actual or expected, by one community on the other. I gave up trying to think. Telling my servants that I was not to be disturbed, I shut myself up in my bedroom and, for ten minutes or quarter of an hour, lay down and read an Edgar Wallace 'thriller'.

My moment of weakness and indecision soon passed. With mental control restored I re-read the telegrams and decided that it would be unwise to alter my carefully planned disposition of police and magistracy on the strength of uncorroborated information from dubious sources. Late in the afternoon reports began to come in by telephone from my officials to say that so far, though communal tension was still acute, there had been no outbreaks of violence. And the following morning I was able to report to Mr Thomson that the day had passed off peacefully.

For a long time I kept copies of all those telegrams that had led to such confusion of mind on my part, and even to temporary panic. In peaceful retrospect it is easy enough to envisage the circumstances in which frightened people, in the hope of obtaining police protection, send alarmist reports to their District Officer. But it is not easy for the recipient of such reports, with the burden of responsibility which he bears, to judge whether they are true or not; and to ignore a report that happened to be true could have serious consequences. I was interested to learn at a later date that Mr Thomson had received many telegrams similar to those which had been sent to me. He, with his greater experience, had not been alarmed. At the top of each he had scribbled the one word 'File'.

At this time my Lyallpur protegé, Lahori Ram, was writing to me almost daily asking that I should use my influence with the Railway Administration to obtain for him a better paid post. When I declined to do this he reproached me for ignoring the obligations of friendship. Neither then, nor at any time, was he able to appreciate the reasons for my diffidence in soliciting favours for him. He certainly could not understand my view that it was up to him, having secured an appointment on the Railway through my good offices, to earn his own promotion. I, for my part, failed to appreciate the view commonly held in India that those who occupy positions of authority are under a moral obligation to help, and to go on helping, their relatives and friends. The two points of view still seem to me to be irreconcilable.

In the latter half of February I was spending a weekend in Delhi when I received the following telegram:

SUBCOMMR PALWAL C/O CHIEF COMMISSIONER DELHI PRIORITY YOU ARE PLACED ON SPECIAL DUTY SERCY FORESTY COMMITTEE FOR TWO MONTHS HAND OVER CHARGE TO PARTABSINGH PROCEED DEHRA DUN IMMEDIATELY REPORT TO SIR CHUNILAL MEHTA CHAIRMAN BEFORE DEPARTURE TELEGRAPH TO EXPANDS NEW DELHI WHEN YOU WILL JOIN DEHRA DUN YOU WILL RECEIVE ALLOWANCE Rs 300 PLUS HALTING AND TRAVELLING ALLOWANCE AND TIME SCALE PAY – PUNJAB

Fortunately for me Sir John Thompson was at hand to elucidate the meaning of this puzzling communication. It appeared that the Government of India had recently appointed a Committee, under the chairmanship of Sir Chunilal Mehta, a Minister of the Bombay Government, to inquire into the activities of the Forest Research Institute at Dehra Dun in the United Provinces and to make recommendations for its future. And here was I suddenly appointed the Committee's Secretary!

I arrived at Dehra Dun, 120 miles to the north-east of Delhi, within twenty-four hours of receiving the telegram. Sir Chunilal Mehta seemed dubious about my qualifications to act as Secretary of his Committee. Nevertheless, he gave me a friendly welcome and, handing me a dozen or more bulky volumes on such topics as Silviculture, Forest Products, Wood Technology, Timber Seasoning and the like, he suggested that study of these would be of help to me in the performance of my new duties. I was also introduced to the other two members of the Committee, Professor Lindemann (later Lord Cherwell) and Mr Wroughton, Manager of the Bombay Burma Trading Corporation.

Initially the members of the Committee slept and ate in the Circuit House. But after a couple of days there Professor Lindemann moved over to the residence of the President of the Institute, Mr Rodger. I have no doubt that Professor Lindemann's change of residence was motivated solely by considerations of personal comfort. In such matters he exhibited an almost feline fastidiousness. But Sir Chunilal Mehta confided to me his apprehensions that the Professor would be unduly influenced by Mr Rodger's supposed conservatism. I myself slept in a tent in the grounds of the Circuit House. I say 'slept', but sleep often evaded me for long hours. The grounds of the Circuit House had been appropriated as their courting ground by several pairs of nightjars. Far into the night I would be kept awake by the breeding call of these birds. Sometimes the call seemed like the sound of a stone skimming over ice; sometimes it sounded as if a telegraph wire had been struck by a stick; but always it went on and on and on. . . .

The Committee spent a fortnight at Dehra Dun recording evidence and discussing various problems with the staff of the Institute. Returning to Delhi, they worked out the main headings for their report but failed to agree on their recommendations. Sir Chunilal Mehta, a politician, was anxious to ensure that more of the top posts at the Institute were held by Indians. Professor Lindemann, a scientist, was insistent that in no circumstances must the high standard of the work done at the Institute be placed in jeopardy. Mr Wroughton, a business man, was concerned to make better provision for industry to be kept in touch with the results of research work done at the Institute. After a day or two of rather aimless discussion, Professor Lindemenn decided that he would like to see the sights of Northern India, Sir Chunilal Mehta said that he had to return to Bombay for a Council meeting, and Mr Wroughton found that he had business arrears to attend to. I was instructed to have a draft report ready in ten days' time. I was aghast. What was I to say in the report? The Committee's discussions had seemed so inconclusive. They had seemed to agree on almost nothing. But Professor Lindemann, sensing my distress (clever and cat-like, he was also kind), took me aside. 'I warned you,' he said, 'that you would have to write the report. But don't worry. It won't be as difficult as you imagine. Say what *you* think should be done and don't bother about us. In particular, avoid saying anything about the matters on which we disagree. Don't say anything, for instance, about the pace of Indianisation of the Forestry Service.'

I set about writing the report and managed to complete a draft of some 20,000 words within the ten days allotted. For two days the Committee discussed the draft and incorporated a number of amendments. On the third day, March 30th, 1929, they all signed the report and left me with instructions to add a chapter giving a brief history of the Forest Research Institute. I was also to see the report through the press.

The five weeks that followed were blissfully idle. They were also happy as I had just become engaged to be married. Early in May, however, I was back at my post in Palwal. One of my former worries had disappeared. The riot case which I had dealt with so ineptly had been transferred to the court of a magistrate specially deputed to try it. But there was plenty of other work on hand. I had to investigate the misappropriation of public funds by the clerk of the local municipal committee: one of my police officers, a trusted Sub-Inspector, had committed a murder while I was away at Dehra Dun: plague and cholera were both raging within a few miles of Palwal; and on my Court file (as I recorded in a letter I wrote home on May 14th) there were pending 45 criminal and 108 revenue cases. Yes, there was plenty to do. But I did not do it. Within a week of my return to Palwal I had been summoned to Simla to assume responsibilities of a very different character.

CHAPTER 3

*A Journey to Western Tibet**

WESTERN Tibet, though cut off from India by the formidable mountain barrier of the Himalayas, was nevertheless visited every summer by Indian traders who bartered grain and cloth for wool and borax. Under the Anglo-Tibetan Trade Regulations of 1914 a British Trade Agency had been established at Gartok, the capital of Western Tibet, to protect the interests of these Indian traders. Unfortunately the two Garpons, joint Governors-General of Western Tibet, had for some years refused the British Trade Agent facilities to carry out his duties. Representations to the Tibetan Government at Lhasa had proved ineffective and the Government of India had decided to send a British officer to Gartok to negotiate direct with the Garpons, to survey the whole field of Indo-Tibetan trade relations and to make recommendations for the future of the Trade Agency.

The Punjab Government, who had been asked to depute one of their officers to carry out this exacting assignment, initially selected an I.C.S. colleague of mine, Maurice Ormerod. He had gone to Simla and had begun to assemble stores and equipment for the expedition but, to his bitter disappointment, the doctors found that his heart would not stand the strain to which it would be subjected at altitudes of 18,000 feet or more. I had been selected to replace him and, on arrival at Simla, I set about completing the preparations which he had begun.

My chief difficulty at this stage was to estimate the quantities of food required over a period of four or five months for myself, my servants and the eleven Gurkhas (Havaldar and ten Riflemen) who were to accompany me as escort. Dr Kanshi Ram, the doctor attached to the British Trade Agency, had already set off for Gartok with the Agency staff and I was

*See the map of Western Tibet between pages 36 and 37.

deprived of the advice and guidance that he could have given me. I could not expect to find in Western Tibet any food other than milk, tea and, with luck, a little barley. I calculated that the weight of stores I would have to carry exceeded by a considerable margin the capacity of the transport that would be available to me – mules for the first fifteen stages, coolies for the next few stages and thereafter such yaks as could be secured from scattered Tibetan settlements. So I cut down the number of my staff and, in particular, reduced the strength of the Gurkha escort.

I left Simla on foot on June 4th, 1929, accompanied by a bearer and a cook, a Gurkha escort of one Havaldar and four Riflemen, and a baggage train of eighteen mules. For the first fifteen marches, about 190 miles, I followed the mule track, known as the Hindustan-Tibet road, which, starting at Simla, runs along the Sutlej valley in an easterly direction as far as Pooh, near the Tibetan border. The mules presented an attractive picture as they wound along the twisting track with bells jangling, with three Gurkhas in front to set the pace and two behind to maintain it. To the villagers along the Hindustan-Tibet road mules were a familiar sight but Gurkhas a rare one. The Gurkhas therefore attracted more attention than the mules. Indeed, with scout hats cocked to one side, wearing grey-blue shirts and khaki shorts, with kukris in their belts and with rifles slung across their shoulders, they looked both picturesque and workmanlike.

At Sarahan, seven days' march from Simla, I found Dr Kanshi Ram waiting for me with the Agency staff and their baggage train, also of eighteen mules. Here I discovered that the newly-appointed Agency interpreter had no knowledge of the Lhasa dialect of the Tibetan language, which was the one generally employed in dealing with officials throughout Western Tibet. I therefore replaced him with a local trader, Raghu Das by name, who was recommended to me by the Rajah of Bushahr, the ruler of the Indian State through which we were passing.

Raghu Das knew no English but both of us could speak

and understand Hindustani and he could speak fluently the dialects both of Lhasa and of Western Tibet. When it came to writing Tibetan, Raghu Das was not so fluent. With a look of intense concentration on his face, with his head on one side and his tongue continually circling the inside of his mouth, he would carefully draw each character of each word he was writing. It would take him a whole morning to write even a short letter. When the letter had been completed, however, it would be a masterpiece of calligraphy.

At Sarahan I had the pleasure of meeting my cousins-by-marriage, the hereditary Wazir of Bushahr and his family. John Howard Wakefield, younger brother of one of the founders of the British Commonwealth, Edward Gibbon Wakefield, had joined the Bengal Army in 1825. In 1831 he was stationed at Kotgarh, midway between Simla and Sarahan. Like his brothers Edward and William he had an eye for feminine beauty, and his attention was attracted by the singular loveliness of a girl of high birth, a Rajput, who lived in the neighbouring township of Rampur. Disguising himself as a camel-driver, so the family legend runs, he would gaze at her over the wall of the compound surrounding her home. Eventually he made her acquaintance, courted her, and won her; and, after she had been converted to Christianity, he carried her off to Bareilly and there married her.

I was interested to learn from the hereditary Wazir of Bushahr that the memory of this unusual marriage was still preserved in his family; and I was able to tell him how the marriage had prospered and how this lovely girl from the hills had become the mother of a son and three beautiful daughters, one of whom had married Mr Justice Tyrrell, father of Lord Tyrrell of Avon, and another a member of the Prussian aristocracy, Prince Hugues de Radolin.

As we came nearer to Pooh we began to overtake flocks of sheep and goats loaded with small bags of grain. To the south, across the Sutlej river, we had superb views of the Bushahri Kailas mountain. Studying it through field-glasses I came to the conclusion that it could be climbed, but it was so sacred that no porters – certainly not local ones – would have given their assistance. It was the seat of a powerful Devta (god) and I was told that, as a sign that the god lived there and had a garden, apples occasionally fell down into the valley below.

At Pooh I encountered the last remote traces of British influence and the first real signs of Tibetan culture and customs.

Deva Ram, the leading local official, paid me several friendly calls. He showed me a rifle, made by Richardson of London, for which he asked me to obtain cartridges. I could not make out what the bore was and asked him to show me his licence. Later he brought, not a licence – he had never had one – but a letter from the Englishman who had presented the rifle to his great-grandfather. The letter was dated 1849, was written by a Lieutenant Strachey, stationed in Ladakh, of the 'Tibet Border Force', and stated how much the writer owed to the loyalty of this Bushahri.

In appearance and habits the villagers of Pooh were Tibetan rather than Indian. Round their necks they wore small metal cylinders containing the mystic invocation 'Om mani padmi hum' ('Oh God, the jewel in the heart of the lotus') written out many hundreds of times. Every time the cylinder was revolved a prayer was offered up to Heaven – or, rather, multiple prayers were offered up as each separate 'Om mani' was believed to have its individual potency. At Pooh, as at other villages in the neighbourhood, I saw prayer wheels ingeniously devised and artfully located. The invocation had been written out countless times on rolls of paper which were then placed in a wooden drum, the size of a five-gallon cask. To the bottom of the drum was attached a wooden propeller with four blades; and the drum was then set above the channel of a stream. The action of the water on the propeller blades made the drum revolve continuously. And so, as the water in some of these mountain streams never fails, the villagers who had contrived and erected this machinery were being prayed for at every moment of their lives.

I halted three days at Pooh in order to examine the Agency files and equipment, to convert heavy mule-loads into lighter coolie-loads, and to make plans for the immediate future. The tent supplied for my use was entirely unsuitable, being too large and too heavy to be carried without great difficulty over the rough tracks and high passes which lay before us. I finally decided to take a shouldari (small, single-fly tent), and this, though it was more than once carried bodily away by the wind and offered small protection against the cold, served my purpose well enough until I found a bigger and better tent in storage at Gartok. The tents to be used by the Gurkhas and orderlies were less inadequate.

The track from Pooh to Gartok, sixteen marches away, ran due east over the Shipki Pass. But several Bushahri traders had begged me to visit Rudok, to the north of the Indus, to secure the removal of the excessive dues which, I was led to believe (wrongly, as it turned out), were being levied from traders by the Jongpon (Governor) there; and I had also been asked to represent to the Governors both of Chumurti and of Rudok the urgent necessity of suppressing the gangs of dacoits (robbers) which were said to infest various localities within their jurisdiction. So I decided that, instead of travelling eastward to Gartok by the direct route, I would make my way in a north-easterly direction to Chagrachan in Chumurti and thence travel northwards, across the Indus, to Rudok. From Rudok I planned to retrace my steps southwards to the Indus and then follow the line of that river and its tributary, the Gartang, until I reached Gartok.

The journey I proposed for myself would take at least a month and probably longer. It was obviously impossible to undertake this expedition with the whole of the Agency staff and baggage as the few villages en route would be unable to supply the required transport. It was equally impracticable to send on the main part of the baggage direct to Gartok without a responsible officer in charge; and I accordingly decided that Dr Kanshi Ram should take the major part of the staff and baggage to Gartok by the normal Shipki route whilst I set out with as few encumbrances as possible on the longer and more strenuous journey to Rudok.

I left Pooh on June 24th with my Gurkha escort, a cook, a bearer, the interpreter and one orderly. Thirty coolies were also engaged to carry our baggage.

From the Sutlej valley we could see, several thousand feet above us, two tiny spots of green, one above the other, high up on a bare, brown, boulder-strewn hill-side. When we had toiled up to the lower of these green patches we found it to consist of fields of beardless barley, hedges of rambler roses in full bloom and a few clumps of birch trees. In the surrounding expanse of barren, stony hill-side there was no trace of water; but a spring at the top of this oasis was the source of several crystal-clear streamlets which spread out from it to make this little Eden.

A few hundred feet higher was the other oasis, fed by a second spring. There was a monastery here, built in ancient times by an ageing Rajah of Bushahr in gratitude for the birth of a son and heir. He attributed his good fortune, not to hormones, but to the prayers of the Tashi Lama in distant Lhasa whose aid he had invoked in his despair; and the monastery, founded and endowed to commemorate the happy event, was given the appropriate name of Tashi-gong.

The village and the whole of the hill-side were monastery property. It was holy ground. No bird or animal might be killed there, no wrongdoer arrested, and no disturbance must break the holy peace. The monastery itself, tenanted by a single Lama and an attendant, was dirty and evil-smelling though it contained valuable articles of copper and brass and silver. In its structure the monastery was like the houses of the village. It was built into the hill-side, of stone, with timber supports and a flat roof to act as a threshing floor. It was enveloped by an atmosphere of indescribable tranquillity. Birds were tame. Two pigeons were courting within ten yards of me by the side of a stream and took no notice of my cumbersome attempts to photograph them. A rose finch sat on a spray of briar within a few feet of me. A stonechat clinked at my side; and a pair of meadow buntings drank from the stream only a yard or two below me. The only disturbing element in the whole scene was a lammergeyer which flapped its way over the hill-side, hunting.

From this point we followed, at a high altitude, the line of the Spiti river as far as its junction with the Para river. Then, following the Para river, we crossed from Bushahr into the Tibetan Province of Chumurti on the morning of June 30th. On the way I had been compelled to dismiss my bearer who, not being a teetotaller, had begun to adopt undesirable methods, which might have proved infectious, of fortifying himself against the cold. We also had to halt for a day to give one of the Gurkhas time to recover from what I took to be an attack of mountain sickness. He had a temperature of 102·5 degrees and I gave him quinine and aspirin. After I had treated him the local medicine-man was called in (I did not know this at the time) and bled him.

I took advantage of the day's halt to go after game. I failed to get a shot at any Ram Chukor (Himalyan Snow Cock) though I saw and heard them. They have a haunting call which begins like the crowing of a pheasant and ends like the cry of a curlew. I did, however, succeed in shooting a burrhel (Blue Wild Sheep), a six-year-old beast which provided an excellent meal for our party.

It was in the course of this little shooting trip that I noticed my interpreter Raghu Das and the local shikari preparing their morning smoke. They selected a level piece of ground about 9 inches by 9 inches. Over this they spread a layer of earth about 3 inches thick which was well patted down so that it became fairly compact. Into one side of this little platform of packed mud was inserted horizontally a stick about 6 inches in length, the size of a rather thick pipe stem. The stick was then withdrawn and they blew down the tunnel it had made in order to remove any loose particles of earth. Two balls of tobacco, each the size of an acorn, were then set alight on a fire of twigs nearby. When they were well alight they were inserted into the tunnel in the earth, the hole at the end of the tunnel was stopped up and another hole made in the upper surface of the layer of earth. Raghu Das and the shikari then leant down, one after the other, put a half-clenched fist over the hole and through this drew the smoke into their mouths. It seemed to me an uncomfortable proceeding, but at least it showed how greatly tobacco was appreciated.

On July 2nd we reached Samlakar, the camping ground to the west of the Bodpo Pass. Here I learned from a party of Tibetans who had crossed the pass on the previous day that the Governor of Chumurti was away on pilgrimage and there was no chance of my meeting him at Chagrachan, the capital of his district, as I had intended. Chagrachan lay on the route to Tashigong on the Indus. But a shorter route to Rudok would be via Demchok, also on the Indus. I decided therefore that, after crossing the Bodpo Pass, instead of travelling eastwards to Chagrachan as I had previously planned, I would make my way northwards, over the Himi Pass, towards Demchok.

The cold at Samlakar was severe and a biting wind blew up the valley. No fuel was available, and yak dung, with which we were to have a long and unpleasant acquaintance, had to be used for cooking the food.

The Gurkha who had so quickly recovered from an attack of mountain sickness a few days earlier was now suffering again from the same ailment as well as from the cold. But it was impossible to stay for more than a night at a place as cold and inhospitable as Samlakar and I determined, if the Gurkha were no worse the following morning, to push on over the Bodpo Pass and give him a chance of rest and recovery in a more sheltered spot.

We set off from Samlakar on the morning of July 3rd. The sick Gurkha had enjoyed a good night's rest and, wrapping him up as warmly as we could, we set him astride a large and quiet yak. The height of the Bodpo Pass is shown on maps as

19,412 feet. The approach to the summit from the west was by quite gentle slopes. There was no difficulty with rock and, at the time of year when we made the crossing, there was little snow on the western slopes. The height, however, proved very distressing to a party not yet acclimatised to such altitudes. The cook, a Ladakhi hill-man, went ahead with the Tibetans driving our loaded yaks; but, in spite of the assistance he received from holding on to a yak's tail, he collapsed twice on the way. In the second group came Raghu Das, the Havaldar and myself. Both Raghu Das and the Havaldar suffered severely from cold and exhaustion but, by taking turns to ride on the one pony with the party, they managed to reach the summit successfully.

When Raghu Das, the Havaldar and I arrived at the summit we were some way ahead of the other Gurkhas and the orderly. Though the cold was almost unbearable I thought it would be wise for us to wait for the others as they might need help. We had to wait for about an hour before they arrived. The sick Gurkha had lost consciousness, and our efforts to revive him proved fruitless. The other three Gurkhas were also in a state of utter exhaustion and one of them actually collapsed while I was speaking to him. Only the orderly was capable of giving any help.

A Mr Calvert who crossed the Bodpo Pass in 1906 described the descent to the east as being 'very difficult and quite impassable for any laden animals whatever'. Beyond the summit the track descended steeply over deep snow and ice penetrated here and there by jagged rocks. Then, after following a rock ridge for half a mile at an easier gradient, it again descended steeply and debouched on to a rough boulder-strewn slope beside a frozen lake.

The orderly and I carried the unconscious Gurkha down the most difficult portion of the descent while his yak, relieved of its burden, slid or stumbled down behind us. When the going was easier again we tied the Gurkha on to the yak, but it was difficult to make him secure and, in the end, I put up the orderly also on the yak and made him support the Gurkha from behind.

The rest of the party made their way along as best they could. It was dusk before we had all reached the night's camping ground on an exposed and fuel-less hill-side, being greeted on our arrival by a furious storm of rain and hail. I gave everybody some rum, to keep out the cold; and the cook, brave fellow, who had suffered more than most of us, managed to prepare a hot meal for me. For fuel he had only tent pegs and sodden yak's dung!

The sick Gurkha was still unconscious the following morning; but as he needed warmth even more than rest I decided to move on a few miles and camp in a sheltered valley beyond the Himi Pass. Here, four days later, to our great sorrow, he died without having regained consciousness.

Meanwhile, the other Gurkhas had lost their usual cheerfulness and appeared to be nervous and depressed. I spoke to the Havaldar and discovered that partly they were frightened of the altitude (they knew that we had more mountains to cross) and partly they were frightened of the gods who inhabited this lonely splendid region on the roof of the world. We were trespassers, and the gods resented our intrusion. I assured the Havaldar that the gods were friendly, not hostile, and I told him that, to prove it, I would next day climb the lofty snow-capped mountain which towered above us to the west.

At 6.30 a.m. the next morning, putting two slabs of chocolate and a dozen ginger biscuits into my pockets and handing my field glasses to the Havaldar so that he could watch my progress, I started on the climb. I set my barometer at 18,025 feet but the needle had reached its limit, 20,750 feet, before I first got a clear view of the top of the mountain, a rounded summit of snow. A ridge of rock ran up to within 150 feet of the summit. This ridge formed the dividing line between the sharply angled snow slope and a perpendicular rock precipice which descended sheer 1,000 feet or more to a glacier far below. I decided to make my way along the ridge as far as I dared; but at places the carpet of snow extended, at an alarmingly steep angle, to the very edge of the precipice, without any intervening rock, and I had to move very cautiously. Fortunately the snow was of good quality and held perfectly. But one step I took released an avalanche of loose stones just below me, and it was not pleasant to hear them bounding down the precipice and thudding on to the glacier far below. I progressed a considerable way along the ridge but eventually my courage failed me. I simply dared not leave the comparative safety of the rock ridge to make the final ascent to the summit over the intervening snow. Instead, I sat down and gazed at the awe-inspiring array of snow-clad mountains to the west, beyond the Para river, and at the dark chain of hills to the north-east, in the direction of Demchok and the Indus river.

I got back to the camp exactly twelve hours after I had started, tired but not exhausted. I wondered what the Havaldar would think of my exploit. Would he consider that the gods had defeated me? I need not have worried. He had watched me disappear from view along the rock ridge at a point which (to him, so far away) seemed a negligible distance from the summit. When I re-appeared half an hour later on my descent he had assumed without question that I had reached the top. And when he ran out to welcome me on my return to the camp I could see from his smiling cheerful face that all his fears had vanished.

On July 9th we made a long march and camped on the further side of the Nerbad Pass. We were now only some fifteen miles as the crow flies from Demchok on the Indus. But we were not crows and we could not fly; and a chain of high mountains, without a break in them, lay between us and the Indus valley. The track we had followed across the Nerbad Pass led north-west to Bemkhar. But to travel to Demchok via Bemkhar involved a detour of fifty miles, and I was reluctant to waste time on such a long, and perhaps unnecessary, deviation.

Examination of a small-scale map, the only one I had of this part of my journey, showed that there was, or had been, a pass across the mountains to the south-east; and it was obvious that, if we could find this pass and get our yaks across it, we would come down on to the Deboche-Demchok route and be at Demchok in two days' time. Inquiries made from a passing party of traders were not encouraging. These men had never heard of a pass to the south-east. If there were one, they said, it would certainly be used as it would save travellers to or from Demchok a full day's march. I made further enquiries from some Tibetan shepherds grazing their flocks on the lower slopes of the mountains. They had heard that, many years ago, two traders had come over the mountains from the direction in which we were anxious to go; but they had lost their one pony on the way and had not repeated the experiment. Nor could these shepherds tell us exactly where this pass was to be found.

Raghu Das and I spent the whole of July 10th exploring the mountains to the south-east in the hope of discovering some break in the huge barrier. Our investigations were fruitful only to this extent, that they eliminated a great number of possibilities. I came to the conclusion that, if there was a pass, it must be at the head of one particular stream which flowed down in a north-westerly direction from the range above us. Rejoining the main party, which had been waiting for us in the valley below, we marched up-stream along the chosen route for several miles and camped beside the stream for the night.

The next morning we followed the stream to its source, a perpendicular wall of solid snow which was clearly insurmountable. There was, however, a rough track made by Kiang (wild asses) up a steep and stony hill-side to the east. Up this we laboured and found, at the top, a broad open space, snow-covered and surrounded by steep hills, but with an outlet to the south-east, as I had hoped, down which a stream flowed. We followed the stream downward for several miles, the yaks clambering with difficulty over the rough rocks, but precipitous hills to the north and east gave us no chance of breaking away to join the Deboche-Demchok track. We were only a mile above Deboche before we were able to leave the line of the stream; and then we learned with disgust from the two inhabitants of the tent which constituted the village of Deboche that there was, in harsh reality, no Deboche-Demchok 'route' and that the track leading from Deboche to Demchok was impassable for animals – impassable, indeed, for any but active men unencumbered with luggage.

One route was, however, left to us. The Sershang Pass, though not leading directly to Demchok, provided a passable track across the mountain range which still separated us from the Indus valley, and I decided to follow this track. We camped on the night of July 11th beside a frozen lake below the Sershang Pass, and began the ascent of the pass the following morning before dawn. There was no snow on the southern slopes of the pass, but there was deep snow on the summit, and the descent was made down a rock ridge at the side of a steep slope of frozen snow. Only one large patch of snow had to be crossed and this was frozen so hard that even the laden yaks did not break the crust but slithered down with their forelegs firmly planted in front of them and a look of pained surprise in their eyes as they gradually gathered speed. It was 9 p.m. before the last of the party had arrived at Demchok, but fatigue was forgotten in the general delight at having reached, after so many delays and disappointments, the low-lying valley of the Indus.

CHAPTER 4

Rudok and Gartok

RAGHU DAS told me that the Indus was often a serious obstacle to traders, who sometimes had to wait for weeks before the waters subsided sufficiently to allow them to cross without danger. 'Yaks and ponies,' said Raghu Das, 'swim strongly, and when men cannot cross by themselves they hang on to the tails of these animals. Sheep, and especially rams, are also comparatively strong swimmers and display more cunning than other animals in crossing flooded rivers. Instead of spending their strength in battling against the current they swim with it, gradually edging their way across to the further bank and, in the case of a broad river, they will often land half a mile below the point at which they started. Goats are poor swimmers and generally have to be helped across. But the chief difficulty is with mules, and traders, to get them across a river which is out of their depth, tie a stout rope to their ears and, launching them on the waters, drag them across wholesale.'

We crossed the Indus by a ford two miles below Demchok. The water was not more than waist-deep and the crossing would have been easy if the bed of the river had not been covered by rounded slimy boulders which made it difficult for us to keep our footing.

The marches to Rudok were long but easy, first across a stony plain and later over grass meadows which fringed a winding rivulet of clear water. From above Demchok the view of the Tibetan plateau to the east of the Indus had not been what I expected. I had expected to see a rolling table-land covered with grass, where sheep and goats could range at will. Actually I saw little of any plateau. There were only broad bare spaces at the foot of mountains equally bare. The colours were all browns and blacks and purples with no trace of green;

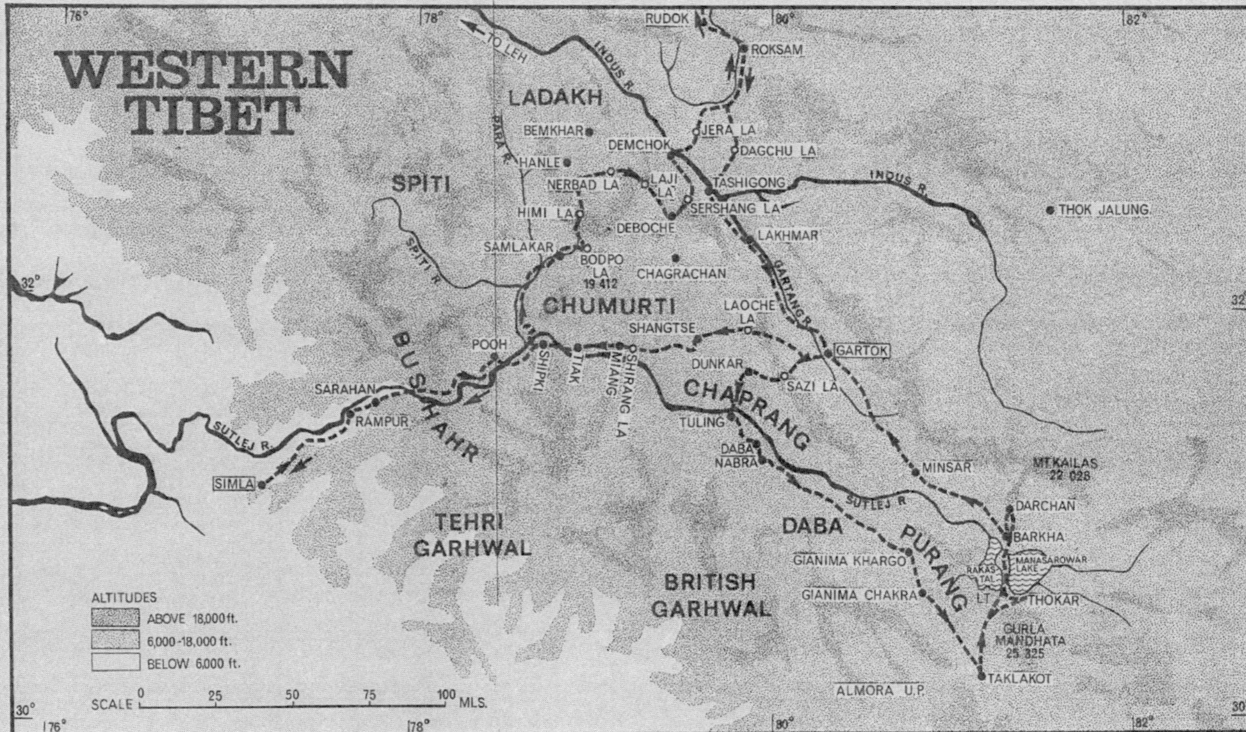
WESTERN TIBET
LADAKH
SPITI
CHUMURTI
BUSHAHR
CHAPRANG
DABA
PURANG
TEHRI GARHWAL
BRITISH GARHWAL
ALMORA U.P.
TO LEH
INDUS R.
PARA R.
SPITI R.
SUTLEJ R.
GARTANG R.
RUDOK
ROKSAM
BEMKHAR
DEMCHOK
JERA LA
DAGCHU LA
HANLE
NERBAD LA
LAJI LA
TASHIGONG
SERSHANG LA
HIMI LA
DEBOCHE
LAKHMAR
THOK JALUNG
SAMLAKAR
BODPO LA 19 412
CHAGRACHAN
LAOCHE LA
SHANGTSE
POOH
SHIPKI
TIAK
MIANG
SHIRANG LA
DUNKAR
GARTOK
SAZI LA
SARAHAN
RAMPUR
TULING
DABA
NABRA
MINSAR
MT KAILAS 22 028
DARCHAN
BARKHA
SIMLA
GIANIMA KHARGO
GIANIMA CHAKRA
RAKAS TAL
MANASAROWAR LAKE
LT
THOKAR
GURLA MANDHATA 25 325
TAKLAKOT
ALTITUDES
ABOVE 18,000 ft.
6,000-18,000 ft.
BELOW 6,000 ft.
SCALE 0 25 50 75 100 MLS.
76°
78°
80°
82°
32°
30°

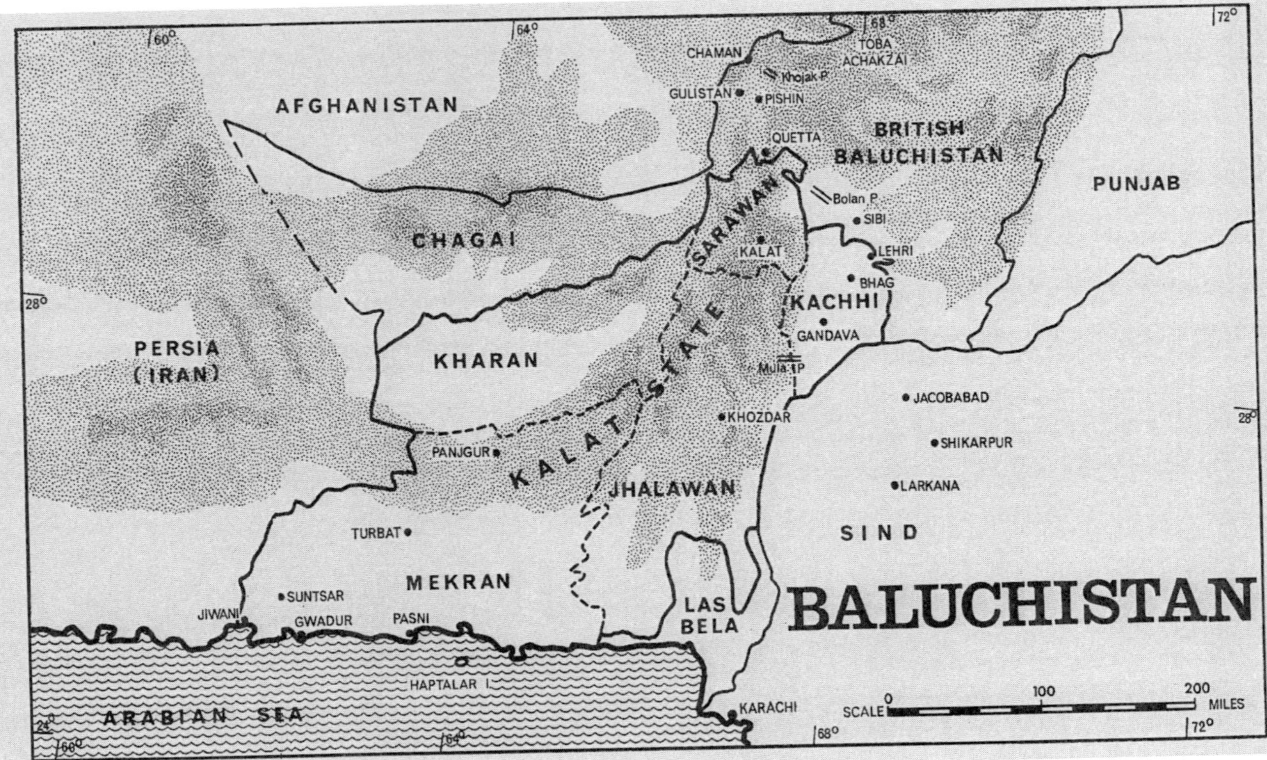
BALUCHISTAN
AFGHANISTAN
PERSIA (IRAN)
CHAGAI
KHARAN
MEKRAN
KALAT STATE
SARAWAN
JHALAWAN
KACHHI
BRITISH BALUCHISTAN
PUNJAB
SIND
LAS BELA
ARABIAN SEA
CHAMAN
TOBA ACHAKZAI
Khojak P.
GULISTAN
PISHIN
QUETTA
Bolan P.
SIBI
LEHRI
BHAG
KALAT
GANDAVA
Mula P.
KHOZDAR
JACOBABAD
SHIKARPUR
LARKANA
PANJGUR
TURBAT
SUNTSAR
JIWANI
GWADUR
PASNI
HAPTALAR I.
KARACHI
SCALE 0 100 200 MILES

and the mountains looked as if they had been casually deposited by some celestial Power who had not had time to arrange them in any order or sequence. The marches to Rudok, however, proved my first impressions to have been misleading. There really was a plateau, of a mean elevation of 15,000 feet above sea level, and from this plateau rose, to varying heights and with their spurs running in different directions, the array of mountains which I had seen from my vantage point to the west of the Indus. Moreover, we had not left the Indus more than fifteen miles behind before we came to the pasture lands, previously hidden from our view, which clothed with green the lower slopes of the mountains and the shallow depressions between them.

It was on the road from Roksam to Rudok that I had my first interview with a Tibetan of the upper class. He was the head Lama of the Rudok monastery and was on a tour of inspection of the flocks of his monastery, which owned many of the valley pastures through which we had recently passed. When I met him he had halted for his mid-day meal of tea and curds and was seated, clothed in a robe of scarlet and gold, beneath a large black umbrella planted in the ground at his side. He proved to be very friendly and nearly two hours had passed in amiable conversation before I was able to get away without appearing to be discourteous. He displayed great interest in the oddments which I happened to be carrying with me – compass, barometer, field glasses, shot-gun and rifle. But he was chiefly delighted with the map which I showed him, and he marvelled at the knowledge of his country which I seemed to display when I read from it the names of villages in the neighbourhood of his home near Lhasa. Everything that I had with me he wanted to buy, at my own price; but he was in no way annoyed at my refusal to sell. Before we parted he insisted on taking me aside with my interpreter, away from the rest of the party, and giving me a piece of advice: 'Never trust the word of a Tibetan. If a Tibetan makes a promise, see that it is written down on paper and signed.' With these words, and with a parting salutation which was too akin to an embrace to be entirely pleasing, he allowed me to go on my way.

Our party arrived at Rudok after nightfall on July 17th. From several miles away I had seen it, a rocky hill, purple and black in the fading light, rising high above the level of the surrounding plain. But in the bright sunshine of the next morning this rugged eminence of rock, crowned by the palace of the Jongpon (Governor), white and brown against a background of blue sky, seemed yet more beautiful and impressive. It seemed, indeed, worthy of the sanctity, greater than that of Lhasa, to which it had always laid claim.

On the morning after my arrival the Jongpon, Mondo by name, came to call on me. He proved to be a young man of about thirty who, with three other boys of his own age, had been sent to school in England in 1914 by the Tibetan Government as an experiment. He had spent some years at Rugby before returning to Tibet, and was delighted to meet someone who knew his school and took an interest in hearing about his experiences there. He spoke English hesitantly and with difficulty, but it was perfect English when it did arrive; whilst I, no less than he, took pleasure in speaking that language again.

Familiarity with the British seemed to have bred in Mondo great respect for them. When the British Trade Agent had complained to him about the 10 per cent tax which he, like his predecessors, had been levying from Indian traders, he immediately reduced it to 2 per cent and had made no subsequent attempts to increase it. Traders, indeed, had nothing but praise for his moderation and fair treatment of them, and it was fear for the future rather than present distress which had made the Bushahris so anxious that I should visit Rudok. His own subjects, however, had a different tale to tell, and spoke of him as the most oppressive of a long succession of tyrannical Jongpons. He told me that he himself had been beaten at Rugby for failing to do his 'prep' properly, and this was the reason, perhaps, why he seldom had his subjects beaten. But this appeared to be the one form of despotic abuse of power in which he did not indulge. His subjects were ground down by excessive taxes imposed or withheld at will. When he came from Lhasa to take up his appointment at Rudok he brought with him 300 mule-loads of tea for which, of course, he had free transport. This was sold at ten times its proper value to his poorer subjects and at twenty times its value to the richer ones. Every year he bought sheep at 1 rupee each from one section of his subjects and sold them to another section at 6 rupees each. When he made a purchase he paid in rupees at the rate of 8 tankas to the rupee; when he sold, he demanded rupees at the rate of 2½ tankas to the rupee, the buying and selling price in each case being fixed in tankas. No means of extracting money from impoverished subjects had been neglected by this avaricious Jongpon. To me, however, he was charming; and on the second day of my stay at Rudok he showed me over his palace and entertained me to lunch with a grace and courtesy which were unexceptionable.

Lunching with a Tibetan official of high rank was a novel experience for me. I was entranced by the Gyakhi (Tibetan spaniel) which was his constant companion and shared his bed and board. It was literally a lap-dog for, when he was sitting, it lay across his hands concealed in the broad sleeves of his robe. An animated hot-water-bottle, it kept him warm by day and by night. The lunch itself consisted of Chinese dishes. The rice came from Ladakh but the rest of the food had been brought from Lhasa, a two months' journey. Eight silver dishes containing concoctions of fish and vegetables, and two silver bowls filled with rice, were placed in front of us. With the aid of chopsticks the Jongpon took morsels from each of the various dishes, put them into his bowl of rice and proceeded to eat. I followed his example, copying carefully but unskilfully his method of manipulating the chopsticks. From time to time a servant would refill our bowls with hot rice and, later, we drank the mixture of clarified butter, flour and tea which was the common drink of the country.

The Jongpon's palace was a lofty, rambling structure made, for the most part, of mud, but with foundations of stone and layers of stone at irregular intervals throughout the walls. The ceilings were supported by large beams of wood said to have been brought from Leh. From the roof of the palace there was a fine view of the great freshwater lake, the Nyak Tso, while directly below, on the southern slope of the hill on which the palace stood, were the two hundred desolate and fifty tenanted houses which now constituted the town of Rudok. Once upon a time, Mondo told me, Rudok had contained a thousand houses, all within an encircling wall: but most of the inhabitants had lost their lives in a great war and the town had never recovered its former prosperity.

History records that in 1627 a Jesuit priest, Fr Andrade, established a mission at Rudok. But it did not last long and for 300 years the town had been closed to Europeans. That I had been allowed inside the town at all was a unique privilege and I did not imagine for a moment that I would be permitted to visit the monastery. Mondo, however, had different views.

'Would you like to have a look at the monastery?' he asked me, quite casually.

I was dumbfounded. 'Surely I wouldn't be allowed in there,' I replied. 'Isn't it very sacred?'

'Indeed it is. But the chapel at Rugby is also sacred and I was not only allowed to go to chapel, I was compelled to go!'

So we all visited the monastery. First we passed through a narrow, stone-flagged passage into a courtyard, where we were confronted by a massive locked door. After a short time a Lama came and opened this door and we entered a circular chamber whose walls were covered with richly coloured frescoes portraying the figures of gods and devils and all kinds of imaginary animals. From this chamber a short, wide passage led to another locked door. On either side of this passage, seated in galleries 6 feet above the level of the floor, were two human figures, three times life size, crowned and armed, with fat, bulging faces. The figures were of mud, with a brightly painted waxen exterior. They were there as guardians of the sacred parts beyond the second locked door. But Mondo was himself a Lama of a high order and, sponsored by him, we were allowed to pass beyond the second door into a spacious low-roofed cavern hung with splendid tapestries which gleamed in the dim wavering light of countless candles. We moved on, past lines of cushioned prayer-stools and beneath rows of Chinese hangings swaying gently in the draught from the open door, until we came to the innermost shrine of all. Here were trestle tables covered with elaborately-chased silver ornaments. In the centre was the dominating figure of Buddha, while beyond, as far as the eye could penetrate into the dim recesses, were rows and rows of draperies and tapestries suspended from the roof. As we returned to the entrance I noticed that the side walls of this mysterious and holy cellar were lined from top to bottom with sacred books.

On the last evening of my four-day stay at Rudok Mondo came to bid me farewell and I managed to elicit from him a good deal of information about his work. The Jongpons of Rudok and Chaprang were personally appointed by the Dalai Lama, and before they came to Western Tibet to take charge of their districts they had to serve for three years in one of the big monasteries at Lhasa. This was an expensive occupation as they had to provide the food, consisting mostly of tea, for all the Lamas there. The money spent in this way they were expected to recoup, with interest, out of the inhabitants of their districts during their three-year tenure of office. The district of Rudok was the biggest in Western Tibet, and the Jongpon collected all the dues payable on the extensive pasture-lands which belonged to the Lhasa Government and were vested in the Jongpon during the term of his administration. The Jongpon had to send about Rs 2,000/- (£150) annually to the Lhasa Government, and this sum was raised partly from taxes, partly from fines imposed in civil or criminal cases, and partly from other dues payable in accordance with custom or the Jongpon's will. The Jongpon also engaged in trade, and the sum total of his annual income from these combined sources must have been very great. Letters for Lhasa were sent by special messenger to Leh, a journey of ten days. Thence they went by Indian post to Gyantse, via Darjeeling; and from Gyantse by Tibetan post to Lhasa. Only on very special occasions were letters sent direct to Lhasa through Tibet by relays of mounted messengers; and the custom of sealing the despatch to the messenger and the messenger to his horse was one, I was told, which had long been discontinued.

In Rudok there appeared to be little criminal work for the Jongpon. He had power to beat (and in cases of murder or armed robbery the complainant, as well as the accused, was always beaten as a preliminary to judicial proceedings), but could only punish by cutting off feet or hands with the previous sanction of the Lhasa Government. In practice the punishment was inflicted first and the Lhasa Government informed later. There was much gold in the Rudok district, but the Jongpon had no power to interfere in the administration of the gold fields. These were controlled by the Sarpon, an officer specially appointed from Lhasa to collect dues from gold diggers and hear civil or criminal cases in which they were involved.

Mondo parted from me with many expressions of goodwill and gave practical demonstration of his concern for my welfare by sending one of his servants in advance to ensure that I would suffer no delay in obtaining transport.

We left Rudok on July 21st. Marching in a southerly direction we reached the right bank of the Indus opposite the Tashigong monastery on July 24th, my twenty-sixth birthday, which I celebrated by treating myself to half a tin of sweetened condensed milk. The river was in flood and could not be crossed, so we camped for the night and hoped that the waters would have subsided by the following morning. In the course of the night a north-westerly gale blew all our tents away; fortunately they were recovered before they had been blown into the river. On the next morning it was obvious that the river was less turbulent but, owing perhaps to the wind of the previous night, it had not subsided as much as we had hoped. When the sun was well up I decided to test for myself the depth and force of the river, which was about 85 yards wide at the so-called ford. Only 40 yards proved to be in any way difficult, and the water never rose above my shoulders. The bed of the river was smooth and the main current, though strong, was not irresistible.

I had often thought that, though a ford may begin as the shallowest part of a river, the tread of thousands of men and animals must, in the course of centuries, wear away the bed to such an extent that the ford could become actually deeper than other neighbouring parts of the river. To test this admittedly improbable theory I went 200 yards upstream and tried to re-cross the river there. But I was soon out of my depth and had to swim at least 50 yards before I touched bottom again. In covering this distance I was carried some 150 yards downstream by the force of the current.

I decided that a crossing by the ford was perfectly feasible and set about making the necessary arrangements. Certain items of our baggage, such as flour, guns, ammunition and official papers, had to be kept dry at any cost, and these were made up into separate bundles of not more than 30 lb. weight. Other articles, such as tents, bedding and tinned stores, were either waterproof or could be dried later in the wind and sun, and these were loaded on to the yaks. These animals swim very low in the water and their loads were bound to get wet. My first plan was to place four men at 10-yard intervals across the deep part of the river while two or three others carried the light bundles across the comparatively shallow water between them and the bank. This plan proved, in practice, to be completely futile. The Gurkhas whom I stationed in the deep part of the river could not hold their ground but were forced downstream by the current; and the Tibetans in charge of the yaks, on whose help I had relied, could be induced neither by threats nor persuasion to enter even the shallowest part of the river. The one orderly with the party, though courageous enough, was so small and light that he could only get across the river by clinging to the pony. The Ladakhi cook got half-way across, found himself being carried downstream, and scrambled back again to safety in a state of ludicrous terror; and one of the Gurkhas got across with such difficulty that he would obviously be useless for the task of carrying the bundles across.

It was clear that I could expect effective help only from Raghu Das and the other three Gurkhas. So, abandoning my original plan, I decided that each of us, taking one bundle at a time, should cross and re-cross the river until all the bundles had been landed on the further bank. This we did. I and the three Gurkhas each crossed the river four times with bundles balanced on our heads; and the pony, led by Raghu Das and with two bundles loaded at such a height above the saddle that they did not get wet when the animal swam, also crossed the river to the further bank four times. The yaks, loaded with the heavy baggage, gave no trouble. They were driven into the river by the Tibetans and pelted with stones from behind until they came to a point where the further bank appeared to them to be also the nearer one. The pony had behaved splendidly, the cook badly; and so, to please the one and annoy the other, I rewarded the pony with a liberal portion of my small remaining stock of sugar.

We had succeeded in crossing the river. But disappointment awaited us on the further bank. The Tibetans of Tashigong, thinking that we could not cross the river for at least another two days, had no fresh yaks waiting for us. To take on the same yaks for another stage, especially when their owners were stranded on the further bank of the Indus, would have been a gross breach of custom; and the Tashigong yaks, grazing high up on the mountains, could hardly be collected in less than a day and a half. The head Lama of the Tashigong monastery supported my efforts to make the local headman use every endeavour to provide some sort of transport that day. A passing trader offered to lend us some of his baggage animals for the next stage, and by 5 p.m. we had collected three yaks, six bullocks and two ponies. These, with the addition of Raghu Das's pony, were sufficient for our requirements; and we had started on the next stage to Lakhmar by 5.30 p.m. The light lasted for one and a half hours; there were then two hours of pitch darkness, during which we stumbled over rocks and through streams or plodded stolidly over soft sand and shingle; then, at last, at about 9 p.m. the moon rose, and the latter part of the march was completed in bright moonlight. By the time that the whole of the party had arrived at Lakhmar it was past midnight.

The Tibetan Government, I was told, had issued an edict forbidding the killing of birds or animals on the ground that such practices would shorten the life of the Dalai Lama. On the last stage of our journey to Gartok, however, I was persuaded by the Gurkhas to disregard this edict. Not being Buddhists, the Gurkhas were unable to see any connection between the life of the Dalai Lama and the life of a bird or animal. Between the track we were following and the Gartang river we saw a lake some 500 yards in length and 400 yards in breadth. Feeding on it were many hundreds of ruddy sheldrake and about 150 bar-headed geese. We were carrying with us three shot-guns and two rifles. I and the Gurkhas took up positions at different points round the lake and together we converged towards the centre. The water was shoulder high but, even so, we managed to bag eighteen geese. Since the rifle bullets and shot-gun pellets were discharged at a flat angle they ricochetted over the still surface of the lake and were almost as dangerous to ourselves as they were to the geese. I myself received a charge of shot in my broad-brimmed unfashionable topee, and blessed the day when, on my voyage out to India, I had saved it from the Rushton purge.

We arrived at Gartok on the evening of July 28th, having completed the journey from Rudok, upwards of 150 miles, in eight days. There we found Dr Kanshi Ram with the rest of the Agency staff waiting for us. Their journey from Pooh had been uneventful.

Gartok, the capital of Western Tibet, seat of the Garpons (Governors-General of Western Tibet) and headquarters of the British Trade Agency, consisted of some fifteen squalid mud huts huddled together on damp ground in the middle of a bleak plain perpetually swept by cold winds. The Garpons made Gartok their headquarters for five months in every year. Without special permission from the Lhasa Government they were not allowed to leave their headquarters; and only on one or two occasions during their annual period of residence at Gartok did they emerge for a short time from the malodorous warmth of their dingy hovels. The Senior Garpon's house was also the Court of the two Garpons, and there they administered injustice impartially to all. The mentality of the Senior Garpon was of particular interest. Normally people speak the truth unless there is some particular object to be gained by telling a lie; but *his* conversation followed the reverse principle; and he only swerved from falsehood on the few occasions when truth seemed more likely to serve his purpose. The secular power of the two Garpons in Western Tibet was absolute, though theoretically appeals from their judicial decisions could be preferred to the Dalai Lama at Lhasa. The two Garpons were of equal rank, and the terms Senior and Junior customarily applied to them were mistranslations of the Tibetan words Gong and Hog, which mean Upper and Lower and had reference only to the relative positions of their houses. Socially the elder of the two Garpons took precedence, but officially neither could do any act without the concurrence of the other, and the common seal was kept under double-lock.

Relations between the Garpons and the British Trade Agent had been strained for some years. The Garpons had, contrary to the provisions of the Anglo-Tibetan Trade Regulations, refused to admit the Trade Agent to their Court when trying cases in which British subjects were involved. They had, indeed, refused to try any case instituted by a British subject in which Tibetans were accused or defendants. They had also, in disregard of the Trade Regulations, imposed a 2 per cent tax on Ladakhi traders; and were much incensed when the Trade Agent had directed the Ladakhi traders not to pay the tax until it had been sanctioned by the Government of India. I had been authorised to inform the Garpons that there was no longer any objection to the payment of the 2 per cent tax by Ladakhi traders; and I had hopes that, when the Garpons were informed of this concession, they would agree to dispose of the pending cases.

When I arrived at Gartok on July 28th I expected that the Garpons, following the procedure customary in their country, would call on me. But on July 29th they neither called on me nor sent any message of welcome. So, on the morning of July 30th, I sent Raghu Das to inquire from the Garpons' servants at what hour the Garpons were likely to call as I should like to make adequate preparations to receive them. The reply came back that the Garpons had no intention of calling. I decided to ignore the discourtesy and sent a politely phrased note to each of the Garpons asking them if they would give me the pleasure of their company at tea the next day. I sent the notes by the hand of Raghu Das who was to explain that this was a friendly invitation which had no connection with the official business which would have to be discussed later. The Junior Garpon declined the invitation in courteous terms to which it would be impossible to take exception. But the Senior Garpon sent a downright refusal, remarking that he was the ruler of Western Tibet and if I wanted to see him I would have to go to him; he added that business should come first and tea parties could follow. These replies were not committed to paper but communicated to me verbally through Raghu Das.

My staff deeply resented these insults. The Havaldar, in particular, was itching to seize the Senior Garpon and bring him captive to my tent. I was more realistic, and came to the reluctant conclusion that, as the Garpons would not come to see me, I must go to see them. Accordingly, on July 31st, I asked them to fix a time the next day at which I could attend their Court. They replied that noon the next day would be convenient; and at that hour I rode over to their Court with an escort of Gurkhas and orderlies.

In previous years British Trade Agents had given complimentary presents to the Garpons with little result. I decided that this year presents should only be given if the Garpons proved friendly and amenable to reason. The Senior Garpon's son-in-law had been hanging about our camp the day before and had been allowed to get glimpses of the rich array of presents laid out there. I had hopes that the prospect of winning these might induce the Garpons to accede to my requests; and when I attended their Court my senior orderly brought and laid beside me two magnificently embellished ceremonial swords, with hilts of gold and ivory.

The Garpons received me politely. The Senior Garpon, indeed, was in high good humour, and had collected quite a large crowd to witness this, for him, proud moment. Omitting preliminary small-talk, I told the Senior Garpon that the object of my visit was to secure from him an explanation of his failure to hear cases in which British subjects were involved. He denied categorically that he had refused to hear such cases; and he also denied having refused to acknowledge the right of the British Trade Agent to attend his Court during the hearing of such cases. At this point I produced copies of the letters he had written to the Trade Agent the previous year; and at this point, too, he gave orders that the crowd which had collected at the door of his court and in the yard outside should be dispersed.

The Senior Garpon had to admit that he had written the letters but did not seem in the least put out at having his previous assertions proved utterly false. Again I asked him why he had failed to observe the Trade Regulations; and this time I received the answer I expected, that it was due to the objections raised by the Trade Agent to the 2 per cent tax on Ladakhi traders. I then told him that I had been authorised by the Government of India to inform him that they agreed to the levy of this tax. He expressed his pleasure at this news, and I told him that I too was pleased as the cause of past misunderstandings had now been removed: he had only to give a written undertaking to settle pending and future cases as they had been settled in the past and all would be well for the future. There followed a long discussion between the two Garpons. I saw that they meant to refuse to give an undertaking in writing, and I was not prepared to accept verbal assurances. I had to consider what my next step should be. The Senior Garpon was a vain man, and flattery or subservience on my part might have induced him to give the written promise. But I would not stoop to conquer. Rejecting this alternative, I addressed the Senior Garpon sternly. A British envoy, I told him, was even now on his way to Lhasa. The Lhasa Government and the Government of India were on the most friendly terms. If he refused to comply with the Treaty Regulations, the British envoy would, under instructions from the Government of India, represent to the Dalai Lama the impossibility of maintaining friendly relations with him when one of his officials openly refused to observe the terms of a sacred agreement between the two countries. The Lhasa Government, I pointed out, would have no alternative but to recall him and appoint another Garpon in his place. Eventually the Garpons said they would give me their reply the next day. I left their Court, taking the swords with me.

The Garpons' reply arrived next day. It was, substantially, a refusal to hear any cases brought by British subjects until orders were received from Lhasa.

My mission had failed. But I had the last laugh. Not only was the Senior Garpon, in fact, recalled to Lhasa, but the presents which I had brought for him were, to his bitter chagrin, distributed to other officials, at Gartok and elsewhere, who, without exception, showed themselves friendly and co-operative.

CHAPTER 5

The Trade Marts of Western Tibet

AFTER a week at Gartok I set off, with a full staff and with better tents, to inspect the Trade Marts to the south of the Sutlej river, which I planned to cross at Tuling. My map showed two routes to Tuling. The first crossed the mountains to the west of Gartok by the Ayi Pass (18,700 feet) and continued southwards to Tuling via Dunkar. The second crossed the same range of mountains by the Bogo Pass (19,220 feet) and followed a more direct line to Tuling. On the advice of the Tibetans who were to supply our transport animals I decided to cross the range by a third pass known locally as the Sazi Pass. I was the more inclined to adopt this course as the Ayi Pass had been crossed by Captain Rawling in 1904 and the Bogo Pass by Mr Mackworth Young in 1912, but there was no record of the Sazi Pass ever having been crossed by a European traveller. Indeed, there was no record even of the existence of the pass.

Our first problem was to cross the flooded Gartang. The banks of this river were not high, and the water brought down by recent heavy rains had spread far and wide over the Gartok plain. It was only through the skill of our guide that we reached the high land to the west of the river without loss or damage to our baggage. At one point we waded through water for more than half a mile, and those who did not follow exactly in the footsteps of the guide soon found themselves labouring in deep water and quicksands.

The ascent of the Sazi Pass two days later was accomplished in ideal conditions. The sun was warm, the wind was not too cold, and the snow was crisp and firm under foot. It never occurred to me that any of the party would find difficulty in crossing the pass, and I took advantage of the splendid conditions to climb the Sazi mountain, a snowy dome which rises above the pass to the east. It was only later that I learned that some members of the main party had had to have assistance in reaching the top of the pass. The descent to the south was exceedingly steep but, as it was over screes devoid of snow, it presented little difficulty. That night Raghu Das, who had accompanied me to the top of the Sazi mountain, suffered so severely from snow-blindness that he had to be forcibly restrained from attempting to knock out his brains against the rocks. Dr Kanshi Ram treated his eyes with a solution of cocaine, and eventually, though the poor man got no sleep, he did get some relief from pain.

The country in the neighbourhood of Dunkar consisted of large fantastically-shaped ridges and mountains of mud, intersected by water-made channels several hundreds of feet in depth. The action of rain-water had pitted these mud-mountains in such a way as to leave a forest of pinnacles standing up vertically. The Dunkar monastery, once a fort, crowned the summit of one of these ridges of mud, while the inhabitants of Dunkar lived either in houses on the banks of the stream below or in caves tunnelled into the side of the ridge. The stream, until about 2 p.m. each day, was a gently flowing rivulet of clear, fresh water; in the afternoon, however, melted snow from the mountains above turned it into a muddy torrent resembling nothing so much as a Westmorland beck in spate.

From Dunkar we followed a well-used track to Tuling, the ecclesiastical capital of Western Tibet. We crossed the Sutlej one and a half miles above Tuling by an iron chain suspension bridge said to have been built by divine agency some 300 years ago. The monastery possibly dates from the eleventh century, but I could discover nothing about its real history. The monks averred that it had been built by a god in a single night, but the factor of the monastery, an official appointed from Lhasa every three years, assured me that this was only a pious invention on their part. The truth of the matter was, he said, that men had started building the monastery and found that, for every foot they built by day, another foot was added mysteriously by night.

The monastery was not a single building, but a collection of them. They were solid structures of stone and mud and, for the most part, painted red. There were four large temples with the entrances guarded, as at Rudok, by grotesque human figures three or four times life size. The inner walls of the temples were covered with frescoes representing gods and men, angels and devils, and everywhere there were statues and statuettes, in brass or gold, and often studded with turquoise, of the seated Buddha. Outside the four main temples were some twenty chapels. These, too, were filled with images of Buddha while their walls were covered with frescoes. In one of these chapels was a pile of demoniac masks; in another was a collection of high hats surmounted with miniature imitation skulls; and we also saw a cupboard full of human skulls which were used by the Lamas to drink from on certain festivals. One of the images of Buddha which we saw was quite 50 feet high. Some images of gods or devils were given multiple arms and legs – one of them had thirty-two arms and sixteen legs – and there were several representations of a huge and unpleasant-looking black devil trampling humans underfoot. Clearly many members of the Hindu pantheon had intruded into this sanctuary of Lamaist Buddhism.

The magnificent wooden beams which supported the roofs of the four largest temples were said to have come from Bushahr. But I saw also a store of wood containing one or two large, expertly-sawn tree trunks; and I was told that this wood had been taken from the Sutlej, and that the store was renewed every year with wood salvaged from the river. I am still unable to conjecture where this wood can have come from, for I saw no trees near the Sutlej above this point; but the truth of what I was told was vouched for by one of the monks who had himself assisted in the work of salvage.

The abbot of the monastery was not in residence when I was there, but I was hospitably entertained by his deputy, the factor, who had pleasant recollections of his last meeting with Europeans. He had been a small boy when the British Expedition had gone to Lhasa in 1904, and he and his friends had followed the soldiers, collecting souvenirs and being given novel dainties to eat.

The track from Tuling led us in a south-easterly direction through a countryside of gigantic castles and towering pillars of mud such as we had seen near Dunkar; and after nightfall on the second day we arrived at Daba. In Tibetan Da means Arrow and Ba means Place. The tradition was that a Lama of the neighbourhood, on being consulted about the location of a new town that was to be founded, drew a bow at a venture, and the place where the arrow fell became the centre of what was now the town of Daba. The houses were built on ridges along the face of high mud cliffs, whilst on top of the cliffs were the monastery and the Jongpon's residence. The plain below, watered by a broad stream of snow-water from the mountains to the south-west, was marked out by white boundary stones into a number of fields in which barley was grown. There were no traders at Daba that year and I only stayed there long enough to interview the Jongpon's agent before starting off for Nabra, a grazing ground in a lonely valley where the traders from Niti in British Garhwal had all congregated.

There were no houses at Nabra, only two lines of white tents, perhaps fifty in all, where the traders lived, and a few of the black tents of woven yak hair used by Dokpas (Tibetan shepherds). I arrived just before sunset and, while my own tent was being pitched, I waited in the commodious tent of a Garhwali trader, surrounded on all sides by stacks of cloth (to sell) and wool (just bought). Many traders collected in and around the tent and retailed to me stories of oppression by Tibetan officials, of whippings and fines and other injustices. But that year had been a good one for trade and the Garhwalis were well pleased with the business they had done. Later in the evening I was surprised to see a number of girls dressed in bright colours dancing in front of one of the tents. Apparently they came every year from India as camp followers of the traders and (I was told) did very well for themselves when the trade in wool was good.

While I was at Nabra there was much excitement over the capture of three Tibetan thieves. It appeared that for some ten days a party of beggars, three sturdy men with their women and children, had been loitering about the camp and living on the bounty of the traders. Three days before I arrived at Nabra they had all disappeared, and with them had gone a large quantity of wool, food and other articles. The traders reported their loss to the Jongpon's agent at Daba; and he, probably on account of my impending visit, had zealously armed some servants and sent them in pursuit of the thieves. The thieves had been captured and were brought in custody to Nabra on the day after my arrival there. The three men, haled before the Jongpon's servant who was temporarily in charge of the mart, had confessed their crime and, when I arrived on the scene, were on their knees in front of his tent, swaying to and fro, with hands bound tightly behind their backs and tears streaming down their faces, crying out every few seconds, 'Ponbo chu chakor; Ponbo chu chakor' – 'Master, have mercy, please have mercy.' Behind them were the women and children of the party, shrieking and wailing, throwing themselves into attitudes indicative of the deepest despair, and endeavouring by every means in their power to kindle a spark of pity in the heart of their judge. The wretched prisoners had, indeed, much to fear. As soon as the sanction of the Jongpon's agent at Daba was received, each of the thieves would, in turn, be stripped and tied face downwards on to a framework of wood; on either side of him would stand a man with a leathern thong; and these two men would give each thief alternate lashes on the tender part of the thighs. After the first pair of strokes the number 'One' is called, and so the beating goes on, each pair of strokes counting as one until the tally of strokes ordered by the judge has been completed. Men who are beaten lose consciousness before the hundredth stroke and are unable to walk for weeks afterwards. I was surprised that the thieves I saw had confessed their guilt;

but I was told that if they had not taken this course they would have been beaten until they did and, at the end of it all, would have received just as severe a sentence; so confessions were generally made at an early stage of the proceedings. When thieves or dacoits (armed robbers) were captured, members of their family were also punished, a custom which ensured that family influence would invariably be exercised on the side of law and order. The thieves whom I saw in custody were not beaten until after I had left; and I declined a subsequent opportunity of seeing this form of punishment administered.

We set off from Nabra on the morning of August 15th and arrived at Gianima Khargo four days later. There were no houses at this place, which was entirely uninhabited for ten months in the year. At the time of my visit, however, hundreds of tents belonging to Johari traders were pitched there, and a lesser number belonging to Tibetans. To the north of the tents I was surprised to see a large lake, many miles in circumference, which was not marked on my map. A river which was marked on my map could, I found, be jumped across with ease!

I spent three days at Gianima Khargo and made many new Tibetan acquaintances. The local official who was administering the mart on behalf of the absentee Daba Jongpon was a small, bearded man, officious and obsequious. Of higher rank was the Chachho, a young man from Lhasa of good birth and exceptional intelligence, whose duty it was to collect taxes from the Dokpas. The traders from Lhasa were big men with hard faces, but they were openly delighted at the interest I displayed in them and their possessions and took a childish pride in showing me their treasures. Some of these traders were armed with powerful modern rifles. At Gianima Khargo I saw guns or rifles from England, America, Germany, India, Russia, China and Japan. Those who could not afford guns of western pattern carried matchlocks of Tibetan manufacture with prongs of wood attached on which the barrel was rested when aim was being taken; and the Dokpas who could not afford to buy a native matchlock carried, to frighten off dacoits, wooden poles fitted out to look like guns.

On August 23rd we moved on to Gianima Chakra, the mart of the Darma traders. Here, too, there were no permanent houses. The traders pitched their tents on the shore of a large lake (also unmarked on my map) for the period of the trading season. A number of Nepalis also visited this mart, not to trade, but in charge of yaks used for transport. The people of Nepal are racially akin to the Tibetans, and many mixed marriages took place. The male offspring of such marriages became Nepalese subjects and the female offspring Tibetan subjects. This arrangement was probably an ancient one, dating from the days when Nepal, an independent, fighting nation, wanted men, while Tibet, as was evident from the almost universal practice of polyandry, had always been short of women. My four days at Gianima Chakra were almost entirely occupied in the settlement of disputes between traders. The Darma men were a dissolute set of drunkards, but endowed with unexpected tenacity of purpose; and they prosecuted with vigour, when sober, the quarrels they had started in their cups.

We left Gianima Chakra on August 28th and, still travelling in a south-easterly direction, arrived at Taklakot two days later. This was the biggest mart in Western Tibet, and the traders from Chaudans and Biyans who frequented it stayed there for six months in the year. Their houses had stone walls but were roofed with canvas, and the traders lived in comparative comfort. There were several thousands of acres of cultivated land round Taklakot, more than in the whole of the rest of Western Tibet, and on this land barley and field peas were grown. Taklakot, probably because of its proximity to the Indian border, was by far the most advanced district in Western Tibet. Fields were separated by walls. There were bridges across the rivers and streams. The houses of the wealthier Tibetans were solidly built, of stone. There were smooth tracks across the hills. And the whole place reflected a prosperity which I had seen nowhere else in Western Tibet. There were, too, other signs of alien influence. The uses of soap, unknown further north, were familiar to Taklakot Tibetans. The women painted their faces. And the institution of false law-suits was far more common than elsewhere in Western Tibet. The Tibetans of the Purang district (of which Taklakot was the capital), and those of the Rudok district, differed markedly in many of their characteristics. The southerners were smaller in build, more agile of wit, quick to anger, seldom truthful and never reliable. The northerners, on the other hand, were large-bodied, dull-minded and easy-tempered, slower both in the making and breaking of promises.

The Purang Jongpon had returned to Lhasa the previous year and his agent, suffering from an attack of inflated 'ego', hesitated about calling on me. However, curiosity overcame pride and, having sent a number of servants in advance to make certain that due preparation had been made to receive him, he arrived at my tent with an air of rather self-conscious condescension. He soon thawed, however, under the influence of a few tots of brandy, and before he went he assured me that he would come and see me every day until I left. Further good feeling was created by an impromptu shooting match between his servants and the Gurkhas, and he was genuinely grateful for my offer to clean his rifles and those of his staff which, he admitted, were so choked with dirt and rust that it was dangerous to use them.

My work at Taklakot, where I stayed for six days, was not made easier by the reluctance which Indians and Tibetans alike displayed to telling the truth. In judicial cases the examination of Tibetan witnesses led to continual surprises. No Tibetan of lower class had the least idea of his age, and on many occasions their guesses must have been quite twenty years wrong. Again, it was impossible to find out the name of a witness's father if he were dead, as no Tibetan would provoke the anger of Heaven by speaking the name of a dead man. An oath to speak the truth appeared to be violable at will unless the words were spoken into the empty barrel of a gun pointing upwards; and witnesses who did not propose to speak the truth invariably refused to take an oath in this form.

Leaving Taklakot for the return journey northward to Gartok we followed the pilgrim route which crosses the high plain to the west of Mt Gurla Mandhata (25,325 feet) and descends to the shore of Lake Rakas Tal at a place known as Langak Tunkang. I myself made a detour to visit the mart at Thokar on the southern shore of Lake Manasarowar; but my Tibetan guide could not manage the whole distance, the going was more difficult than I had expected, and I did not complete the twenty-eight mile march to Langak Tunkang until long after sunset.

From Langak Tunkang we set off at dawn for Barkha, to the north of the two lakes. On the way we all bathed in the cold but holy waters of Lake Manasarowar and thus obtained remission of sins past, present and future. From the shore of the lake we collected many treasures: pebbles, to be sewn up in a bag and hung round the necks of ponies before they were left to graze on the mountains, so that they would not stray, or be attacked by wild beasts, or stolen; remains of fish, which were a sure remedy in every case of sickness; water which, drunk by the dying, ensured their immediate entry into Heaven; and sand, to be placed in the mouth of a dead man to prevent his being re-born into the body of an animal. Near the Jiu monastery we crossed the stream, deep and fast flowing after recent rains, whose existence has so often been disputed by geographers and which empties the surplus water of Manasarowar into the neighbouring lake of Rakas Tal; and thence we pressed on to the village of Barkha, hidden in a shallow depression in a dreary plain.

The following day I paid a visit to Darchan as I wanted to see the monastery at the foot of Mt Kailas which marked the beginning and end of the pilgrims' circuit round the Holy Mountain. The monastery was a Bhutanese endowment and claimed complete independence of Tibet. It was normally administered by a Bhutanese official, but the post had been vacant for the last two years and control of the monastery was temporarily in the hands of an elderly Tibetan Lama. This Lama, a handsome, well-built man with a refined face and a short beard slightly touched with grey, entertained us with grace and courtesy. I presented him with a few small gifts on behalf of the Government of India and gave him Rs 4/–, the price of a sheep, on my own account. The other members of the party also gave him small sums of money. Thereupon, having lit candles in front of the shrine, he said prayers on behalf of each of us individually as well as for the benefit of the Government of India. Later, our names were written in a large book so that he might remember to pray for us every day for a period of time proportionate to the amount of our contributions. There were only four Lamas resident in the monastery, but at least twenty children were playing in the precincts. Children, except in the vicinity of monasteries, were rarely seen in Western Tibet, and the rate of infant mortality must have been very high. Each family was expected to supply one boy to be trained, from the age of about ten, for the monastic life, but I was told that, in practice, recruits for the monasteries were only compulsorily conscripted from families in which there were at least two other sons to help the parents in looking after their flocks and herds.

At Barkha we had joined the main Lhasa-Leh trade route, and from there to Gartok we were able to follow a well-defined track. On September 10th, the day we left Barkha, some of the party were involved in an exciting incident. Dr Kanshi Ram, with two unarmed orderlies, had ridden on ahead of the main party. Suddenly he heard the report of a gun, and a bullet passed within a few inches of his head. Immediately afterwards a rough-looking Tibetan emerged from concealment and, approaching the Doctor, asked him who he was and what he had with him. The Doctor replied that he was a member of the staff of the British Trade Agency and that the rest of the party, well armed, were following close behind. The Tibetan now began to reload his matchlock, so the Doctor rode off with all speed, closely followed by the orderlies. The Tibetan pursued him for a short way and then, thinking better of it, turned aside to look at a Kiang which had been pulled down by his dogs and was now being mauled by them. It was only when the Doctor had gone some way that he remembered the revolver with which he was armed. Recovering his courage, he returned and, accompanied by the orderlies, crept up quietly behind the Tibetan. When they were only a few yards away the Tibetan, hearing their footsteps, turned round and raised his gun; but the Doctor fired first, to one side of the Tibetan, and the latter, now thoroughly frightened, allowed himself to be disarmed without more ado.

Travelling with our party for purposes of security was an official of the Lhasa Government, and he and I held a joint enquiry into the matter on the spot. We decided to keep our prisoner in custody till the following day when we could ascertain from local Dokpas what they knew about the man. The next day we were fortunate enough to meet a servant of the local official in whose jurisdiction the offence had been committed. Anxious to display his zeal in the cause of justice, he begged me to stay for another hour and see punishment inflicted then and there. This, for many reasons, I was unwilling to do. I told him that I appreciated his kind thought but that I was perfectly content to leave the case in the hands of his master who would, I had no doubt, deal with the delinquent as he deserved. And I thereupon handed over the dacoit into his custody. More serious in Tibetan eyes than the attempted dacoity was the slaughter of the Kiang; and I heard subsequently that the wretched man was sentenced to 100 stripes.

Arriving at Minsar I was surprised to learn that the inhabitants of the district owed allegiance not to the Dalai Lama but to the Maharaja of Kashmir. Formerly, I was told, the forty families resident there had to supply eight men to the Tibetan Army, but now, being subjects of the Maharaja of Kashmir, they were exempt from this obligation, though they still had to provide free transport for Tibetan officials travelling through their territory. Every year a Ladakhi official came to Minsar to collect the tribute due to the Maharaja of Kashmir. The tribute consisted of sixty sheep, twenty goats, ten kids, six yaks and sixty lambskins; and a sum of Rs 60/- was paid, half in rupees, half in tankas, to defray the official's travelling expenses.

Though the men and women of Minsar were subjects of the Maharaja of Kashmir, a Tibetan Government official, the Tarjum, was in administrative charge of the district. The Tarjum was an extremely intelligent man who had travelled both to India and China to trade on behalf of the Lhasa Government. In his present appointment he received no salary but was expected to make what he could by hiring out the 106 Government yaks which were under his control. In the terrible winter of 1927, he told me, all but eight of these yaks had died, and he would have to replace them at his own expense before he was relieved of his post. He explained to me that when an official handed over charge to his successor he was expected to account for every item included in the list which he had himself signed when he entered on his office. This list contained details of the lands and flocks and herds which were vested in the official for the time being. But the most important item was that which concerned population; and each official was bound, under penalty of a heavy fine, to hand over to his successor as many head of men, women and children as had been entrusted to his care by his predecessor. There was little doubt that the population of Western Tibet had decreased greatly in the course of the last hundred years, and these provisions were probably designed by a Government which viewed the decrease in population with anxiety and hoped, by these means, to check the evil. But the provisions were entirely ineffective. An official taking over charge was paid a round sum by his predecessor to overlook the discrepancies between the actual number of the inhabitants within his jurisdiction and the number recorded in the charge sheet; and when this official's term of office expired he paid a similar sum of money to his successor for the same indulgence.

We arrived back at Gartok on September 17th, the day before the opening of the great Annual Fair known as the Char-chan. It was six weeks since we had left Gartok. During that period we had completed a circular tour of nearly 400 miles; and I had learnt by heart the greater part of Housman's 'Last Poems'.

CHAPTER 6

Return to India

THE great event of the Charchan was the horse-race, which was run on the morning of the first day of the Fair, after the moon had set and before the sun had risen over the neighbouring hills. I was determined to see the race and, early on September 18th, I set off with Raghu Das across the Gartok plain. The starting point of the race was at Nakyu, some seven miles to the south-east of Gartok. The course, which was about seven miles long, began over a boulder-strewn plain but continued over a smooth service of gravel and sparsely-growing grass. It ended at a point about three miles from Gartok, beneath the mountains to the north-east.

It was a still, cold morning and the moon was full as we made our way across the plain to the end of the course. As we went I was told stories of the great race and its long past. There were prizes for the first five ponies to come in. The owner of the winning pony received Rs 300/–, presented by the Lhasa Government, and a pony, presented by the Governor of Chumurti. The owner of the last pony to arrive was given a basketful of dung, a prize symbolic of his pony's position in the rear of the field. The contest was open only to officials, though whether this rule was really ancient, or whether it was a limitation imposed comparatively recently by the Garpons to restrict the entry and ensure that only those officially subordinate to them could compete, I do not know. On this occasion the twenty or thirty ponies entered for the race certainly belonged exclusively to members of the official class. The ponies were ridden by small boys twelve or thirteen years of age, mostly from Rudok, where they were specially trained for the occasion. Their clothes were bound tightly to them to prevent them from flapping in the wind. The racing colours of the owner, however, were not worn by the jockey but were painted on his mount.

The first prize was so valuable that the Garpons made great efforts to win it and used every means, scrupulous or otherwise, to achieve their object. Sometimes their retainers were stationed near the end of the course to prevent other competitors arriving first; more often, other ponies were not allowed to start until those belonging to the Garpons had already covered a mile or two. The pony with the most celebrated history was a chestnut from Minsar which, after winning the race two years in succession, appeared so likely to win in the future also that the Garpons attempted to buy it. The owner was naturally unwilling to part with it and for a time, while the two Garpons quarrelled as to which of them should have the privilege of buying it, he managed to keep the pony for himself. Eventually the Garpons settled their difference by a compromise; each was to own the horse in alternate years. And now the real owner had no longer any chance of keeping the pony for himself. The bargain finally driven was that the Garpons should hire the pony each year, for the day of the race only, for Rs 16/–. The pony actually won the race for five more years, so the Garpons' investment was a profitable one. It was said of this pony that in the race it used to lead the rest of the field by such a distance after two or three miles that it could afford to stop and graze off favourite patches of grass. Another celebrated pony, which belonged to the Senior Garpon, had run in the race several times. On the last occasion that it ran its girth broke, its rider was thrown and killed, and the pony finished the course on its own, coming in an easy first. As it belonged to the Senior Garpon, it was awarded the prize.

As we walked across the plain I heard these and many other legendary stories about the race; but soon, guided by the flare of torches, we arrived at the winning-post; and there, in the gathering light of the dawn (for the moon had set while we were still on our way), collected about a small pavilion in which the two Garpons were sitting, a crowd of about seventy men and horses came into view. The men were dressed in picturesque clothes, donned only on this great annual occasion, and wore elaborate, gaily coloured head-dresses. We had not waited more than ten minutes, and the sun had not yet appeared above the neighbouring hills, when the first of the competing ponies came in sight, closely followed by a second. Dismounting near the Garpons' pavilion the boy who had ridden the winning pony received the congratulations of the Senior Garpon, who owned the animal. The second pony, which belonged to the Rudok Jongpon, arrived, tactfully, some 50 yards behind the winner. Eight ponies completed the course; two others were seen careering across the plain in the direction of their grazing ground near Gartok itself, while the rest had given up after covering only part of the course. When the race was over, a procession was formed and the Tibetan spectators (the Garpons referred to them as their 'Army') rode back to Gartok, now in line, now in file, while the boy jockeys circled round them or made dashing displays of galloping in front. Before Gartok was reached a monument, built round bundles of prayers and other sacred charms, had to be passed. Round this the boy jockeys rode perhaps a dozen times, very slowly, and with heads bent. Nobody knew why this was done. It was the custom, I was told.

At about noon of the same day began a display of riding and shooting which lasted for several hours. The Garpons sat on a dais or platform made of dried mud and overhung by a large canopy, while below them, at a height above the ground proportionate to their rank, were seated the officials of Western Tibet or the agents whom they had sent to represent them. Members of the 'Army' which we had seen at the race earlier in the day, still in the same ceremonial dress, performed feats of horsemanship in front of the Garpons and the assembled crowd. Some, armed with bows and arrows and galloping on fast ponies, shot between two marks set up opposite the dais. Others performed the same feat with Tibetan matchlocks. At frequent intervals the Garpons were provided with refreshment by women chosen, I was surprised to hear, for their beauty. Finally, all the performers passed before the Garpons in review, each bowing low as he went by.

The main feature of the second day of the Fair was the dancing in the evening, which took place in front of a pavilion erected for the Garpons at one end of the Senior Garpon's house. I had seen a troupe of Tibetan dancers giving a performance at Gianima Chakra. On that occasion masks had been worn, men and women took part in the same dances, the steps had been vigorous and the music lively. At Gartok we saw a different style of dancing. The steps were uniformly slow, rhythmical and dignified; a reed pipe and a drum provided the simple musical accompaniment; the parties of men and the parties of women never joined in the same dance, and the different dances were given by groups of people from different districts. The costumes of the dancers were picturesque in the extreme, the head-dresses being particularly striking. The men from Purang, for instance, wore high conical hats of white cloth; while their women wore, hanging over the forehead in front and coming down to the neck behind, sheets of finely-chased silver studded with turquoise and fringed with tassels of silk from which depended small silver coins. At the end of their performance the dancers were rewarded with white scarves, the presentations being made, on behalf of the Garpons, by the senior member of their scarlet-robed staff.

During the ten days that we stayed at Gartok our little camp attracted many visitors. Dr Kanshi Ram was indefatigable in extracting decayed teeth and treating other physical ailments. But the chief attraction was our gramophone. When we played it for the first time a group of Dokpas quickly gathered round. It was interesting to watch their reactions when we put on a recording of a Tibetan song. First they stared intently at the gramophone, the actual source of the music. Then, as they recognised the tune, their faces lit up with surprise and pleasure. Next, they looked at their neighbours to see whether they too realised the miracle that was happening. Then, sitting with rapt faces, they beat time to the music. When one record was finished they did not wait for another. Bowing low to me, and putting out their tongues in token of respect, they hurried away to tell their friends of this extraordinary phenomenon.

The most interesting of my visitors was the Sarpon. The Sarpon's rank was equal to that of the Garpons, though they took precedence over him in their own territory. He administered the gold fields and was one of the two principal Government traders. Those to whom he wished to sell had to buy at his price. Not even the Garpons could refuse to buy what he offered them. The Sarpon, unlike the Garpons, was a permanent Government official, and he was allowed to take, as his annual salary, goods to the value of Rs 600/- from the Government stock. He was also allowed free transport and food. On the other hand, the taxes which he collected from the gold diggers (each man paid 6 annas weight of gold per year), and the fines which he imposed in criminal cases, went to the Government and not into his own pocket. The Sarpon himself was a young man of twenty-six, well educated and with pleasant manners. He told me that he went to Lhasa every year for the winter months and returned to Western Tibet in the spring with fresh supplies of cloth and tea for sale.

Another welcome visitor was the Governor of Chumurti through whose territory we had travelled on our way to Rudok. The ponies of his district were famous throughout the hill country for their powers of endurance. He told me that their numbers varied between 200 and 225, half of them being owned by residents of Spiti. The Spiti men paid R 1/- per pony per year for the privilege of grazing their animals on the Chumurti uplands. Half this sum, 8 annas, went to the Governor of Chumurti, and half to the Tibetan who looked after the pony. In addition to the pony which he presented to the winner of the annual horse-race, the Governor of Chumurti also gave a prize to the winner of the archery competition. That year the victor was one of the Senior Garpon's servants. The master, however, claimed the prize, the servant was not in a position to object, and my visitor had been compelled, much against his will, to present the prize to the Senior Garpon.

I was anxious to make inquiries from the Governor of Chumurti about certain dacoities which had been taking place in his district, but he assured me that there were now no dacoits left. Recently two dacoits had been robbing and looting extensively and had terrorised the whole countryside. He, however, had sent a band of twelve armed men after them. The dacoits took refuge in a cave at the top of a precipitous mountain and waited there till their pursuers came within earshot. Threatening to shoot if anyone came nearer, they disclosed the place where the looted goods had been concealed and promised that, if they were now allowed to go on their way, they would never again rob a resident of Chumurti. Their terms were accepted; the stolen goods were recovered, and the dacoits were escorted peacefully beyond the borders of the district.

One of the most interesting traders I met was a Ladakhi whose brother was that year in charge of the Lapchak Mission, an advance party of which I had met near Minsar bound for Lhasa with fifty yak-loads of dried apricots. This trader travelled every year from Leh to Lhasa, a journey of two and a half months, and sometimes returned through India. He had agents in Khotan and Yarkand who supplied him with the jade cups which were so highly prized at Lhasa. He told me, with what truth I do not know, that in 1921 a party of European archaeologists had made excavations in Khotan and, when they left, had taken away with them everything belonging to a Buddhist monastery there. Since that time the Buddhist inhabitants of Khotan had been steadily losing faith in their old religion and 800 of them had recently been converted to Islam. The trader assured me that the dismantling of their monastery was the sole cause of these Buddhists' dissatisfaction with the old faith and their conversion to the new one.

We left Gartok early on September 27th on our return journey to Simla. Travelling due west we made a long march to a camping ground on the further side of the Jongchung Pass. I had provided the majority of the party with ponies and I myself followed last on foot to ensure that nobody got left behind. The sun had set by the time I reached the camping ground. I found that the acting Chaprang Jongpon, who was on his way to Gartok, had also camped at the same spot and I spent an hour in his tent, drinking tea and talking, before I moved on to my own tent. I was then told that two of the Gurkhas had not yet arrived. This was a serious matter as it was a dark night and very cold, we were at a high altitude, and the Gurkhas did not know the way. I ordered rifle shots to be fired immediately and got ready to go out and look for the missing men. However, just as I and two others were setting off, a hail from the distance announced the Gurkhas' safe arrival. One of them had been unable to stand the strain of the ascent over the pass and the other had remained behind to help him. When I had crossed the pass they had been sheltering from the wind under cover of some rocks and had thus escaped my notice. In spite of the darkness they had not wandered far from the track and the rifle shots finally showed them the way to our camp.

We crossed the Laoche Pass (18,500 feet) on September 29th. The gradient on the ascent was steep but the surface was excellent and, though the march was one of twenty miles, there were no casualties on the way. On the following day we reached Shangtse, the summer headquarters of the Chaprang Jongpon. The village, a cluster of mud huts on level ground by the side of a broad stream, was surrounded by fields of barley stubble and, for the first time since we had crossed into Tibet three months earlier, we saw vegetables growing. The Jongpon's wife (who had the cosy title of Chum) sent us a welcome present of butter, cheese and vegetables. I was interested to learn about the marriage customs in this locality. Among the wealthier families, of whom there were very few, the girl made her own choice of a husband and a wedding took place in the customary fashion. But for the majority of girls there was no wedding ceremony. They lived in their homes and were visited there by the young man of their fancy. If children were born, girls remained with the mother, while boys, as soon as they were old enough to look after themselves, went to live with the father.

The first stages of our journey westward from Shangtse were relatively uneventful. The country was intersected by high ridges and deep gorges and the tracks which we had to follow were execrable. The villages we passed through showed signs of a prosperity which, except at Taklakot, I had not seen anywhere else in Tibet. The truth was that these villages, being sparsely scattered about a remote district where travel was both dangerous and strenuous, were rarely visited by officials, and signs of wealth, such as the possession of a stone house, were not so fatal as they were at places on the main Tibetan plateau where travelling was easier and officials could make frequent visits of inspection to see whether anybody was acquiring riches of any kind.

October 6th was a particularly arduous day. As a long and difficult march was in prospect I had given orders that baggage animals were to be ready for loading at sunrise. Long before dawn, however, I was woken up by the chattering and squabbling of the owners of the animals which, that day, included ponies and donkeys as well as yaks. The squabbling was, of course, about distribution of the loads. Normally dice were thrown, or lots drawn by means of straws, to decide this question. The person who threw lowest at dice, or the person who drew the shortest straw, took the heaviest load. But the system can produce anomalous results, as a light load can fall to the lot of a massive yak and a heavy load to the lot of an ancient, weedy pony. On this occasion, ignoring custom and tradition, I made the strongest animals carry the heaviest loads; and I silenced the protests that ensued by promising to pay a bonus to the owners of the more heavily-laden beasts.

At this point of my journey, a few miles east of the Shirang Pass, my maps were blank. They showed neither the Shirang Pass itself nor the range of mountains which it crosses. Our guides, however, were quite confident about the track to be followed. In the early afternoon, when only a single ravine separated us from the top of the pass, I descried, far away on a slope to the south, a herd of twenty-four burrhel (wild sheep). I doubted the wisdom of going after them so late in the day, with the high Shirang Pass still between us and our next camping ground. But meat was badly needed, so I and Raghu Das and one of the Gurkhas set off to stalk the burrhel. Seven pages of my diary are occupied with an account of the prolonged and exciting pursuit that followed. I shot two full-grown burrhel, had the carcasses loaded on to ponies, and still managed to reach the top of the pass in daylight. But there followed, while the light grew fainter and fainter, a long and hazardous descent down a track which, seldom more than 2 feet in width, wound between rocks or across precipitous slopes of shale. However, by the time it was completely dark (the moon was only two days old) we had reached the lower slopes of the range and the last two miles to our camping ground were comparatively easy.

On the following day we completed the descent to Miang. The track made a steep, zig-zag descent of 2,000 feet, was very rough and was much too narrow for laden animals. Bedding rolls were torn to ribbons by jagged, projecting rocks, and several items of luggage were broken or lost when loads fell off, as they frequently did, from stumbling or frightened animals. From Miang to Tiak, on the right bank of the Sutlej, the route was again difficult for the baggage animals. The track followed the course of a small stream which it crossed and re-crossed at frequent intervals. The stream flowed between high sandstone cliffs, and at times the passage between the cliffs was so narrow that the track disappeared into the stream.

Beyond Tiak the baggage animals followed one route, the rest of us another. The baggage animals crossed to the left bank of the Sutlej about a mile below Tiak. The yaks swam across first and the ponies followed with men clinging on to them. The rest of us crossed the Sutlej by a bridge, but our route, until we reached the bridge, was fraught with peril. I quote from my diary:

> It is a very rough and dangerous track. Where the cliffs – and the cliffs are rock now and no longer sandstone – come down sheer to the water's edge, the track rises up and finds a way along ledges in the rock face; where there are no ledges, there are rough wooden galleries which serve the purpose of a track. These wooden galleries are in the form of scaffolding, the interstices between the wooden poles being filled in, or rather covered over, with slabs of rock. In more than one place the track ascends or descends huge slabs of slanting rock with cracks in them which afford foothold enough for a man but none for a pony. When we came to such places, the ponies were grasped firmly by the bridle, near the mouth, by one man, and by the tail by another man, and with this support they managed to scramble across somehow or other. At one such place an orderly tried to pull up the Doctor's pony before seeing that it was supported from behind; the animal of course slipped and came slithering down nearly on top of me as I followed behind. It very nearly went over the edge (there was a drop of 200–300 feet), but fortunately regained its balance just in time.

We were now separated from Indian territory only by the Shipki Pass, which traversed a cliff face high above the Sutlej. Having crossed this pass, not without difficulty and danger, we arrived at Pooh, where the Trade Agency records were stored, on October 13th. There, for the first time for three and a half months, I enjoyed the luxury of sleeping under a roof and in a bed. Having halted at Pooh for six days, we left for Simla on October 19th. Marching by the usual easy stages and doubling only one or two of the shortest ones, we arrived at Simla, nearly five months after we had left it, on the morning of November 2nd.

Lalage Thompson, whom I was to marry on December 7th, was in Delhi with her parents. Accompanied by Raghu Das I left Simla by train on November 3rd and arrived in Delhi on the morning of November 4th. If Lalage expected to meet a bronzed and handsome explorer she must have received a severe shock. To protect my face from the ravages of fierce sun and icy winds I had grown, while I was in Tibet, a large and bushy beard. This I had shaved off when I reached Simla and now, when I stepped on to the platform of the railway station at Delhi, my appearance was far from prepossessing. My forehead was scarlet, my lips were cracked, my nose was a chunk of raw meat; the rest of my face, where it had been protected by the beard, was a sickly white. I looked exactly like a clown.

If Lalage was dismayed by my appearance, she kept her disappointment to herself. And she welcomed the odd assortment of presents I had brought her – earrings of turquoise and silver, jade cups from Khotan and Yarkand, bowls of rosewood from Nepal lined with silver from Lhasa, the Court dress of a Jongpon, saddle rugs woven in China from the wool of Tibetan rams and the fine under-hair of Kashmiri goats, an amber necklace from Burma, skins of stone marten and snow lynx. My own great delight, however, was to have named after my bride (however cryptically) the pass above Deboche which I had discovered and crossed on July 11th. This was to be known thenceforward as the Laji La.

Raghu Das, in his full-length lambskin tunic with its purple girdle, attracted as many curious glances in Delhi as I had done at Gartok in my sports coat and flannel trousers. For him the visit to Delhi was a visit to Wonderland. Delhi was as full of marvels for him as Tibet had been for me. Once, as a small boy, he had visited Dehra Dun with his father and had seen railway trains and motor cars. But he had never travelled in them. Now he was to travel, not only in trains and cars, but in an aeroplane.

As we motored to the Delhi aerodrome, an aeroplane flew over us. At first he thought it was a bird. When he saw that it was a machine, 'How does it know where to go?' he asked. I explained that it had a pilot to control it. A Gipsy Moth was waiting for us on the aerodrome. As I strapped him into the passenger's seat he asked whether he was to go up alone. He had no fear, only curiosity. After his flight he was quite speechless with happy excitement; and I felt that I had found a means of rewarding him, however inadequately, for the faithful service he had given me.

Before Raghu Das left I presented him with a rifle and 200 cartridges and a firearms licence. This, I knew, would raise his status in his native country of Bushahr. But the story of Raghu Das has a sad ending. Returning to his home in the highlands of Bushahr, he told such improbable stories of his flight in an aeroplane, of motor cars speeding along tarred roads, of cinemas and telephones and other strange phenomena, that he suffered the fate of many who have travelled in foreign lands: people simply did not believe him. And, as his credit suffered, so his business as a trader declined until, when I last heard of him, he was living in sadly straitened circumstances.

Having lived for so many months at an altitude of 15,000 feet or more I now found it difficult to acclimatise myself to normal conditions, and I suffered for a time from headaches and insomnia. I also had to relearn the uses of a knife and fork. My week's leave in Delhi was soon over and I returned to Simla for three weeks' concentrated work on the numerous reports that I was submitting to the Government. One of my recommendations resulted, I am glad to say, in the appointment of Dr Kanshi Ram, the Agency Doctor, as British Trade Agent in Gartok for the ensuing year; and he carried out his duties so efficiently that he continued to hold the appointment for many years to come.

CHAPTER 7

Transfer to the Foreign and Political Department

LALAGE and I were married in St James's Church, Delhi, on December 7th, 1929. In a letter to my parents I wrote: 'I was in a state of terror before the wedding just as I used to be before house-matches at school, but the best man comforted me.' As the bride came up the aisle, the best man had whispered to me, not very gallantly, 'I wouldn't be in your shoes for a thousand pounds!'

We spent our honeymoon as the guests of H.H. the Nawab of Rampur in his country palace at Shahabad. We had the palace to ourselves though there was a large staff of servants to wait on us and the approaches were guarded by armed sentries. Beyond the palace grounds was an ornamental lake, some fifty acres in area. There were, too, extensive orange groves, the home of peacock and partridge but also the haunt of leopards. It was a romantic spot well suited to the occasion of our stay there.

After spending Christmas at Delhi I returned to Simla, where I worked for a fortnight on the topographical material I had collected in Tibet. Before I had started on my journey the Survey of India had provided me with outline maps of areas of which geographers knew little or nothing. These I had filled in to the best of my ability, and I had supplemented these records with detailed barometer readings and with numerous photographs. By myself I could have done nothing with this material. But a brilliant young officer of the Survey of India, Captain Crone, knew exactly how to interpret the data I provided; and his skilled craftsmanship converted my raw material into the finished product of Maps.

From mid-January until July 1930 I was in Delhi undergoing

judicial training. Gandhi's 'Passive Resistance' movement was at its height, and I was able to watch its progress in Delhi from a good observation post. A letter which I wrote on June 29th to a cousin, Maisie Fletcher, gives a brief description of my activities during this period and contains some pertinent reflections.

> Since January [I wrote] I have been undergoing a course of what is known as Judicial Training. In practice I spend the day in my own Court trying civil cases, and the only supervision I get is indirect, when cases decided by me go before the District Judge on appeal. During the first fortnight of May, however, when riots in the city caused a good deal of excitement, I attached myself to Mr Johnson, the officiating Chief Commissioner, as a kind of unofficial Personal Assistant and helped, as well as I could, in the cyphering and decyphering of telegrams and other confidential work. I mayn't have helped much, but at least I was in the interesting position of being at the centre of affairs and knowing what plans were being concerted by Government to meet local difficulties.
>
> Executive officers have been having a dreadful time. Their every action has to be justified to the Government of India who, in turn, have to justify the action of their officers to the Government at home. The result of this is that executive officers have continually, in the interests of higher policy, to countenance loss of life when such loss could certainly be avoided. At Delhi, for instance, a clash between the crowd and the police on May 6th resulted in 30 deaths and at least 200 seriously injured. On the morning of that day there was a small crowd which had openly declared its intention of picketing the Law Courts and preventing the transaction of any Government business. (This was to show sympathy with Gandhi in his arrest.) This could not be tolerated: and it was obvious that if the police had charged that small crowd with 'lathis', and this action had been followed up by an order prohibiting the holding of any procession, all the subsequent trouble would have been averted and the matter would have ended with a few bruises and a lot of talk. But, in spite of all its advantages, that action could not be taken as the crowd had not, at that time, shown any violence, and the Chief Commissioner could not have justified his

> action *on paper*. So the day wore on; the crowd grew bigger and bigger; it got more and more excited, and finally attacked the Deputy Commissioner and the Superintendent of Police. The police made lathi charges; the crowd retaliated with brick-bats; and the day ended with an order forbidding processions – and peace, or comparative peace, ensued. But the tragedy is that those lives were lost, and all those people injured, without any necessity. Every one of us realised that it could all have been avoided by firm action at the beginning of the day; but that action could not have been defended on paper. Whereas, by waiting till the crowd had become violent, the Chief Commissioner had his political justification for taking action against the crowd. The fact of the matter is that it has become impossible for an executive officer, without being censured by the Government, to keep order; he is only allowed to restore it!

Complaints such as this must have come from District Officers in Africa in the 1950's as frequently as they came from India in the 1930's. The next paragraph of my letter contains a criticism of the British Government of the day which, I now see, is too harsh. But it contains also a true appreciation of the nature of the dilemma which confronted, and still confronts, British Colonial Secretaries. This is what I wrote:

> The root of the trouble lies in this, I think – that we have a Democratic Government at home which has inherited an Imperial policy abroad. The Labour Government cannot afford to dispense with that policy and dare not, for fear of being untrue to its own ideals, enforce it. And the muddled, middle policy which it has adopted – of leaving Lord Irwin to carry the whole load on his own shoulders – may indeed relieve it of the responsibility of making a decision, but only embarrasses officials charged with actual administration out here.

In July I was posted to Lahore as Additional District Magistrate. In the Punjab, as in Delhi, there had been widespread disturbances. The Courts were overloaded with cases of sedition and unlawful assembly. Worst of all, the Sikhs, a militant race, had been told that the Delhi police had fired on a

Gurdwara (Sikh temple) and in protest they were refusing to pay their land revenue.

My first duty was to tour the Lahore District and enforce the collection of land revenue. It was a difficult task, partly because the Sikhs themselves, unless one knows them well, are difficult people to deal with; partly because the heat was intense and tempers are always frayed in the weeks immediately preceding the monsoon. But my plan of campaign worked well. Wherever I went I summoned the village headmen and told them the true story of the Gurdwara incident, and of how ne'er-do-wells had used the Gurdwara as a base from which to attack the police. Their anger, I told them, was justified: but it should be directed, not against the Government, whose agents, the police, had acted in self-defence, but against those evil men who had first violated the sanctity of the shrine. As I myself had been in Delhi at the time of the incident, and as I had visited the Gurdwara and seen the actual damage done by police bullets – it was only trivial – my words carried conviction. The agitation soon died down and payment of land revenue was resumed.

Returning from my tour I attacked the arrears of work that had accumulated in my Court. I stayed at the Punjab Club, which was cool even in the hottest weather. The furnishings of the Club, it is true, were gloomy and drab and unrelieved by any touch of lightness or colour, of taste or fancy; and the heavy air of the public rooms was permanently tainted with a slightly acrid smell compounded, probably, of stale sweat and furniture polish. But in July, when the midday sun scorched the skin and its glare oppressed the eyes, to escape from the blazing heat outside into the cool darkness of the Club was truly a blessed relief.

One morning I went down to my Court as usual but found the premises deserted. No police with their prisoners, no pleaders taking instructions from their clients, no petition-writers, no groups of witnesses discussing the evidence they were going to give. I sent for the Court watchman and asked him what had happened. He told me – what I had stupidly forgotten – that the Courts were closed as it was a Mohammedan holiday. Gratefully I returned to my room at the Punjab Club to make up arrears of work in comparative comfort.

I was not the only person to forget that the Courts would be closed that day. Twenty-four hours earlier a group of Hindu youths, pledged to rid India of foreign rule, had met in a secluded spot on the banks of the Ravi river. They had with them a small stock of hand-made bombs. They tested one or two of these and found the results satisfactory. Having discussed various plans they finally decided that on the following day one of their number would go to the Court of the District Magistrate and throw a bomb at him while another would visit my Court and similarly dispose of me. Lots were drawn to determine which two of this little group were to do the actual deed; and fate chose Ram Swarup and Narain Das.

On the following day these two youths, each with a bomb under his arm, made their way to the Courts shortly before noon, only to find the doors closed and the precincts deserted. Disappointed, they started to walk home. But the day was hot, and excitement had made them dry-throated. They stopped to buy some milk. As Ram Swarup raised his arm to take his glass of milk he accidentally released the bomb he was carrying. It fell and exploded, killing him and wounding his companion. Half a mile away, in the Punjab Club, I had given up the struggle to work. As Ram Swarup was ordering his milk, I was sipping a long iced lime-juice-and-soda, idly turning over the pages of *The Field* and day-dreaming, as exiles do, of sights and sounds of Home.

I had not been many weeks in Lahore when I received orders to report for duty in Simla, the summer headquarters both of the Punjab Government and of the Government of India. I had been appointed Under-Secretary to the Punjab Government in the Department of Local Self-Government, later known as the Transferred Departments. The first Minister under whom I served was Dr Gokal Chand Narang, but his place was taken, shortly after my arrival, by the young and rising political star,

Sir Firoz Khan Noon. The Secretary of the Department, and my immediate superior, was Mr Mitchell, who had been so kind to me at Lyallpur.

As an Under-Secretary I had nothing to do with policy. But an immense volume of detailed administrative work came to my office table every day. Mr Mitchell had impressed on me the virtues of accuracy, and I spent long hours laboriously and conscientiously checking Municipal Regulations and Bye-Laws, lists of local tariffs and the like. I was at the office by nine o'clock every morning, studied files while I ate my sandwich lunch, had no tea, and seldom left before seven o'clock in the evening. I might have been a civil servant in Whitehall. It was a miserable life, for Lalage as well as for me, but at least I was spared the heat of the Punjab plains.

In October the Punjab Government moved down, and I with them, to their winter headquarters in Lahore. The work remained heavy. However, there were compensations. I could see from my office window the famous field-gun, Zam-Zammeh, round which Kipling had played as a child; and I was encouraged by Sir Firoz Khan Noon to take time off for hunting. Indeed, I saw more of my Minister on the hunting field than I did in the office. But a change in my fortunes, a change of great consequence to my future, was even then imminent.

In 1926, after I had passed the open competitive examination for the Indian Civil Service, I was required by the India Office to fill in a form which contained the following question: 'To what Province do you wish to be posted? State your preferences in order of priority: 1. .... 2. .... 3. ....' I consulted Sir John Thompson and he strongly advised me to make the Punjab my first preference. One of the reasons on which he based this advice was that the Punjab Government and the Government of India both moved to Simla for the summer, and their close association, he said, would make it easier for me to obtain a transfer to the Foreign and Political Department if I so desired at a later stage.

When I filled up the India Office form I had stated my

preferences thus: 1. Punjab. 2. Punjab. 3. Punjab. I had been summoned to the India Office and there interviewed by an indignant Assistant Secretary.

'You must give the names of three Provinces,' he told me, 'in the order of your choice. You may certainly put the Punjab first. But what are your second and third choices?'

'I have no second and third choices,' I replied. 'My only choice is the Punjab.'

'But what if you can't be sent to the Punjab? Have you no preference among the other Provinces?'

'No,' I said. 'If I am not sent to the Punjab I shall not go out to India at all.'

The Assistant Secretary was much put out. He argued with me, but I was obdurate. It was only when I had left his office that I had qualms. Had I, perhaps, gone too far? Had I been too uncompromising? However, all was well. Sir John Thompson suggested to Sir Malcolm Hailey, the Governor of the Punjab, that I would be a useful recruit to the Punjab cadre; Sir Malcolm Hailey asked the India Office to send me to his Province, and the India Office duly, perhaps reluctantly, agreed to do so.

While I was in Tibet I had thought much about my future. The Punjab was certainly a magnificent Province. But members of the Services in British India were the target of incessant vilification, abuse and insult by nationalist politicians. The prospect of being endlessly humiliated was not alluring. The Foreign and Political Department, on the other hand, opened up a pleasing vista of possibilities and uncertainties. I might be sent to an Indian State anywhere from Travancore to Kashmir. I might be sent to Persia or Afghanistan, to Nepal or Sikkim or even Aden; or I might be given an administrative post in the North-West Frontier Province, Baluchistan or Ajmer-Merwara. In any case, I reflected, I would be out of range of irresponsible criticism from a hostile Legislative Assembly. And so, for better or worse, I had decided to apply for transfer to the Foreign and Political Department; and in August 1929 I had sent in my application from (of all places) Tuling.

The Punjab Government had replied promptly and bluntly. They were not prepared, they said, to recommend my application to the Government of India. They were already short of officers and could not spare another one.

When I returned to India I consulted Sir John Thompson. He told me that, though the Punjab Government were fully entitled to say that they could not spare me, they were at fault in refusing even to forward my application to the Government of India. Accordingly, when I told the Government of India what had happened, they directed the Punjab Government to send on my application, and later informed me that my desire to join the Foreign and Political Department had been 'noted'.

There the matter had rested for nearly a year. But the first week of November 1930 brought two surprises. On November 1st I received a letter from the Punjab Government informing me that I had been appointed to officiate as Deputy Commissioner, Dera Ghazi Khan, and that I was to hand over charge of my duties as Under-Secretary on November 15th. This was exciting news. Such rapid promotion was all the more gratifying for being entirely unexpected. I began to make preparations for the move when, later in the week, the Chief Secretary rang me up on the telephone. The Foreign and Political Department, he told me, had asked for my transfer. The Governor was not prepared to let me go. He was sorry to have to stand in my way but the shortage of trained I.C.S. officers was such that he simply could not spare me. Had I anything to say?

'Yes, Sir,' I replied. 'I have a lot to say. My only reason for joining the I.C.S. and coming out to India at all was to enter the Foreign and Political Department. If I cannot do that I might as well resign and go home.'

'Do you really mean that?' he asked. And he went on to reproach me for ingratitude to the Punjab Government which had taken so much trouble to train me as an administrator and had treated me so generously in every way. I hadn't really meant what I said, and might have weakened in my resolution if he had appealed to my better nature or, indeed, to my vanity.

But I didn't like being scolded, so I re-affirmed my intention of resigning if I were not allowed my transfer.

A few hours later the Governor, Sir Geoffrey de Montmorency, sent for me. Tall and distinguished-looking, his dark hair tinged with grey, this gifted man, by his industry and intelligence, had built for himself a great career in the wake of another great servant of the State, Sir Malcolm Hailey. Now he looked at me and said, quite quietly, 'Do you really mean that you are going to leave us if we don't let you go to the Foreign and Political Department?'

'I am afraid so, Your Excellency,' I replied. Unless I had been prepared to make the humiliating confession that I had been bluffing when I spoke to the Chief Secretary, I could make no other reply.

Sir Geoffrey did not remonstrate or argue with me. He simply said that he would think the matter over. And the following day the Chief Secretary told me over the telephone, very huffily, that His Excellency had agreed to my transfer. He added some uncomplimentary remarks of his own, but his exact words have (I am glad to say) long since passed from my memory.

I did not have to travel far to join my first post in the Foreign and Political Department. I was appointed Under-Secretary to the Agent to the Governor General for the Punjab States, Sir James Fitzpatrick, whose headquarters, like those of the Provincial Government, were in Lahore. The post I was to fill had been vacant for some weeks and, when I entered my new office, I found it stacked from floor to ceiling with files requiring attention. It seemed to me that I would have to work unremittingly for many weeks before I could clear away so many hundredweights of paper. I was mistaken. Some of the files contained prima facie evidence in extradition cases, and these required a modicum of scrutiny; but the rest were applications for passports, gun-licences and the like, and so speedily did I dispose of them ('dispose them off' my babu would have said) that in a couple of days my office table was clear. Nor, when I called for more work, was any forthcoming. 'This,' I thought to myself, 'is fine. Already I am halfway to achieving the Roman ideal of "otium cum dignitate". I have the "otium" and the "dignitas" will follow soon enough.'

My rejoicing was premature, for the period of my leisure lasted less than a week. The Secretary, Gyan Nath, had been despatched by Sir James Fitzpatrick to Bilaspur State to deal with civil disturbances there. Now he returned in a condition of great distress. Insurgents had attacked the Central Gaol, he reported, and had released all the prisoners. He himself had been fired on by the rebels and had barely escaped with his life.

Sir James Fitzpatrick realised that prompt action was required if the trouble was not to spread. The Lahore Command promised a detachment of troops from Coke's Rifles; and the Punjab Government agreed to place at his disposal a force of 100 Special Armed Police provided that they were put in the charge of a British Officer. This stipulation, of course, let out Gyan Nath, and brought me in.

I found out what I could about Bilaspur State. The ruler, H.H. Raja Anand Chand, was still a minor and, since 1927, the State had been run by a Council of Administration under the supervision of the Agent to the Governor-General. The State itself, about the size of a small English county, nestled in the foot-hills of the Himalayas and was divided by the Sutlej river into two portions of roughly equal size. The capital, also called Bilaspur, was situated on the left bank of the Sutlej and was thirty or forty miles away from the railhead at Rupar. The scattered population of the State numbered little more than 100,000, while the local security forces (troops and police combined) amounted to fewer than 200.

My instructions were simple enough: to restore order. But to carry out the instructions was not so simple. On the march up from Rupar I began to realise that the officer in charge of the detachment from Coke's Rifles, an Indian Army Captain with a good deal of seniority, was not at all the sort of person whom I myself would have chosen for an expedition of this kind. He took exception to my walking with the men instead of riding. An officer, he asserted, has a duty to be fresh at the end of the day's march. I, for my part, protested against his rigid application of the rule of fifty minutes' marching, ten minutes' rest. Such a rule might be reasonable enough in the plains: in hilly country its enforcement was absurd.

As we planned our campaign in our headquarters at Bilaspur, our mutual antipathy blossomed into open enmity. He refused to take his troops into the hilly northern portion of the State, where the seat of the trouble lay, without a guarantee that supplies of water, fuel and food (eggs, milk, meat, vegetables) would be available at every prospective camping-ground. I could, of course, give no such guarantee. Deadlock ensued. But a night's rest, and the common sense of Lieutenant Lewis, the second-in-command, who was as co-operative as his Captain was recalcitrant, broke the deadlock. The Captain, it was decided, should take the majority of his own men on a flag-march through the southern part of the State, where the terrain was relatively easy and supplies were readily available; Lewis and I, with all the Special Police and the remaining few troops, would undertake the much more arduous expedition into the hilly tract to the north.

At the end of ten days one or other of the two small forces had visited practically every village in the State. In the south there was no trouble – there never had been. In the north we made a few arrests of wanted men, but many of the principal agitators had already fled the State. The cause of the revolt, I soon discovered, had been gross maladministration by the Council. I was sorry for the men we arrested. If I had been a subject of the Raja of Bilaspur in 1930 I would certainly have been one of the rebels. They had to be punished severely, of course. But I was confident that when, in two years' time, the young Raja assumed full ruling powers, he would grant a general amnesty. And this, in fact, he did.

We completed our mission in the first week of December. Order was now restored, and I submitted to Sir James

Fitzpatrick proposals for the complete reorganisation of the administration. The Captain was in good humour after his successful flag-march, and we had a happy reconciliation. Leaving Bilaspur on December 3rd I arrived at Delhi on December 5th where, the previous day, Lalage had given birth to her first child, our daughter Imogen.

CHAPTER 8

Ajmer—Locusts and a Leopard

I HAD been little more than a month in the Punjab States Agency when I was transferred to Ajmer as Assistant Commissioner. Ajmer was the capital of the small but strategically important Province of Ajmer-Merwara, in the heart of Rajputana. It was an ancient city with a romantic history. There, in the year 1615, in a marble pavilion on the shores of Lake Anasagar, the Moghul Emperor, Jahangir, had received Sir Thomas Roe, Britain's first Ambassador to India. There, too, was the Dargah Sharif, shrine of the Muslim Saint, Muin-ud-din Chishti; and only a few miles away were the temples and sacred lake of Pushkar, as famous a place of pilgrimage for Hindus as was the Dargah Sharif for Mohammedans. Ajmer was also a centre of worship for the Jains, the Hindu sect who hold all animal life, even of insects, to be sacred.

In the actual city of Ajmer there was much religious intolerance, and communal clashes were frequent. In the surrounding district, however, Muslims and Hindus got on together well enough, and it was a common sight to see Hindus leaving offerings at the shrine of a Pir (Muslim holy man). At Beawar, indeed, thirty miles south-west of Ajmer, both Hindus and Mohammedans would annually gather at the tomb of a Christian, Colonel Dixon, to strew flowers on his grave and pray for his soul. Forgotten by his countrymen, Colonel Dixon is yet remembered by the descendants of those whom he saved from drought and famine more than a century ago. As Superintendent of Ajmer-Merwara in the 1830's he was responsible for the administration of a tract of arid, hilly country whose inhabitants depended for their livelihood on the cultivation of monsoon crops. When the rains failed, or when they came unseasonably, the inhabitants starved; or, rather, the women and children starved while the men formed themselves into robber gangs which went marauding and foraging far afield. Colonel Dixon taught these people how to build dams and so conserve the rain-water which had formerly gone to waste. It was said, with what truth I do not know, that the tragedy of the Mutiny so affected this much-loved man that he died of a broken heart. But his dams survive, as does his memory in the land where he built them.

The Assistant Commissioner exercised substantial criminal powers as a magistrate and was also responsible, under the Commissioner, for the collection of land revenue, of excise duties and of income tax. The Commissioner, Mr Gibson, was a middle-aged bachelor of independent mind and means. At an earlier stage of his life he had published a small book of poems. I learned some of these by heart but never quite dared to quote from them in any of the official reports that I submitted to him. He was much loved by the people of Ajmer, and those who served under him were devoted to him.

Mr Gibson told me, as soon as I arrived in Ajmer, that I would become involved in two disputes that had been going on for decades. One concerned rights in the endowments of the Dargah Sharif; the other was between two factions of Brahmins at Pushkar, each of which claimed the major share of pilgrims' offerings. Mr Gibson told me that, if I liked, I could try to effect a compromise between the contesting parties though I would only be wasting my time. What I was not to do was to force a decision in either case. If I did that, he warned me, bloodshed would certainly follow. I took Mr Gibson's wise advice and, when I left Ajmer in the spring of 1932, the two disputes were still simmering like kettles. I had done nothing to bring them to the boil.

I have said that those who served under Mr Gibson were devoted to him. This was at least partly because he did not hesitate to give them his protection whenever need for this arose. In 1931 the Government of India embarked on an economy drive. Not content with cutting salaries, they also sought to impose a 10 per cent reduction in the strength of revenue establishments. As soon as we in Ajmer received orders to this effect, I worked out a scheme to make them operative. My proposals involved the discharge of some twenty Government employees whose work would be redistributed in a manner which seemed to me fair and practicable. Mr Gibson sent for me.

'You don't really suggest, do you,' he said, 'that we should sack twenty men like this?'

'Well, Sir, I don't see any alternative. These are the Government's orders and I suppose we have to carry them out.'

'No, no,' Mr Gibson replied, 'we can't treat our people like that. How can we expect loyal service from our subordinates if we let them down the moment there is a bit of trouble?'

'What can we do, then?'

'The Political Department know that we have this locust invasion on our hands. Go back to your office and draft an Express Letter asking for sanction to employ forty additional revenue staff. Say that twenty of these will only be required temporarily, until the locusts have been dealt with, but that the other twenty will be needed permanently as we are already under-staffed on the revenue side and collections of land revenue are beginning to fall into arrears.'

'Very well, Sir,' I replied. 'But what are we to do about these other orders for the 10 per cent cut in establishment?'

'Forget about them.'

I was dubious then, and am still dubious, about the morality of Mr Gibson's expedient. Should loyalty to subordinates take precedence over loyalty in carrying out Government policy? However that may be, the result was what Mr Gibson had foreseen: though we got no extra staff, we also had to surrender none.

As a probationer in the Foreign and Political Department I now had to pass a Departmental examination. The papers were to be set by Mr Gibson but the answers would be marked in Delhi. I expected no difficulty in 'satisfying' my examiners in most of the subjects. But one paper was on Tod's *Annals and Antiquities of Rajasthan*, a formidable encyclopaedia of information on everything that concerned Rajputana and the leading Rajput families, including genealogies that went back to the Sun and the Moon. I went to Mr Gibson.

'Must I really read all this?' I asked. 'It would take me days and days, and my work would suffer.'

'You mean,' he said, 'that I would have to do some of your work for you?'

'Yes, Sir.'

'Well, I don't propose to do that. I think that, when the time comes, you will not find the questions unanswerable.'

I took the hint. The pages of my copy of Tod's great work are still uncut. But I passed the examination with flying colours. It was not difficult to answer such questions as: 'Tod says the Rajputs are a very gallant race. Do you agree?'

If Mr Gibson was an unusual man, so too was my principal assistant in the field of Excise and Income Tax, Diwan Bahadur Pandit Pyarai Lal. Small and bearded, with twinkling eyes, a shrewd face and a nervous manner, he had two disparate ambitions in life; to serve God and to serve the Assistant Commissioner. Of a long line of Assistant Commissioners the one whom he most revered was a certain Captain Shuldham who, I was told, would dress up in native costume when on the hunt for dope smugglers. The one whom he least revered was my immediate predecessor, Captain Bedi, who, to Pyarai Lal's great disappointment, had preferred to spend his energies on the pursuit of partridge and sandgrouse rather than of smugglers. To my family and me Pyarai Lal was a true friend, and we grew to love him dearly for his quite exceptional qualities of fidelity and unselfishness. And yet, high-principled as he was, he unashamedly used his official position to ensure that his personal servant, Neola Ram, was annually given contracts for a number of remunerative opium and liquor shops. In such matters, as I have already observed, the Western and Oriental viewpoints are poles apart.

My chief Revenue assistant, Rai Bahadur Ram Swarup Rawat, was a dapper little man, honest, industrious and competent. It was mainly thanks to him that I was able to carry to a successful conclusion a campaign which, at times, seemed but a forlorn hope. The campaign was against locusts, which invaded, in their billions, the sandy, semi-desert area to the north and west of Ajmer.

The habits of the desert locust are well known. The mature female insect deposits some 300–400 eggs a few inches below the surface of the ground and dies within a week of doing so. A fortnight or three weeks later the eggs hatch out into tiny ant-like 'hoppers'. These hoppers move slowly across the countryside, in massive armies, devouring wholesale every growing thing that comes in their path. Entomologists distinguish five separate stages in the growth of the hopper, the first four stages each taking about a week and the last stage about a fortnight. To the unscientific observer it seems only that, with every day that passes, the hoppers become stronger and more active. To begin with they have the size and mobility of ants: after a month they are as large and active as grasshoppers: six or seven weeks from the date of hatching they take to themselves wings and fly away, bringing ruin to every peasant on whose land they may chance to settle.

In my war against the locusts I enjoyed a number of advantages that are normally denied to military commanders. In the first place, my enemy was the enemy of all mankind and I could expect full co-operation in my campaign of destruction. Again, the speed and direction of the enemy's movements, once he was located, could be predicted with a reasonable degree of certainty. Finally, the extent of his vulnerability was known precisely. He was most vulnerable as an immobile egg – if he could be found; as a hopper he became progressively less vulnerable; once he had acquired the full strength of his wings he was invulnerable, indestructible. The whole force of the attack had, therefore, to be concentrated on the locusts during the first stages of their life cycle.

Ram Swarup and I organised an information service throughout the many hundreds of square miles for which we were responsible, and plotted on field maps the areas where eggs had been laid. Where water was available these areas were flooded and the eggs rendered infertile. Where there was no water, we arranged for the land to be cross-ploughed by teams of oxen from adjacent villages.

In spite of all these efforts we heard, when the incubation period was over, of the emergence of countless swarms of hoppers. We had distributed many tons of sodium fluosilicate which, mixed with bran, was supposed to provide an effective poison bait. But the Ajmer hoppers of 1931, at least in the first stages of their life, seemed only to thrive on the poison. We soon found that the most effective way of destroying the hoppers was by driving them into trenches and there burying them. It would be seen, at dawn, in which direction the massed hoppers were moving. All available labour would be mobilised to dig, across their line of advance, deep, broad trenches, and to set up canvas screens on the flanks of the moving army to guide it in the desired direction. When one line of trenches was filled to overflowing with hoppers it would be earthed over and stamped down and another line prepared further on. And so, while the hours of daylight lasted, the work of destruction continued. It continued all day and every day for several weeks until, in the end, I was able to claim that no single hopper had survived.

My best allies were birds. Kites, rosy pastors and bee eaters never ceased devouring hoppers. Villagers whose crops were in imminent danger co-operated enthusiastically. Others were less keen and had to be given threats or promises as seemed appropriate. Jains refused to help at all as it was contrary to their religious beliefs to take life. Under pressure, however, they agreed to pay for the labour which I hired to do their share of the work.

The villagers in the locust-affected areas were mostly peasant proprietors who paid land revenue to the Government. To the south of Ajmer, however, most of the land was owned by petty Rajput chiefs, known as Istimrardars, who held a privileged position vis-à-vis both the Government and their tenants. Some of these Istimrardars were responsible men who carried out their magisterial duties efficiently and were solicitous of their tenants' welfare. Others had succumbed to the temptations of idleness and comparative wealth. Living in isolated fortresses, exempt from those tests of courage and leadership which clan warfare had formerly imposed, the worst of them had degenerated into arrogant, lecherous, drunken bullies. Such men made rapacious and oppressive landlords, and their tenants were easy prey for the Congress agitators who were, in 1931, fanning the flames of agrarian revolt. But the Istimrardars, however debauched some of their number might be, were entitled to the protection of their rights, and I had the distasteful task of affording them that protection. If I had little sympathy for the more worthless of the Istimrardars, I had even less sympathy for the town-bred agitators who, without real interest in the peasants or any genuine desire to improve their lot, were simply using them as pawns in the game of Nationalist politics. My sympathies lay wholly with the oppressed peasantry and, where the law gave me scope to do so, I did not hesitate to relieve them of their burdens.

Much of my time was spent in Court. The work was never monotonous but, in the hot weather, could be trying to the temper. On one occasion, I regret to recall, I flung a heavy glass paper-weight at an inattentive orderly. Fortunately for him – and for me – my aim was bad, and the paper-weight crashed through a glass partition into a neighbouring room. I punished myself by paying for the repairs. On another occasion my Court was flooded by an unruly mob of demonstrators waving Congress flags and shouting Nationalist slogans. They filled the whole of the body of the Court but refrained from invading the dais on which I was sitting. They made a deafening uproar but I affected to take no notice and continued to record notes on the case I was trying. Luck, the Superintendent of

Police, was in his office only a hundred yards away. To him I sent a brief note. 'Dear Jim,' I wrote, 'my Court is crammed with a howling mob of Congress-walas. Could you clear it for me, please?' Within a couple of minutes Luck himself, accompanied by three or four constables, burst in through a back door. He did not have to use force. His sudden appearance and resolute mien so dismayed this sorry band of timid patriots that, one and all, they took to their heels and fled.

My predecessor, Captain Bedi, was such a keen 'shikari' that he had never scrupled to adjourn the proceedings of his Court when he heard that there was promise of getting a few shots at sandgrouse, partridge or duck. I was a less determined sportsman but did one day adjourn my Court at noon when the headmen of a village fifteen miles away arrived with news that a leopard had been disturbed immediately after killing a goat that morning. The leopard, they said, would certainly return to the kill later in the day, and they begged me to shoot it for them. 'We are poor men and this robber has already taken more than a dozen of our goats.'

I arrived at the site of the kill armed with a rifle and a shotgun. At that time I knew nothing about the art of shooting leopards, but the terrain, even to my unpractised eye, looked singularly unpromising. The dead goat was lying on level ground in an open space with no suitable cover, and certainly no tree, anywhere near. I had no idea how, or where, to conceal myself. But the villagers had a plan. Some 12 or 15 yards from the goat they dug a pit about 4 feet deep. Round this they arranged a light screen of thorn scrub. I was to wait in the pit and shoot the leopard when it returned to the kill!

It did not seem to me to be at all a good plan. I could not see clearly through the thorn screen which, while it obstructed my view, offered me no protection. If the leopard came in daylight it would almost certainly see me before I saw it. If it came after dark I would not be able to use the rifle as I could not see its sights, having only a hand-torch with me. Finally, whether there was light or no light, the pit might well be directly in the line of the leopard's approach to its prospective meal. What would happen then? No, it did not seem to me to be at all a good plan. But I could not think of a better one, and so, as I could not disappoint the villagers' expectations, I decided to give it a trial.

I crouched in the pit, my rifle pointing in the direction of the kill. The air was hot and heavy. Insects pestered me. So intense was the silence that my slightest movement to ease cramped arm or leg produced sounds which seemed magnified a hundred-fold. Gradually the sun sank. Soon it became too dark to see the sights of my rifle, so I took the shotgun instead, both barrels of which I had loaded with ball cartridge. As I made the change I heard, or imagined that I heard, a sound to my right, but I could see nothing. A little later I heard another faint sound, immediately behind me. I did not dare to turn and look. I listened intently, but now I could hear only the pounding of my own heart. The minutes passed and I began to feel very lonely. By now it was completely dark, and I was on the point of giving up the uncomfortable vigil when, suddenly, I became aware of a foul smell. It came in waves, and it could only come from disturbance of the goat's carcass. I had still heard nothing and could, of course, see nothing. But then there came a sound, a squelchy sound, from directly in front of me. I pressed the button of the torch and there, in the centre of the beam of light, was a full-grown leopard. Broadside on to me, with its head turned in my direction, it seemed strangely white in the light of the torch. In a moment it streaked away to the right. I fired one barrel at it as it disappeared from sight and another in the direction in which it was moving. Again there was silence; and I did not know whether I had hit and killed, hit and wounded, or completely missed. Re-loading my gun with No. 2 shot cartridges I put on the torch and set off to follow the line of the leopard's flight. I had covered perhaps 30 yards when I saw the beast, a few yards away, crouched in the grass and facing me. As the light fell on it, it made a convulsive effort to spring at me. But it only moved an inch or two. One of my shots had damaged its spine, and it was helpless. Quickly, with another shot, I put it out of its misery.

Ajmer, being a railway headquarters, had a population of several thousand Anglo-Indians of mixed European and Asian descent. Theirs was an unhappy lot. Despised by the British and Indian communities, it seemed that, most of all, they despised themselves. Sometimes I met them socially but most often, alas, I met them in my Court, where I had to deal with many distressing cases. The presence in Ajmer of such a large English-speaking community led Indian shopkeepers to frame their advertisements in a language with which they were not fully conversant. Here is a tailor's appeal to prospective customers.

GOLDEN OPPORTUNITY!!	GOLDEN OPPORTUNITY!!
WELL CUT CLOTH ARE A BEAUTY	CLOTHES MAKE THE MAN LOOK DECENT

A MAN IN UP TO DATE APPARELS AND
WELL DRESSED LOOKS GENTLEMAN

An Ajmer tobacconist, advertising a cigar as 'A typical Rolls Royce in the entire cigardom', appended a quotation. I do not know where the quotation comes from but it has always given me pleasure to read it:

> There is nothing to beat a good cigar for the nerves. At the Battle of Saarbrucken the Brunswick Hussars galloped into action behind good strong Havana cigars. They staggered the enemy!

In the autumn of 1931 it was discovered that Ajmer was the headquarters of a small group of terrorist revolutionaries. Sentries were put on guard at my house day and night and I never moved out of doors without being accompanied by at least one armed detective in plain clothes. I soon learned the simple rules necessary to survival. In the evenings, for instance, lights were never put on in any room in the house until the curtains had been drawn. Sitting in Court, I always had my own loaded revolver handy on my desk. If I had to go through a door, I first opened it cautiously. In the end it all became a matter of routine. But the danger was real, as events proved. Early in 1932 the police arrested a man whom they believed to be a revolutionary. He was charged in my Court with conspiracy to murder and, after recording preliminary evidence, I committed the case to a senior Court, the Court of the Sessions Judge. As the charge was such a serious one I refused to allow the man to be released on bail, though the evidence against him was not strong. The man appealed to the Sessions Judge against my refusal to allow bail, his appeal was accepted, and he was released. Within forty-eight hours of his release he walked up to Mr Gibson and fired a revolver at him at point-blank range. Fortunately the first shot misfired, and the second went wide. Mr Gibson went unscathed and I, by the time this happened, had left for England on a year's leave.

CHAPTER 9

A Murder in Quetta

WHEN I first set sail for India in November 1927 I was a bachelor, and my luggage consisted of a single trunk, a gun-case and two suitcases. On my second voyage to India, in March 1933, our party consisted of Lalage and myself, our two daughters, Imogen and Xanthe, and their Scottish nurse. Imogen was nearly two and a half years old and Xanthe was a baby of four months. Our baggage was mountainous, and we were bound for Quetta where I was to take up my new appointment of Assistant Political Agent.

From Karachi we travelled north by rail. Dawn was breaking as the two engines pulling our train laboured up the Bolan Pass. From our carriage windows Lalage and I looked out on a new world, a world that had nothing in common with the India we had known before. Here were rugged, barren, sun-browned mountains, cleft by deep ravines and gorges. Forbidding of aspect in the full light of day, the hills were now, in the first light of dawn, clothed with a gentle effulgence that made them seem welcoming and friendly. The air, too, was different from that of India. It was fresh, cold, bracing. It was the air, not of India, but of the Central Asian plateau. Simply to breathe such air in such surroundings was exhilarating.

Baluchistan, of which Quetta was the administrative centre, was a territory greater in area than the whole of the British Isles. Occupying the extreme western corner of the Indian Empire, it was bounded on the south by the Arabian Sea, on the west by Persia and on the north by Afghanistan. Strategically the territory was of great importance. In Quetta itself were stationed some 12,000 troops, while the frontier tracts were guarded either by Pathan tribesmen, who were paid subsidies for the purpose, or by locally-raised militiamen known as levies. In some outlying areas the levies were organised into military units called Levy Corps, but in the districts of Quetta, Pishin and Chaman the levies were under the direct control of the Political Agent, Quetta, and performed the functions of police rather than soldiers.

My first task on arrival at Quetta was to learn Pushtu, the language of the Pathan tribesmen. Pushtu is a derivative of Persian, which I had studied during my probationary year at Cambridge, so I made good progress with the vocabulary and grammar of the new language. I was slow, however, at speaking it, and so, to give me practice in this, Mr Todd, the Political Agent, sent me on frequent tours of inspection of the levy posts in the district. It was while I was on such a tour of inspection, to the west of Gulistan, that news arrived early one morning of a large-scale raid. During the night marauders from beyond the Afghan border had raided a neighbouring village and driven off all the sheep and goats they could lay their hands on. Our little force of levies assembled quickly. Armed with rifles and mounted on tough ponies, we followed the tracks of the raiding party over a boulder-strewn river bed for mile after mile, hour after hour. Early in the afternoon we emerged on to the plateau on the Afghan side of the border. Here the droppings of the sheep and goats were quite fresh, and we pressed on the faster for this encouragement. The tracks were now leading us in a northerly direction, parallel to a line of low hills on our right. We were urging on our flagging ponies when two things happened in quick succession. A keen-eyed levy suddenly shouted and, pointing forward, drew our attention to a small cloud of dust on the horizon in front of us. There, without doubt, were the animals we were pursuing; and they were not more than a couple of miles ahead of us. We were still peering ahead at the cloud of dust, and the levy's shout was still in our ears, when two rifle shots rang out and we heard the whine of bullets passing uncomfortably close to us. The reactions of fear are instantaneous. In a moment I was off my pony and behind some rocks. The levies also took cover, but with greater deliberation than I had shown.

The council of war that followed had its humorous features though I was not capable of appreciating them at the time. My knowledge of Pushtu was still elementary, and I could not explain in words exactly what I wanted done. Nor was it easy for me, lying flat on my belly, to explain my wishes by gesture. In the end, however, the levies understood my instructions well enough. The main body, about a dozen men, were to go after the stolen animals, round them up, and bring them back to where we were. Four men, leaving their ponies with me, were to engage the raiders who had fired at us from the hills on our right. I would stay where I was, with two other men, in concealment, guarding the ponies. I hoped that the ponies would act as a bait to one or more of the raiders who, seeing them apparently unguarded, might be tempted to try to steal them.

During the hour and a half that I waited in ambush I heard some desultory firing from the hills to the right but nothing else disturbed the peace of my vigil. Then the main body returned, driving before them the stolen flocks and herds, which they had recovered without encountering any resistance. The raiders had not waited to engage them but had fled to the adjacent hills. As we turned homeward we were joined by the party of four who had been sent to clear the hills. They had seen in the distance the two men who had fired on us, and had exchanged shots with them, but had not been able to approach them more nearly. We spent that night in the hills and the next morning, taking a guide with me and going ahead of the main party, I returned to the levy post from which our expedition had started. The same evening I was back in Quetta and dining at The Residency in a dinner jacket, stiff shirt and patent-leather shoes.

It was possible to enjoy at Quetta a very active social life. The Agent to the Governor-General, Sir Norman Cater, was a bachelor, but he had living with him two vivacious nieces, Mary Stevens and Betty Chubb, and they ensured that parties at The Residency were always lively and entertaining. In a mixed society of soldiers and civilians there were, of course, many jealousies, many snobberies; and gossip, spicy rather than malicious, abounded. But European life in Quetta, in the spring of 1933, presented, on the whole, a picture of gay and happy activity. In our own house, No. 25 Lytton Road, we did our share of entertaining. And Lalage, characteristically, soon collected round herself and the children quite a menagerie of animals. There were our two horses, Jorrocks and Music, and Imogen's pony Bucephalus; there were the two fat-tailed sheep, Diocletian and Tamerlane; there were three rabbits, Pericles, Aspasia and Heliogabalus; and, finally, there was Ptolemy, the tortoise. If some of the names seem unusual, even extravagant, I can only plead that they were the carefully considered choice of our elder daughter, Imogen, who, though she was shaky on her aspirates, took great delight in articulating sonorous words of many syllables.

A society such as that at Quetta – gay, frivolous, absorbed in its own pursuits – will happily ignore tragedies of the world outside: but it can be shocked into stillness and fear when tragedy invades its own little world. Such was the effect in Quetta of the murder of Major and Mrs Abbott in the summer of 1933.

At seven o'clock one morning Hussain, Major Abbott's bearer, reported to the police that his master and mistress had been murdered during the night. He had found them, he said, dead in their bedroom when he had taken them their early morning tea. The police went at once to Major Abbott's bungalow. Mrs Abbott was lying on the floor of the bedroom, near the door, with her head staved in. Major Abbott was lying in bed, also with his head staved in. But – and this was the most puzzling feature of the case – Major Abbott's head was swathed in bandages applied after he had received his injuries.

The police made the most thorough investigations but could find no clue to the murderer. All the servants were of good character. Nothing had been stolen. Major Abbott had risen from the ranks and he and his wife, though not particularly popular with their neighbours, had no special enemies. There seemed to be no motive for the murder. It was impossible, moreover, to reconstruct the crime. Who had been killed first, Major Abbott or Mrs Abbott? Where was the weapon with which the murder had been committed? Neither the police nor anyone else could answer these questions.

The days dragged on. Weeks passed by. The shock of the Abbotts' murder was forgotten, and people resumed their normal social round. Then, one day, as I was sitting in my Court, the police brought a man before me. It was Hussain, the Abbotts' bearer. Short, square, with slightly Mongoloid features, he had the open countenance of a transparently honest and honourable man. He came from a village near Leh, in that remote hill-tract which lies between the Himalayas and the Karakoram range of mountains. The police told me that Hussain had confessed to the murder of Major and Mrs Abbott and that he wanted to have his statement recorded by a magistrate.

This is the substance of what Hussain told me:

> From the beginning the day was a bad one. The Sahib complained that his early morning tea was cold. Then, when he was dressing, I could not find the shirt he wanted. The dhobi had not brought it back from the wash. The Sahib said I was to blame. All day I was busy doing things for Memsahib, and then, when the guests arrived for dinner before the Sahib was ready, he was angry with me. After the dinner was over I helped to serve the drinks. I had no food all day. When the Sahib was undressing to go to bed he called me bad names. He called me 'su'ar ka bachha' (son of a pig). When I went to my quarters I could not sleep. I kept on thinking that the Sahib had insulted my father, who is dead. I did not mind what the Sahib called me, but he should not have said bad things about my father. So I went to the kitchen and took a chopper and crept very quietly into the Sahib's bedroom. Sahib and Memsahib were both asleep. I struck the Sahib and was leaving the room when Memsahib woke up. 'Hussain,' she cried, 'Oh Hussain, what have you done?' Then she got some bandages

from a drawer and I helped her to bind up the Sahib's head. When we had finished, she suddenly started to run from the room. I knew she was going to telephone to the police, and I was frightened, so I struck her too. I am sorry, and I am ashamed, that I struck Memsahib. But there was no alternative. I cleaned the chopper in the kitchen sink and went back to bed. No one had heard anything.

I only asked Hussain one question. 'Why have you now decided to tell the story of what you did?' 'Because,' he replied, 'the police were troubling all the servants and no one was allowed to go home. This was very hard on them.'

The case was tried by the Sessions Judge. At his trial Hussain pleaded 'Not Guilty'. But his confession before me provided all the evidence the Court required. He was sentenced to death and hanged in the Quetta Jail.

As Peshawar, in the North-West Frontier Province, stood sentinel over the Indian side of the Khyber Pass, so, in Baluchistan, Quetta guarded the Indian side of the Khojak Pass. In past times military invaders from Central Asia had used both the Khyber and the Khojak Passes. If they came from Kabul, they forced their way over the Khyber; if from Kandahar, over the Khojak. But now, for forty years or more, these passes had been channels of trade, and the Quetta bazaar, like that of Peshawar, while it contained much rubbish, yielded also occasional treasures. There were Persian and Afghan rugs, a great variety of skins, china tea-sets from Russia, exotic jewellery and, most interesting of all, Persian copies of Chinese porcelain.

My most treasured purchase was not, however, made in the bazaar. One day a cipher telegram arrived from the British Consul in Kandahar informing us that a Persian banker was travelling to Bombay via Quetta. We were asked to give him special protection from the time when he crossed the Afghan border at Chaman as he was carrying with him some valuable jewellery. I arranged for an escort to meet the traveller at Chaman. When he arrived at Quetta he called on me to thank me for the arrangements I had made for his safety. He also wanted further assistance. His funds were exhausted, he said, and he still had a long and expensive journey before him. Could I advance him some money? Or could I, perhaps, help him to sell a piece of jewellery in Quetta?

'I should like to help you,' I replied, 'but first tell me something about the reason for your journey. Who does this jewellery belong to and why are you taking it to Bombay to sell?'

The story he told me was a strange one but I did not doubt its truth as he was clearly a man of standing and he carried with him credentials from the Afghan Government. A party of White Russians, he told me, had fled from Siberia and, after enduring incredible hardships, had finally escaped across the Russian border into Afghanistan. They were 'aristocrats', who had started their journey with a good deal of jewellery and still had some of it left. The Afghan Government had given them asylum and had undertaken to sell their jewellery for them to the best advantage. He, the Persian banker, had been commissioned by the Afghan Government to travel to Bombay, the nearest international market for precious stones, and there dispose of the jewellery.

'Can I see the jewellery?' I asked.

'Of course,' he replied; and forthwith, to my amazement, he drew out from under his coat an oblong tin box which had once contained cartons of Scissors cigarettes. From this box he extracted a number of variously-shaped small parcels, undid them, and laid out their contents on a table. A superb diamond necklace must have been worth several thousand pounds. Hardly less valuable were a diamond bracelet and a pair of diamond earrings. Most of the articles displayed on the table were far beyond the means of anyone I knew in Quetta. But there were smaller objects too, less obviously costly. One of these was a marquise ring, with an enamel centre surrounded by diamonds. In the middle of the enamel, traced out in brilliants, was the monogram, surmounted by a crown, of Nicholas II,

Czar of all the Russias! Here, verily, was corroboration of the story of the Russian emigrés. I took the ring to a firm of jewellers in Quetta, obtained a rough estimate of the value of the stones, and offered a price which was accepted. Of course, I could not afford it. But the transaction gave satisfaction to both the parties concerned. The Persian banker was enabled to resume his journey to Bombay; and I possessed an historic ring. I say 'I possessed' the ring. But I did not possess it for long. Lalage borrowed it to wear at a ball at The Residency – and has not yet returned it to me!

Whereas the Khyber Pass led directly into Afghanistan, the Khojak Pass, after crossing a range of mountains which forms the natural boundary between Baluchistan and Afghanistan, descended abruptly into a British enclave in the plain which stretches south and south-west from Kandahar. This enclave, known as Chaman, was surrendered to the British towards the end of the last century. It formed a valuable listening-in post and to it came, sooner or later, news of all that was happening among the tribes in South Afghanistan. In the Chaman bazaar there existed what was, I suppose, one of the world's biggest stocks of second-hand overcoats. The traditional overcoat of the Pathan is the Poshtin. But this, being lined with lamb's wool, is expensive. The second-hand overcoats in the Chaman bazaar were relatively cheap and, because they came from the west, were fashionable. I examined a number of these overcoats. Most of them from the United States of America. Others came from Paris, Berlin and other European capitals. Several bore the name-tapes of tailors in Savile Row and Sackville Street. How they found their way to Chaman I do not know.

Chaman was a railhead, and every summer hundreds of tons of fruit – grapes, apricots, peaches, pomegranates, plums and cherries – were despatched southwards to India. The post of station-master at Chaman was one of the most lucrative in the whole of the Railway Service. The incumbent of this post was credibly reported to earn – or make – upwards of £5,000 a year. There was always, or there could always be contrived, a shortage of railway wagons. Soft fruit deteriorates rapidly. Only the station-master could say which consignment was to be sent off first, which consignment delayed. The post was reserved, I understood, for men nearing retirement who had given long and faithful service. Great was their reward.

To the east of Chaman and running parallel with the Afghan boundary were several ranges of lofty, barren mountains. Concealed in these mountains, and surrounded by them on all sides, was an extensive table-land. In the winter this table-land was deserted. The height and cold made it uninhabitable. In the summer, however, it was the resort of the Achakzai, the most formidable of all the Pathan tribes in Baluchistan. For centuries they had preyed on caravans travelling over the Khojak Pass. During the Afghan Wars they had harassed and spoiled British troops using this route. It was Sir Robert Sandeman who enlisted them on the side of law and order by paying them to guard the border and protect the pass. On the whole the system worked well. Occasionally, however, their predatory instincts would re-assert themselves. Some branch of the tribe, under an enterprising leader, would revert to its traditional way of life and start raiding and marauding on both sides of the border. Such a case had occurred in 1924. Mahmud Khan, head of the Alizai section of the tribe, was a born leader of men, and a strategist of rare ability. With a band of carefully chosen followers he planned and executed a series of successful raids and amassed a great deal of booty. Eventually the Army had to be moved against him, and he surrendered. He was not punished. On the contrary, he was formally pardoned and he and his followers were given land on which to settle and grow crops.

In the summer of 1933 I spent a week on this table-land, known as Toba Achakzai, and was hospitably entertained by the reformed Mahmud Khan. In a letter to my parents I wrote:

> Wherever I go an enormous party moves with me; about 40 armed and mounted levies, my own staff, and a number of local maliks, as well as the men in charge of the 20 camels which carry our tents, food and equipment. But military discipline is observed

> the whole time. There are armed sentries round the camp at night, and scouts in advance and on the flanks when we march anywhere – even when we go out hunting. It shows how near they all are to the days when every man's hand was against them and when they considered everyone not of their tribe to be legitimate prey.

The favourite sport of the Achakzai was hunting, or perhaps I should say coursing. Eighty or a hundred men, most of them mounted on small, wiry ponies, would form a line extending across country for perhaps half a mile. Spaced at intervals of 150 or 200 yards along the line, Afghan hounds would be held in leash. As the line advanced, every man let out the most blood-curdling cries and holloas. The din was terrific; but it redoubled whenever a hare or fox started up. The Afghan hound hunts only by sight and many hares escaped because they were not viewed by the hounds. But when a hound did get a view of its quarry the excitement was intense and everyone joined in the chase. Most of the hares escaped because they are so much faster than the hounds on up-gradients. It was only when a hare was headed downhill that its fate was sealed.

Fishing was another sport enjoyed by the Achakzai, but their methods of taking fish were, by English standards, unconventional. Mostly they 'netted' them, using parts of their clothing for the purpose. But sometimes they 'tickled' them. They did not use the English schoolboy's method of feeling gently for the fish while it is idling under a stone or bank. Their method was quite different. Having stirred up the mud in a pool to make the water opaque, they would enter the water boldly and make sudden snatches at fish as they felt them brushing against their legs or feet. By the netting method they captured large numbers of small fish. By the tickling method they captured small numbers of large fish.

A letter which I wrote home at the time tells of the entertainment provided for me. After describing a wrestling match, the letter goes on:

> After that there was a horse race, of about 6 furlongs, over an open space in a valley. There were nine entrants and they galloped over

the rough ground (with two small water jumps) at a most amazing pace. There was a very close finish, four horses coming in almost together. As a fight seemed likely to break out over the result I had to give several first prizes! And after that there was an Achakzai dance. I imagine that the dance is generally performed round a fire at night; but as it was not yet dark, and as there was no fire, the men put their shoes and waistcoats in a heap and danced round that. As in most folk dances the movements were, to begin with, slow and rhythmical, but they gradually increased in violence and the finale was a most energetic performance – like a Highland Fling done in treble quick time. They also sang a song while dancing – a love song. The words have been translated thus:

You have wounded me sore,
Give me medicine,
Give me the medicine that only you can give
Or I shall die to-day.

I will not give you what you ask.
Your days are numbered by God
And He has decided whether you shall die to-day or not.
If you die to-day, it is no fault of mine.

A heartless reply, to say the least of it, to a lover's plea.

I enjoyed my life as Assistant Political Agent, Quetta. But it only lasted for six months. In September 1933 the Khan of Kalat died and I was appointed Wazir-i-Azam (Chief Minister) to his successor. A new life began for me, strange and exciting and carrying with it responsibilities far greater than any I had hitherto been called upon to bear.

CHAPTER 10

Chief Minister, Kalat State

KALAT, a country the size of England and Wales combined, was a barbarous State which for a century and a half had been misgoverned by a succession of barbarous Khans. Ahmad Yar, the new ruler, often spoke with pride of his famous eighteenth-century ancestor, Nasir Khan the Great, but he seldom mentioned the names of his immediate predecessors.

Ahmad Yar's grandfather, Khudadad Khan, had been an ogre. He counted his toll of human heads as other Indian rulers counted the number of tigers they had shot. He once boasted to the Agent to the Governor General that, while he had been Khan, he had killed 3,500 men and women – 100 for every year of his rule. On one occasion he punished a petty theft from his treasury by having the principal offender stoned to death. Five women connected with the offence were killed with the sword, and two men, minor accomplices, were emasculated. He was warned that such barbarities would not be tolerated. However, he completely ignored the warning. A few months later he caused his Wazir, Faqir Mohammed, to be hacked to death, together with the Wazir's father (an old man of ninety), his son aged twenty, and his confidential servant. It was these brutal murders, personally supervised by his younger son, Mir Azim Jan, that finally led to his forced abdication.

Khudadad Khan was succeeded by his eldest son, Mahmud Khan, who died in 1931. Mahmud Khan's eccentricities were of a different character. Locking himself up in the Miri, his fortress at Kalat, he indulged a mania for collecting things. He collected thousands of pairs of shoes, hundreds of lengths of silk for turbans, dozens of horses, and as many motor cars as the depth of his purse would allow. Fearful lest anyone should steal these treasures he went to extraordinary lengths to protect them.

All the left shoes were destroyed. No one, he must have calculated, could possibly want to purloin shoes that could not be worn. The lengths of turban silk were rent down the middle to render them unusable. The horses were stabled underground, in darkness, where no one could see them. Many of them, alas, went blind. And the motor cars mouldered away with their wheels removed.

When Mahmud Khan died in 1931 he was succeeded by his younger brother, Mir Azim Jan, the man who, earlier in his life, had butchered his father's Wazir. Mir Azim Jan died in 1933. He should have been succeeded by his eldest son, Akram Jan. But Akram Jan's mother, the senior begum, was not as shrewd as the junior begum, Ahmad Yar's mother. Akram Jan was introduced to seductive hemp drugs which gradually destroyed his mental faculties and, when Azim Jan died, it was necessarily the younger son, Ahmad Yar, who was chosen to succeed him.

It was perhaps surprising that a person as young as I was – just turned thirty – should have been appointed Chief Minister of such an important State as Kalat, extensive, primitive and turbulent. The explanation is simple. The Government of India had decided that they could not tolerate the continuance of gross misrule in the State. During the latter part of Mahmud Khan's reign the administration of the State had been conducted by his Wazir-i-Azam, Nawab Sir Mir Shams Shah, a shrewd old man. But Mir Azim Jan had sacked the Nawab, had appointed a mere cipher in his place and, in two short years, had emptied the treasury and reduced the administration to a condition of utter chaos. The introduction into the State of a British officer, for the first time in its long history, was deemed essential. But the State could not afford the services of a senior British officer. A junior officer must do his best. In any case, it was felt, a young man would have a better chance than an older one of winning the confidence of the new ruler, who was still under thirty years of age and, being a younger son, had never been trained in the duties of a ruler or, indeed, given any formal education at all.

For Ahmad Yar the rise in status and fortune was no less dramatic than it was for me. Until recently a subaltern in the Zhob levy corps, he had now become His Highness Mir Ahmad Yar Khan, Beglar Begi, Khan and Wali of Kalat (Prince of Princes, Ruler and Governor of Kalat), head of the third largest State in India and entitled to a salute of nineteen guns.

Kalat was unique among Indian States in that the ruler directly administered through his Wazir only about one-third of his territory; the remaining portion was under the control of tribal chiefs known as Sirdars. The State was divided into five provinces. Their names had a romantic flavour of Central Asia; Sarawan, Jhalawan, Kachhi, Mekran and Kharan. The last of these, Kharan, was administered by its own semi-independent Nawab. Each of the other four provinces contained extensive areas, known as Niabats, for the administration of which the Wazir-i-Azam was responsible. The Sirdars owed allegiance to the Khan but resented interference by him or his Wazir in the affairs of their own tribal territory. For centuries successive Khans and their Sirdars had quarrelled, all concerned being ambitious for greater power, larger estates. Sir Robert Sandeman, in the last quarter of the nineteenth century, had temporarily reconciled ancient enmities and established a *modus vivendi* for the Khan and the Sirdars. But the maladministration of recent years had placed too great a strain on the Sandeman compromises. The old system had broken down and some new relationship between the Khan and the Sirdars had now to be established.

All this I realised later. To begin with, however, I did not appreciate the nature of the political and constitutional problems which confronted me. I was conscious only of the appalling confusion into which the whole administration had fallen. Many State employees had not been paid for months. Cash chests in the more distant Niabats were empty. Corruption was rife. In Mekran the edict abolishing slavery, passed in 1927, was still ignored. There was as yet no written law in the State, either criminal or civil. Prisoners languished in jail untried. The horses in the famous State stud were starving – the grain intended for their use was taken by the syces for themselves and their own ill-nourished families. In the Wazir-i-Azam's office there had accumulated many months of unanswered correspondence, all of it in Urdu, in a script which I could not read without assistance; and none of my staff spoke a word of English. In my first three weeks of office I felt that I was living a nightmare – a nightmare from which I could see no prospect of release. Even so, the first general instructions that I issued were sensible and brought a ray of hope to disheartened officials throughout the State. Breaking into the State's reserve funds, I sent adequate supplies of cash to all the Niabats; and I directed that no head of an establishment should receive his salary until he had certified to me in writing that all members of his subordinate staff had received their arrears of pay in full.

At the end of three weeks' incessant toil I began to suffer from insomnia. The responsibilities of my new office were too harassing for me, the load of unfamiliar work heavier than I could bear. I was on the verge of break-down when relief came in an unexpected and improbable manner. It came in the form of a crisis. Pasni, a small port on the Arabian Sea in the extreme south of the State, more than 400 miles by road from Quetta, had suddenly sprung into prominence. In British India the customs duty on imported Japanese silk was 66 per cent; in Pasni it was only 5 per cent. In the autumn of 1933 a firm of enterprising Sindhi merchants realised that they could take advantage of this disparity. They arranged for silk consigned to Karachi to be trans-shipped in bond at that port and sent on to Pasni. Thence they had it carried overland to Larkana, Shikarpur, Jacobabad and other towns in Sind, where it found a ready sale at prices far below the normal market rate. The pioneers of this new trade route made a quick fortune. Other merchants rushed in to follow the trail they had blazed, and thousands of bales of silk were diverted from Karachi to Pasni. The Government of India, concerned at the loss of customs revenue (there were no customs posts along the Kalat-Sind border), telegraphed to the

Agent to the Governor-General in Baluchistan asking for this illicit traffic to be stopped immediately. Sir Norman Cater sent for me and asked me what action the Kalat Durbar proposed to take to comply with the Government of India's request. I told him that I could not give him a reply until I had accurate information about what was happening. But, I added, I was myself prepared to visit Pasni at once to ascertain the true facts. To this Sir Norman agreed, and I set off the next day by road for Pasni.

It was this long journey by road which gave my harassed mind the respite it needed. For three days I travelled by car, over atrocious roads, through the heart of my new domain. The country was wild, desolate, magnificent in its solitude. The State officials whom I met varied in their attitude to me. Some were glad to meet a superior to whom they could pour out their tale of woe. The administration, they told me, had fallen into such disrepute that they could not collect dues owing to the State; their authority was flouted; the tribesmen, encouraged by their Sirdars, were insolent and uncooperative. Other officials were suspicious of the new Wazir. Taking advantage of the absence of any control from above, they had built up little empires of their own from which they extracted the maximum amount of private benefit. Such men were, not unnaturally, apprehensive of what I might discover and report to the Khan. I dealt with each after his kind. To those whom I deemed to be honest I promised support and gave guidance. To the others I was non-committal: I asked many questions but gave no indication of what I thought of the replies I received.

Somehow, by what means I do not know, news of my impending visit had spread through Mekran. As I made my way from Panjgur to Turbat, from Turbat to Pasni, I found the road blocked at many points by crowds of tribesmen who advertised that they were suppliants by the traditional method of putting on their heads inflammable material – paper or dry grass – and setting it alight. Their grievances were real. They had been oppressed beyond endurance, some by Sirdars, others by avaricious and irresponsible State officials. I promised them redress, though I was still uncertain of the means by which I could carry out the promise.

At Pasni I was surprised to discover that the senior Customs Officer was an honest man who had diligently collected and accounted for the greatly increased revenue brought in by the imports of silk. There are advantages in autocracy. I passed an order doubling the man's salary and raising his status in the official hierarchy. My order was dramatic and was intended to be dramatic. This seemed to me to be an excellent means of demonstrating that, under the new régime, honesty and faithful service would be quickly recognised and liberally rewarded.

While I was at Pasni I revised the whole of the Customs tariff and brought the new schedule into immediate effect. As a gesture of apparent goodwill to the Government of India I raised the duty on silk goods from 5 per cent to 30 per cent. This measure did not stop the trade – I did not expect that it would – but it rendered it less profitable to the merchants while, at the same time, it brought in a handsome revenue to the State. Eventually, after a good deal of haggling, which occupied some weeks, I yielded to pressure from the Government of India and raised the duty to the full 66 per cent. In the intervening period, however, the State treasury had been amply replenished.

During the winter of 1933 my principal worry was the State's financial condition. The Pasni windfall would not be repeated and current expenditure was running at a much higher level than income. A tour of the Niabats in Kachhi confirmed the views I had provisionally formed on my journey to Pasni. Deficiency in the State's revenues was due partly to dishonest officials or incompetent administration, but partly also to encroachment by Sirdars on State rights and on State territory. I determined, unwisely, to deal with both problems simultaneously. My reform of the administration was drastic. From the Baluchistan Government I secured on deputation several competent and reliable revenue officials. The senior of these I appointed as my deputy in Mekran. The others I placed in key supervisory positions elsewhere. I sacked two or three State officials whose misdoings were notorious, I promoted those in whom I felt some degree of confidence, and I transferred to new duties those whom I thought capable of reform. If I had stopped there all would have been well. But I also gave directions for the recovery of rights filched from the State by Sirdars and their tribesmen. These directions, carried out with more zeal than tact, led to difficulties which, if I had possessed greater political experience, I could have foreseen and avoided.

During the winter, which I spent at Sibi, I got to know Ahmad Yar well and to like him greatly. I did not trouble him much with administrative problems. He, for his part, told me little of what the Sirdars were doing and saying. I only knew that there was a constant coming-and-going of Sirdars to and from his residence at Dhadar or the Miri in Kalat.

In the spring of 1934 I returned to Quetta and there, one day early in June, the Bangalzai Sirdar came to see me. He was one of the leading Sirdars of the State and was highly esteemed both by the Baluchistan Government and by H.H. the Khan. I had always found him courteous and friendly. Now, speaking earnestly in a confidential whisper, he told me that the Khan might suggest to me that I should visit Kachhi to see that the earthen dams across the Nari river had been properly constructed. Kachhi was the granary of the State and the autumn crop of Jowar (sorghum) depended on efficient control of the summer floods.

'If His Highness does make this suggestion, don't go. I speak as a friend. The heat in Kachhi is killing. Even I, with all my land there, have never visited Kachhi in the summer. No Sirdar ever has. If necessary, send your Revenue Assistant. But don't go yourself.'

I thanked him for the warning and assured him that I had no intention of visiting Kachhi. I could guess what the heat there was like. In Jacobabad the shade temperature, recorded daily in the newspapers, was in the 120s. Sibi was hotter than Jacobabad. Bhag and Gandava, in Kachhi, were hotter than Sibi.

The next day I received a letter from the Khan instructing me to visit Kachhi and inspect the dams there. I had never before received written orders from the Khan, and I was greatly perturbed at what appeared to be a change of attitude towards me. I decided to motor to Kalat, ninety miles away, to seek an interview with the Khan, find out how the land lay, and secure, if I could, modification of the orders. Then I learned that the Khan, after despatching his letter to me, had left Kalat by car for an undisclosed destination. Knowing the Khan as I did, I was sure that he had anticipated that I would wish to see him, was nervous about an interview with me, and had prudently taken avoiding action.

Puzzled and distressed at the Khan's orders and the change in our relationship that they disclosed, I was inclined at first to act on the Bangalzai Sirdar's advice and send my Revenue Assistant to Kachhi. But I soon saw that, if I did this, I would only be evading the real issue. To obey, or not to obey: that was the question. And I finally decided to obey.

My first difficulty was to find a servant to go with me. Ghulam Mohammed, my Kashmiri bearer, was aghast at the thought of visiting Kachhi at the peak of the hot season. 'Please excuse me,' he said. 'I have a wife and children to think of.' 'So have I,' I replied. But I could not persuade him, and would not force him, to go with me. In the end Azam volunteered to accompany me. Azam, small, dirty, dishevelled, with a hideous squint, had been one of my orderlies when I was Assistant Political Agent, Quetta. My successor, Bazalgette, had justifiably taken exception to Azam's permanently unshaven appearance. 'Do you never shave?' he asked him. 'Kabhi, kabhi (sometimes I do),' replied Azam, honestly enough. But Bazalgette thought the man was being insolent and replaced him with someone who was more of an orderly and less of an eyesore. I had taken the discharged Azam into Kalat State service partly because the children were fond of him, partly because I believed him to possess an independent outlook and a sense of humour. Often, when I was indulging a fit of temper, other orderlies and servants would make themselves scarce. But not Azam. He would stand his ground and face the music and sometimes, I suspected, he would be smiling covertly to himself. So now he repaid what he himself would have termed my earlier kindness to him.

I spent a week in Kachhi inspecting earthen dams built across the dry beds of the Nari and other rivers. It was a week of horror. The heat made it so. The worst day was the one on which we rode from Gandava to Bhag, some thirty-five miles across a treeless, shadeless plain. We set off long before dawn and reached Khudabad, nineteen miles on our way, before the sun became really tyrannous. At Khudabad there were trees and a well. We watered the horses and rested awhile in the shade. When we resumed our journey the sun was scorching, searing. For some miles all went well. Then a horse collapsed, then another. When there were still four miles to go, our party of eighteen had been reduced to ten, and I began to wonder whether I myself would complete the journey. I touched my horse's withers. They were burning hot, too hot to rest my hand on. The track ahead swayed up and down. Was this mirage or hallucination? I didn't know. And then I began to feel myself swelling as though my body were a balloon being pumped up. Gradually but continuously I felt myself being inflated and knew that I must soon burst. And now I saw the tall houses of Bhag, raised by a mirage high above the level of the horizon. In my mind I debated the only question that seemed to me to matter – 'Can I get to Bhag before I burst?' I did get there; but only just. I do not think I could have lasted another quarter-mile. The horse that had carried me so bravely died within an hour of our arrival. Other horses and alas! one of the men, died on the way.

As soon as I arrived at Bhag I took off my clothes and immersed myself in a zinc tub filled with cold water. In a minute or two the water was hot. The tub was refilled with cold water.

This water, too, soon became warm. It was only when the tub had been filled for the third time that the water remained cool. The doctor in charge of the State dispensary at Bhag told me that the thermometer in his verandah registered a shade temperature of 135 degrees. He expressed surprise that any of us had survived the journey.

I was happy to get back safely to Quetta. I was even happier when the Khan summoned me to Kalat and showered me with compliments.

'I am sorry,' he said, 'that I had to ask you to carry out such an unpleasant task. But Wadera Sahib (the Bangalzai Sirdar) made the suggestion. Now you have shown that you really care for my interests and those of my people.'

So the Bangalzai Sirdar had laid a trap for me! And I had very nearly fallen into it! But at least I knew now that Wadera Sahib was my enemy; and I could guess that the Rind Sirdar, hereditary enemy of the Bangalzai, would be my friend.

The rains came, and I decided to undertake another tour of Kachhi in order to see for myself exactly how the irrigation system worked. This time conditions were very different. Where there had been dry river beds there were now torrents of brown water. Much of the arid plain had become a sea of mud. Travel by foot or on horseback was laborious and difficult; by car or camel it was impossible. Nevertheless, I managed to cover a lot of ground. At one point, south of Bhag, where progress by any other means seemed impracticable, I launched myself on to the flooded Nari. Buoyed up by an empty kerosine oil tin I was swept downstream for six exciting miles. The water was warm and muddy. There were no rocks and no rapids. The only hazards were occasional submerged acacia trees whose thorns, if one encountered them, lacerated the flesh.

This was an enjoyable excursion which brought both profit and reward. It was profitable in that I now understood fully the indigenous system of flood control and could envisage means both of improving and extending it. The reward came later in a manner as unexpected as it was bizarre.

Nawab Asadullah Khan Raisani, head of the Sarawan line of chiefs, was the most powerful Sirdar in the State. Comparatively well educated, intelligent, conservative in outlook, he was a pillar of Baluchistan society with an influence that extended far beyond the boundaries of his own tribal territory. I regarded him as a friend and counted on his support in my efforts to restore the fortunes of the State. But he, like the Bangalzai Sirdar, had come to the conclusion that I was dangerous, a menace to the rights of Sirdars where they came into conflict, as they often did, with the rights of the Khan. Determined to get rid of me, he decided to instigate an agitation against me on the grounds that I was an outsider, a Christian ignorant of Islamic law and custom who should have no place in a Muslim State – and certainly no position of authority such as that which I held as Wazir-i-Azam. In furtherance of this plan he approached an influential Mullah of Karachi, told him of the indignity to which a great Muslim State had been subjected, and invited him to visit Kalat and advise the Khan to appoint as his Wazir a man of his own faith.

The Mullah accepted the invitation to visit Kalat. But he had many followers in Kachhi and, on his journey northwards, he spent several days at Gandava and Bhag preaching in the mosques there and, of course, gathering information about recent events in the State. When he arrived at Kalat he disappointed the Raisani Nawab. Not only did he congratulate the Khan on having as his Wazir a man who had the true interests of his people at heart, but he actually preached in the Kalat mosque a sermon in which, taking as his text a passage from the Koran about 'Good Works', he referred to my exploits in Kachhi and expressed the hope that Muslims in the State would emulate the spirit of public service shown by their Christian Wazir.

I spent the winter of 1934 at Sibi. I knew now that certain Sirdars were plotting my downfall. I knew also that, if I tried to counter intrigue with intrigue, I should certainly fail. I possessed no talent in that direction, certainly no talent comparable to that of the Brahui and Biloch Sirdars. But my position was a strong one. The Khan had growing confidence in me. I had the backing of Sir Norman Cater and the Political Agent, Mr Skrine. Most important of all, the administrative reforms I had introduced were now beginning to bear fruit, and the financial year 1934–35 was likely to end with a small surplus instead of the large deficit that had been expected. And so, casting aside any thoughts of counter-conspiracy, I concentrated my attention on plans for the development of the State's still slender economic resources.

CHAPTER II

The Quetta Earthquake

The Quetta earthquake occurred in the early hours of the morning of May 31st, 1935. But no premonition of tragedy clouded the opening weeks of that year. The Khan, returning from an extensive tour of Jhalawan and Kachhi, had seen for himself the conditions of insecurity in which the great majority of his subjects had to pass their lives, and he now became hardly less determined than I was to introduce into the government of his State some measure of order and justice. Moreover, at the Shahi Jirga Darbar, held annually at Sibi in February, Sir Norman Cater, addressing an assembly of Chiefs from the whole of Baluchistan, had congratulated the Khan on the progress made in his State in the past twelve months; and this public acknowledgement greatly encouraged him in his new mood of interested co-operation.

To the world outside Baluchistan Kalat was hardly known except for its stud and racing stables. Not only was the purest Hirzai blood preserved there, stock descended from the famous white horse ridden by Chakar, King of the Rinds, but many thoroughbred English mares had been imported and, with them, an English thoroughbred stallion, Irish Hope, winner of the Irish 2000 Guineas. To have dispersed the stud on grounds of economy would have been a sensible measure and would have released money for roads, schools, hospitals and other accompaniments of a civilised State. But I could not bring myself to break up, expensive though it was, the sole institution in which Kalat could legitimately take some measure of pride. And so, as a compromise, while I substantially reduced the number of animals maintained, I kept the best, and ensured, with Lalage's unpaid but enthusiastic assistance, that the best were looked after as they deserved.

In March 1935 Lalage, accompanied by the family, took a number of Kalat race-horses down to Karachi to supervise their training in preparation for the Spring Meeting there. I followed in April, and we all had a happy fortnight by the seaside. Imogen was now four and a half years old, Xanthe (who enjoyed the pet name of Bold One, or Bold) was two and a half. The mornings were often spent watching the horses at exercise on the sands or swimming with them in the sea, an excellent way of developing their muscle without putting strain on the ligaments and tendons. Some of the horses, especially high-spirited Shirin, enjoyed plunging through the breakers. So did Imogen: Bold was not so bold!

Back in Quetta later in the month our horses – those we owned privately as well as those belonging to the State – enjoyed a run of successes which continued into May. Now at last, with my plans for extended irrigation in Kachhi completed, and with my deputy in Mekran proving an unqualified success, I was able to relax a little and enjoy some of the pleasures of social life in Quetta which preoccupation with my work had hitherto denied me. In particular, I looked forward to the race meeting to be held early in June. Lalage's Golden Helm, a beautifully bred English mare by Bay d'Or out of Helvia by Cicero, was still improving and would certainly win again for us. My own Ambrosia, purchased in Karachi in March, had been handicapped two stone below her true form. In her first race at Quetta, backing her from 3 to 1 against until she was 3 to 1 on, I had more than recovered her purchase price; and she would still win another couple of races before the handicapper caught up with her. At least in the racing world, prospects were bright for us.

Then came the disaster of which the whole world knows. Lalage was injured, Imogen killed. I do not have to tax my memory to recall details of that dreadful night. Here is the letter, written to Lalage's mother three days after the earthquake, which gives a factual, unadorned account of what occurred:

Camp – Residency Gardens,
QUETTA.

3rd June 1935.

My dear Lady Thompson,

First let me put you out of any anxiety you may feel for Lal. Since yesterday evening her condition has greatly improved, and it seems certain now that she has no internal injuries and that, with a few more days' complete rest, she will be quite all right again. Bold One is flourishing, and adapted herself at once to the environment of the house she is staying in.

I am momentarily laid up with a damaged leg, so, for the first time for three days, have a few hours of leisure. Most of them are spent in sleep, but there is still some time left, before darkness sets in, in which to write to you about what happened to us.

On the night of the 30th May, Lal and I dined out with Hugh Weightman, who had a small party to meet Colonel and Mrs Hay, on a visit to Quetta from Kabul. We got back from the cinema late and went to bed at about a quarter to one on the morning of May 31st, the beds being side by side. I was woken up, in pitch blackness, by an indescribable roar of noise. I had time, so Lal tells me, to say, 'My God, what's that?' before the crash came; but to me it seemed that I had hardly woken from a deep sleep and, alarmed, had half turned towards Lal, when the whole world collapsed on me. Everything tumbled on me – beams, rafters, bricks, mortar – from above and from both sides. I was surprised, when all this falling of the house had stopped, to find myself alive. I called to Lal, but she could only groan in reply, asking me how I was. I told her that I was unhurt and she then said that there was a big beam across her back, that hurt her frightfully, and she could not move. I then struggled desperately to move but could not manage to. My head was wedged between two rafters, and the beam that was across Lal's back was also across my thighs. My legs and body were covered deep with bricks and plaster.

My bed was on the right of Lal's, and I was lying on my back on it. Lal had leant over to me just before the house collapsed, and was trapped from above, a beam across the small of her back and her head near my chest. The only part of my body I could move was my right hand, and I tried to remove such bits of bricks and plaster as I could touch with that hand. But the danger of that was soon apparent, as some plaster was dislodged and almost filled the small breathing space that was left to me. Somehow, I do not know how, I again managed to breathe, though not freely, and working again with my hand, more cautiously, I managed to free most of my arm and gradually cleared a space by Lal's head so that she could breathe more easily. My anxiety then was to get the beam off Lal's back, which was causing her agony; it seemed immoveable, but I hoped, if I could remove bricks and plaster from above it, that I might take away some of the weight on it and be able, by straining upwards with my legs, to take some of the strain off her. But alas; I removed what I could with my half-free arm, but still found the beam immoveable.

Meanwhile, I heard Nurse (from a great distance, it seemed) shout for help, and I also heard Bold One crying; but no sound from Imogen.

After I had found it quite impossible to free myself or help Lal, I simply lay still, as did Lal, and we waited. Eventually (after about 10 minutes) I heard sounds of people moving; I shouted, but got no reply. Nurse also shouted, and it seemed that people answered her shouts. After that, things are confused in my mind. I remember feeling relief at the thought that Bold One had got away, with Nurse, though how I knew they had been pulled out I cannot say: perhaps the fact that Nurse's shouts for help had stopped and men's voices were heard made me deduce that they had escaped. Then I shouted again, at intervals, for Ghulam Mohammad, and eventually a voice replied from the infinite distance. Gradually the voices came nearer, and eventually communication was definitely established with our rescuers – one of whom pattered prayers to Allah incessantly. Then the worst period of all followed. I could not move at all: everything was pitch black, and Lalage was silent, in great pain and possibly dying. The rescuers made no headway; they had no light, and no implements, and could only guess where we were. Slowly, slowly, all too slowly, they cleared away bricks and plaster from above us, and at last got to the beam lying across me and Lal. They tried to move it – and failed. I urged them, with entreaties, to try again; again they failed to move it. And, to my despair, they said it could not be moved. And still no light.

Time passed: the rescuers seemed to have despaired of getting us out, and I had that last horror of feeling that Lal and I could not even kill ourselves. Eventually the rescuers (a sweeper, a motor driver and a levy, from our compound, and a prisoner from the lock-up behind the house) tried approaching us from a different direction. They removed bricks and rubble from over our heads, and behind our heads. I urged them to remove the rafter above my head as I thought that, if I could move my head, I could show them how to get the beam off Lalage. But they could not move it. And now a light appeared – a candle. How they got it, or where they got it from, I cannot guess. But at least it showed them where we were and how we were lying. Above my head, however, it was still dark and I could see nothing; though my arm was free enough to help me to clear a space round Lalage's head to enable her to breathe. And now I got cramp – terrible, excruciating cramp – in my neck, but not a muscle could I move to relieve it. At last they got my head and Lalage's free – how, I do not know – and after that I was able to show them how to get Lalage out. They cleared all rubble away from the upper part of her body and legs, took some of the strain off the beam across her and drew her out by the shoulders. When she was out, they half-carried, half-dragged her out into the open through a hole they had cleared under the eaves of the roof. Then they returned to me. Now that I could breathe freely I was quite happy for myself, though I had little hope for Imogen. It was another ten minutes before I was got out, and just as I got on to the drive in front of the house, where Lal had collapsed in a heap, up came O'Connor (the Supt. of Police) with help. They took Lal off in a car to the Hospital, and called a party of the West Yorks Regiment who had come from Cantonments to help in the rescue work.

The earthquake occurred at 3.5 a.m. and the soldiers arrived at about 4.30 a.m. so Lal had been in that frightful condition for an hour and a quarter, and myself for a bit longer. The soldiers divided into three parties. One party I set to work (under an officer) where Imogen had been sleeping, and the other parties at places where our servants or levies etc., had been buried. It was still too dark to see much but the parties kept at work with the help of hurricane lanterns, and, from the servants' quarters, bodies, dead or alive, were continually being extracted. The party looking for

Imogen worked for 2½ hours before they came on one of her feet, and then I did not look any more, but waited near by.

When they got her out, they wrapped her in a blanket and took me and her up to the Hospital. There I found Lal and Bold One, the latter very dirty and cheerful, and Lal only half conscious, after an injection of morphia. Bold One was bothering her, so I looked after Bold, and got water, etc., for Lal for one or two hours, until a Mrs Skeen (wife of a Major in the Gurkhas) offered to take Bold away, give her clothes and look after her temporarily. Mrs Skeen has two daughters aged 10 and 4½, and they have made Bold completely at home and look after her with great tenderness and solicitude. After Lal had been made as comfortable as possible, on a bed in the shade of a tree in the Hospital compound, I was rescued by an officer who lived nearby who told me that I could get a bath, some tea and some clothes at his house. So I made my way along, in my pyjamas, bare-foot, over some very rough ground to his house, where I had a bath and cleaned some of the plaster and dirt from eyes and nose and mouth and ears and had tea and whiskey and toast. I also got some clothes. Then I was given a lift to the Residency, the headquarters for rescue work, and did what I could to help.

After a late lunch I got a baby car (the only one of ours that escaped), borrowed two gardeners from Mr Gould, went up to the Hospital and took Imogen's body which had been wrapped up in a red blanket (with a label on it 'Boy Wakefield') and went up to the Cemetery. There I chose a place next to Humphry's* grave and set the gardeners to work. There was to be a communal burial at about 6 p.m. but the grave for Imogen was completed by about 5.30 p.m. so I got Clayden (the Assistant Chaplain here whom I knew at Cambridge and liked very much) to take the service over her. Only he and I and the two gardeners were present. In a trench not far away over 150 other victims of the tragedy were buried – and they too had almost no mourners present.

I cannot tell you all that I have done since then. Our house and offices and clerks' and servants' quarters are all level with the ground. Ghulum Mohammad, the wonderful bearer that

* Humphry Bland, best man at my wedding and Imogen's godfather; killed in a motor accident at Quetta, April 20th, 1933.

Humphry gave us, was killed; and also Sher Zaman, Imogen's bearer, aged about 13. Indeed, few survived. On the morning of June 1st, as I was going over the wreckage of our house seeing if I could salvage anything in the way of shoes or soap or matches for myself, I heard a slight snuffling noise deep in the ruins. I collected some men, and after 4 hours' work we got Panther, the black Labrador, out. He had been buried there for 35 hours. He has almost recovered now and will be quite all right in a few days' time.

I also examined the places where we had all been sleeping. It was miraculous that any of us escaped. Where Bold's cot had been, the bottom of the wall had stood fast and the top of the wall had collapsed *over*, but not *on* her, the bricks falling into the middle of the room. Where Nurse had been, the wall had fallen outwards, and she had been thrown over towards Bold One. Imogen was in a corner and both walls had fallen right on top of her. She did not utter a sound and death must have been instantaneous. Where Lalage was, the roof had collapsed at her feet mostly, one beam and a huge mass of rubble coming on to her body. But there had fallen on to her pillow a pile of bricks three feet deep, and if she had not leant over to me as she did, when the crash came, there could have been no hope for her. On my bed there were two rafters across the pillows (my head had been wedged between them) and the beam where my thighs had been. The rest was rubble, which had been over my body and legs. Nurse is slightly injured in the back and is in hospital, but should be out in a few days' time.

The last three days I have been busy collecting the survivors of my office and staff, getting them food and drink and so on. Almost all the horses escaped without serious injury, though my own two – Jorrocks and Ambrosia – were killed outright. It has been difficult to get food for the horses, and I cannot send them out to Mastung, as that's worse than Quetta. Four-fifths of the inhabitants killed, food all buried in the debris, and no water. Kalat is also flat, but the Khan and his family escaped.

I have been up to see Lalage at the British Military Hospital at frequent intervals. For two days she was in a state of complete collapse, and could keep neither food nor drink down. Yesterday she took a slight turn for the better: the doctors think that she has no internal injury (though, like mine, her body is a mass of bruises and scars) and were only doubtful if she had the strength to recover. But this morning I found her distinctly better; this evening I could not go to see her as I have got a sore on my leg and I have got to keep quiet for 12 hours or so, but others have been to see her and say the change is quite remarkable. She is nearly her old self again, and hasn't been sick for 24 hours. The nursing at the Hospital (mostly voluntary nurses, wives of officers from the Cantonment) has been wonderful. Skilled and gentle. Lalage could not have pulled through without that nursing. The loss and the suffering have been terrible, and the tragedy is such a general one that one's own personal loss, and the sense of it, are still dulled. Indeed, just at present, you may feel the loss of Imogen even more than we do, if possible. I don't know when I'll be able to write again, but you can take no news to be good news.

With love from Lal and myself,
TEDDY.

Three incidents, unrecorded in this letter, are still fresh in my memory.

One of the four men who had dug us out was a stranger to me. 'Who are you?' I asked him.

'I am a prisoner,' he replied unemotionally. 'The day after tomorrow Your Honour is to try me for murder.'

I recall, too, the shock which I experienced when, as I looked sadly at the long line of bodies which the troops had dug out from the ruins of our servants' quarters, one of the corpses (it was our Goanese cook, Manuel) suddenly rose from the dead, as it were, shook himself, and walked away.

And I remember – how could I forget it – the act of one of the Kalat stable-boys, Sher Mohammed, a tall, loose-limbed, work-shy Pathan. When I returned to the ruins of our house from the Residency camp I was still shoeless; shoeless on a waste of broken glass, fragmented brick and chips of mortar. Seeing my condition, Sher Mohammed took off his own shoes and insisted on my wearing them. . . .

One of my melancholy duties was to collect and record the

personal possessions of Kalat subjects killed in Quetta. Among the victims of the earthquake was Yusuf Ali, the young Chief of the Magasi tribe. Yusuf Ali had received a college education in Sind and had formed political views which were, in the context of Baluchistan society, revolutionary. As leader of a newly formed political party, the Young Biloch party, he had introduced into Baluchistan professional anti-British agitators; and he was heading for serious trouble when, in the winter of 1933, Sir Norman Cater sent for him.

'Sirdar Sahib,' said Sir Norman to him, 'you are young and you have chosen your friends unwisely. I suggest that you leave Baluchistan for twelve months and widen your mind by foreign travel. Why don't you visit Europe and see for yourself what the West is like?'

Yusuf Ali demurred. 'I do not want to leave home,' he protested.

'You will have to leave home in any case,' replied Sir Norman. 'I cannot allow you to stay in Baluchistan stirring up trouble. But if you are wise you will leave voluntarily. No one need know that you are taking my advice in this matter.'

So Yusuf Ali had sailed for England, and when he returned, a year later, he seemed a different man. 'Bilkul "gentleman" ban-gaya,' the Raisani Nawab reported to me. 'He has become the complete English gentleman.' 'But even so,' he added, 'I wouldn't trust him. The change is only on the surface.'

Yusuf Ali had come to see me in Sibi. It was true that he was covered with syphilitic sores, but he was wearing English clothes, professed sentiments of loyalty both to the British Government and the Khan, had given up (he said) his old political associates, and was now prepared to work, under my guidance, for the improvement of social conditions in his own tribal territory. I did not know whether to believe him or not. But I took him at his word and promised to help him with the building and staffing of new schools and new dispensaries.

In the earthquake his body had not been mutilated beyond recognition; and the oddments which he had about his person –

ring, cigarette case, pocket book – were brought to me. The contents of the pocket book showed that his political conversion had indeed been a genuine one; and they disclosed how it came about. He had made the acquaintance, in a London park, of an English girl of poor education and dubious morals. The acquaintance ripened into a passionate and romantic attachment. He had described himself to the girl as a Prince; and he treated her, I have no doubt, with princely generosity. To him the girl seemed the very embodiment of feminine loveliness and charm. Accepted by this girl as her lover, he had been purged of every trace of anti-British feeling. The correspondence in the pocket book told the whole story, oh, so clearly. And I was glad that, when he had visited me in Sibi and told me of his changed feelings towards the British, I had shown no sign of scepticism.

Until the end of June I spent the greater part of every day touring affected villages in the State and organising medical relief and supplies of food. Early in July some of my earthquake sores became septic and I had to have medical treatment. The Khan wrote me a charming letter. Spelling and punctuation may have been open to criticism, but the spirit of sympathy and friendliness which it showed cheered me greatly. Here is the letter, exactly as the Khan wrote it:

Kalat.

12/7/35.

My dear Teerdy,

Thank you very much for your letter, I pray to God for your health and I am sure you will be absolutely alright in a short time, don't worry yourself about State work everything is well here, I don't mine about the excessive work it will be alright when you get better, look after your health very much, because your good health is very valuable to me, as my whole State deppends upon you, I like to see you in Kalat when you are absolutely well and healthy.

Will you please give my salams to your wife and love to my little friend [Xanthe].

I hear that you are getting a Ford V eight for yourself, why not to get this car in bond and instead of your private car it should be a State car in your services, I don't want you spending your money because you have already lost much property in this earthquack, dont think about funds it can be arranged.

Yours sincerely
Ahmad Yar

The earthquake caused damage in the State along a strip of territory ninety miles in length of an average width of fifteen miles. Casualties amounted to some 3,000 killed and more than 1,500 seriously injured. In the course of the first few weeks following the earthquake all possible measures were taken to relieve immediate distress. Camp hospitals were opened at convenient centres, while doctors and nurses visited outlying villages. Labour was provided to open up channels or dig wells where the earthquake had blocked supplies of drinking water. Special levies were engaged to protect property lying in ruined bazaars and to guard standing crops from the depredations of marauding nomads. Food and clothing were issued to the destitute and water-mills were repaired. But these measures were necessarily only of temporary benefit. They preserved life in the local inhabitants but did not give them the means of living otherwise than as animals. Their condition was, indeed, pitiable. They could not leave their homes since, unlike the majority of survivors from Quetta, they had no relations or friends in the Punjab or Sind. Shelterless, they remained near their ruined houses, beside their surviving sheep and goats and cattle, guarding the remnants of their household goods.

The Viceroy had opened an Earthquake Relief Fund which attracted generous support from all over the world. The total of the Fund reached more than 54 lakhs of rupees (over £400,000). From Kalat we asked for a grant of 5¼ lakhs, less than one-tenth of the Fund's resources. I prepared an estimate showing in detail how the money would be used – on houses, on water-channels and water-mills, on plough cattle. Kalat, I urged, had a special claim on the Fund.

> The inhabitants of the earthquake area in Kalat [I wrote] have not, like the majority of sufferers in Quetta, received help in Sind or the Punjab. They have no connection with those Provinces. They have no homes but those they have lost, no land or water but that which has now been rendered useless, and no relatives or friends who are not in a similar plight to themselves.

We received only 1 lakh of rupees (£7,500). Unfortunately the Fund was administered on behalf of the Viceroy by officials of the Finance Department of the Government of India. Like Treasury officials in Britain they were able and conscientious but totally lacking in judgment or imagination. They did not realise, and could not be made to realise, that the real need was for quick assistance on the most generous scale possible.

Years later, in 1938, the administrators of the Fund were actually searching in Sind and the Punjab for earthquake sufferers to whom they could distribute the balance of the Fund. How precious that balance would have been in Kalat in the summer of 1935!

CHAPTER 12

The Khan of Kalat

I SPENT the late summer and autumn of 1935 in a tent pitched outside the ruins of Kalat town. Here, in close touch with the Khan, I wrestled with the State's financial problems. Kalat's total annual revenues did not exceed 15 lakhs of rupees, and we needed fully that amount merely to replace essential buildings destroyed by the earthquake. Necessary replacements included State residences for the Khan, accommodation for State officials, administrative offices, levy posts, schools and hospitals. It was not easy to see how the money could be raised.

At one moment during the summer I had hopes of striking a profitable bargain with the Agha Khan who, though he was entitled to be called His Highness and enjoyed a personal salute of eleven guns, was not a territorial ruler. Followers he had in abundance, but no subjects, as there was no territory over which he exercised sovereign rights. It seemed to me that if, as I had reason to believe, the Agha Khan was in search of a principality, Kalat could easily spare Haptalar, an island in the Arabian Sea lying off the coast of Mekran, which was frequented only by a handful of fishermen. These fishermen made a living by catching sharks, whose fins were exported to Malaya via Colombo. Dried shark's fin, I was told, possessed aphrodisiac properties which were much relished by the Chinese residents of Malaya. But my scheme was still-born. Ahmad Yar would not hear of ceding sovereignty over any portion of his territory. To do so, he patiently explained to me, would constitute a betrayal of the trust that he had inherited from his ancestors and hoped, with the aid of Providence, to hand on to his successors. So that dream faded.

We raised a certain amount of money by issuing prospecting

licences to oil companies. But the most substantial source of new State revenue originated in the steps I had taken during the previous year to revive the agricultural economy of Kachhi.

The province of Kachhi contained some 5,000 square miles of potentially fertile alluvial plain through the middle of which flowed the River Nari. At the beginning of the century the population of Kalat State was estimated to be about 470,000. By 1933 the figure had fallen to little more than 300,000. There was no doubt that the depopulation of the State had been due to misrule so grossly oppressive that even the hardy Biloch and Brahui tribesmen could not endure it. Kachhi had suffered more than any other province. Villages were deserted, land was untilled. The peasantry of Kachhi, fleeing from oppression in the State, had taken refuge in Sind, where the men-folk earned a meagre and uncertain livelihood as unskilled labourers.

Kachhi had not been affected by the earthquake, and the potentialities for its development were almost unlimited. The system of cultivation was traditional and, in my experience, unique. Every summer, before the rains came, the cultivators from villages adjacent to the River Nari collected in groups and combined to construct across its course a series of solid earthen dams. Every village supplied its quota of men and bullocks proportionate to its share of the area to be irrigated. The larger dams might be as much as 250 yards in length, 60 yards broad at the base and 50 or 60 feet in height. Men and bullocks, using only wooden plank-harrows, worked with ant-like discipline and co-ordination to erect these massive ephemeral structures. (What a man and a pair of bullocks did in a day, a bulldozer could have done in an hour.) When the floods came, in July or August, the upper dams would be breached, one after another, as soon as the area commanded by each had received sufficient water. In due course, as soon as their turn came, the lower dams too would be breached. Even so, precious water ran to waste in measureless volume and, as an observer recorded at the beginning of the century, 'the scientific development of this indigenous system would probably result in a very large increase of cultivation.'

Fortunately for Kalat State there was stationed in Quetta in 1934–35 an irrigation engineer of quite exceptional talent, H. L. Francis. He loved water and problems connected with water as others love politics, maybe, or racing. Generously, without remuneration of any kind, he devoted much of his spare time (including long week-ends) to the study of my problems in Kachhi. He advised against constructing permanent dams across the River Nari. These, he thought, might be left high and dry should the river change its course. But he prepared detailed plans for the dimensions and location of earthen dams of traditional design and for the ramification of channels spreading out from points upstream of them. And he encouraged me to invest State capital in the construction of a concrete dam across a smaller river where it debouched from the hills above Lehri in the east of the province. This latter dam was so constructed that the channels leading from it delivered to each of many hundreds of landholders his exact share of the water available.

Francis himself was killed in the earthquake and did not see the fruit of his labours. But his plans proved faultless. In the spring of 1935, attracted by generous revenue concessions which had been widely advertised throughout Sind, hundreds of emigré families returned to their former homes in Kachhi. Money was advanced to them for the purchase of bullocks and seed-grain and, joining with the cultivators who had remained in their villages, they co-operated in building a series of dams to the specifications suggested by Francis. When the floods came, extensive tracts of virgin soil were irrigated and the ensuing harvest proved to be, in quantity and quality, without precedent. The concrete dam above Lehri was also an unqualified success.

Living, as I was, at Kalat during the late summer of 1935, I saw a great deal of Ahmad Yar. From him I received my first initiation into the arts and crafts of practical politics. I was well acquainted with Political Theory as an academic study and could argue with anyone the respective merits of different forms of government. But practical politics, at least in the eyes of Ahmad Yar, were concerned solely with the struggle for power. I myself, brought up against the background of a stable society and trained as an administrator, took for granted the possession of power and was interested only in methods of using it to the best public advantage. But Ahmad Yar was heir to a different tradition, a tradition of craft and guile and incessant intrigue. These, with poison and the sword, were the weapons with which his ancestors had established their position; these, he felt instinctively, were the weapons with which he must maintain his own position. More precisely, as I gradually discovered, Ahmad Yar was concerned, first, to consolidate his existing position of relative superiority to his Sirdars (historically the Khan of Kalat, in relation to his Sirdars, was only *primus inter pares*) and, secondly, to convert that position of relative superiority into one of absolute supremacy.

In administrative matters the Khan left me very much to my own devices and I was able to do as I pleased. In political matters, however, we could not see eye to eye. I believed, and sought to persuade him, that the State as a whole could not prosper unless the Khan and his Sirdars were united. They must work together, I urged, to promote the welfare of all the inhabitants of the State wherever they lived, whether in the tribal territory of the Sirdars or in the Niabats administered by the Khan's Wazir. Only in this way, I argued, could the Khan become the respected ruler of a great State.

But Ahmad Yar would not agree. He probably thought me naïve and ingenuous, my ideas unrealistic. He himself firmly believed in a policy of 'Divide and Rule' and was convinced that, if he did not foster dissension among his Sirdars, they would combine to overthrow him or, at least, to reduce his authority over them. Nevertheless, though we could not agree on policy in relation to the Sirdars, our candid discussions did result in our getting to know each other much better than we had done before.

Hugh Weightman, who had been Secretary to the Agent to the Governor-General at the time of the earthquake, was now Political Agent, Kalat. On October 21st he and his wife and Lalage and I set off on a fortnight's tour of the province of Mekran. I had much work to do there. A dispute between the two leading Sirdars of Mekran had to be settled if bloodshed was to be avoided. Work on a new airfield and seaplane base at Jiwani, at the extreme south-west corner of the State, had to be inspected. The possibility of exporting Mekran dates of the Mazawati variety – the best in the world – had to be explored. Above all, I was determined to stop, by customs patrols or other means, the illicit traffic which was being carried on between South East Persia and the seaport of Gwadur, an enclave in Kalat territory belonging to the Sultan of Muscat.

All this work was of absorbing interest. But letters which I wrote to my parents giving an account of my activities at that time show that Weightman and I did not confine our energies to work alone. Here is a typical extract:

> The next day, October 29th, we left Jiwani at 7 a.m. and got to Dum, near Suntsar, at 8.30 a.m. We spent most of the morning shooting and got quite a good mixed bag – 20 black partridge, 4 grey partridge, 8 sandgrouse and 14 duck. After lunch we set off for Turbat but, 15 miles from home, the darkness came on and our lights wouldn't work. We were still on a difficult road in the hills. However, my driver found out what was wrong and, though he couldn't repair the damage then and there, by lying along the mudguard he was able to hold some connection together which kept the lights going intermittently. So we got along very slowly, and eventually arrived at Turbat at 9.15 p.m.

From Pasni in Mekran we travelled by car north-east to Khozdar in the province of Jhalawan. Our plan was to cross by the Mula Pass the range of mountains which lies between Khozdar and the Kachhi plain. But we could not take our cars more than a few miles beyond Khozdar and, leaving them to their drivers to bring to Kachhi via Kalat and the Bolan Pass, we set off on horseback or on foot for the three-day crossing of the Mula Pass.

This journey was a memorable one for me because I was nearly drowned in the Mula river. Here is the report of the incident written by Weightman when recommending me for the Albert Medal. (In fact I received the bronze medal of the Royal Humane Society, an award much more appropriate to the circumstances.)

> On the 13th November 1935 Mr Wakefield, accompanied by his wife and by my wife, was sitting by the side of a deep pool in a gorge named Chattokh in the Mula Pass in Kalat State. Two Musiani Brahuis were bathing in the shallow water at the head of the pool where there is a very strong flow of water and where the bottom shelves rapidly. One of the men suddenly got out of his depth and, being unable to swim, was sucked under by the strong current and, as was subsequently discovered, was carried under a submerged ledge in the rock face of the opposite cliff. Mr Wakefield, removing only his shoes, dived fully dressed into the pool but was at first unable to find the drowning man. Just as his breath was giving out and he was about to come to the surface preparatory to another dive, he caught sight of an arm which he seized, and attempted to swim to the surface. It was then that he discovered that the man was caught under a ledge of rock, and simultaneously the hand seized his arm in an immoveable grip. By now Mr Wakefield's breath was completely exhausted and he realised that he was in imminent danger of being drowned himself. Fortunately he is an exceptionally powerful man and with a last tremendous effort he succeeded in dislodging the man from the cleft in which he was caught and brought him to the surface. He himself rapidly recovered but he had considerable difficulty in holding the man's head out of water and getting him into the shallows. He was then helped out by other Brahuis and proceeded to apply artificial respiration to the half-drowned man, who soon recovered.

Weightman wrote that the half-drowned man 'soon recovered'. 'Soon' is a relative term. It was several minutes, and it seemed to me much longer, before the aids of artificial respiration (learnt in the Haileybury swimming bath) restored him to consciousness. Then, with a spasmodic fluttering of eyelids, he opened his eyes, looked about him and rose from the ground. Without saying a word to anyone, he walked to his pony, mounted it and rode off. That was the last I saw of him. It was not, however, the last I heard of him. The Musiani tribe were not highly regarded among the Brahuis. When the Khan of Kalat heard that his Wazir-i-Azam had nearly lost his life in saving a Musiani from drowning, he could not at first believe the tale. Assured of its truth, he found it the most amusing story he had ever heard. If I had risked my life to serve some useful purpose – that he would have appreciated and applauded. But he found it laughable that anyone in my position should risk his life to rescue a despised Musiani from drowning; and laugh he did, to my face as well as behind my back.

Arriving in Kachhi, I spent some days inspecting the massed heaps of grain that the bumper harvest had yielded. Ownership of all land in the Niabats was nominally vested in the Khan as head of the State. In British India land revenue was normally collected in cash, but in Kalat the peasant proprietor met the State's demands by handing over a fixed share of the produce of his land. That share, depending on the terms of the occupier's tenure of his land, might be as little as one-tenth or as much as one-third. At every threshing floor in every village the State's share of the grain was set on one side and duly weighed by revenue officials. Later in the season the grain belonging to the State was sold, Niabat by Niabat, to grain merchants, commonly known as 'contractors', who annually gathered for the auction from centres of population throughout Baluchistan and Sind.

The State's share of the autumn crop of 1933, auctioned early in 1934, had been small in quantity and had fetched a low price. The 1934 crop had been larger but the prices were still low. They were, indeed, so much below the true market value that my suspicions had been aroused and I had instituted a thorough investigation into the circumstances surrounding the auction. This investigation disclosed that the contractors who habitually bid at the auctions formed a closely organised ring and agreed among themselves to make only minimum bids for each parcel of grain.

I reproached myself for having allowed the State to be cheated in the previous two years by the conspiracy of crooked contractors and resolved that this should not happen again. With the help of my Revenue Assistant, whose home was in the Punjab, I made plans to break the ring.

Our plans were successful. When the auctions were held, early in 1936, there were several new contractors bidding – men of status from the Punjab, whose travelling expenses we had paid and who were perfectly willing to offer a fair price for our grain. Moreover, we changed the method of auction and instituted what is known as the Dutch system. By this system the auctioneer does not begin with a low figure, raise it as bids are made, and knock down the lot to the highest bidder. He begins with a high figure, gradually lowers it, and sells to the first man to make a bid.

I did not attend the auctions but was astonished at their outcome. The prices realised for our grain were, in the case of some lots, far in excess of the prevailing market rates. I heard later what had happened. There were twelve lots to be auctioned. The first lot was knocked down to a contractor from the Punjab at a fair, but not excessive, figure. The second and third lots also went to contractors from the Punjab. At this stage of the auction the local contractors from Sind and Baluchistan began to get worried. They had to stock up with grain to keep their businesses going. One of their number took the fourth lot. A blackleg? They were not sure. And now there were only eight lots left, with fifteen or more contractors requiring to make purchases. If there had earlier been 'gentlemen's agreements' (or thieves' compacts) they were at this point forgotten, or at least ignored. The last few lots went, competitively, at sky-high prices. Indeed, the purchaser of the last lot, a grain merchant from Bhag, was later forced into liquidation as a consequence of his rash bid.

Those who had most cause for satisfaction at this dénouement were myself and the Punjab contractors. I had succeeded in doubling – almost trebling – the State's revenue from Kachhi. The Punjab contractors, for their part, made a handsome profit by selling, at an enhanced price, the grain they had bought in the first three lots, to contractors from Sind and Baluchistan who had been unable to buy any grain at all. These Punjab contractors returned to their distant homes (with free railway tickets) handsomely rewarded for their enterprise.

I spent the cold weather of 1935–36 at Sibi in constant touch with Ahmad Yar, who was living only a few miles away at his winter headquarters at Dhadar. The Sirdars were now becoming more tolerant of me. At first I must have seemed to them like a Christian bull in a Muslim china shop. What did I know of the subtleties of Islamic law? What knowledge had I of the State's unwritten customs which, as generation succeeded generation, had gradually acquired the full force and validity of law? Or how could I appreciate the intricate interplay of tribal ambitions and jealousies whose roots were grounded in the unrecorded past? In spite of all this the Sirdars were beginning to realise that, while I was 'the Khan's man', I was not necessarily on this account hostile to them and to their order. Indeed, they began to sense that my influence on the Khan was salutary to the extent that I discouraged him, if only with partial success, from taking sides in inter-tribal rivalries and setting one Sirdar against another.

I declined to be drawn into conspiracy and intrigue, not because I was high-principled or priggish, but because I doubted my capacity to play successfully a game with rules so different from those of cricket!

One day the Musiani Sirdar came to see me. Zahri Khan had a crooked nose, a comically crooked face and a crooked mind. He also had a sophisticated sense of humour surprising in a man of his background. In Urdu the word Zahri means 'poisonous'. When I first met him he had told me that I could always remember him as he was 'poisonous by name and poisonous by nature'. I was now to discover that his description of himself did not lack an element of truth.

Before entering my 'daftar' (a convenient word meaning an office or study) Zahri Khan had, as a mark of respect, removed his sandals. After the usual preliminary greetings and standing barefoot in front of the desk at which I had been working, he gave me a searching look.

'Wazir Sahib,' he said, 'I have a proposition to put to you.'

'Go ahead,' I replied. 'What is it?'

'I know that you have the State's interests at heart. You can advance these if you will co-operate with me. I am on intimate terms with Rasul Baksh, the Zarakzai Sirdar, and he has great confidence in me. As you know, he is a temperamental person and has twice crossed the border with his followers.'

Here I must explain that if a Sirdar 'crossed the border', i.e. went over to Afghanistan, he signified thereby renunciation of his allegiance to the Khan. In Parliamentary terms he crossed the floor of the House, as it were, and joined the Opposition.

Zahri Khan continued.

'Twice he has crossed the border and twice he has been pardoned. On the last occasion he was warned that, if he crossed the border again, his lands would be forfeited to the State. I am quite certain that, by promising to go with him, I can persuade him to cross the border again. You see what I mean?'

'No,' I replied, 'I don't.'

I was not feigning stupidity. I genuinely didn't see what he was leading up to.

Zahri Khan sighed at my obtuseness. His game was, indeed, very different from cricket.

He explained further. 'I will prevail on Rasul Baksh to cross the border. I may even have to go part of the way with him myself. Then his lands – and they are rich and fertile lands – can be forfeited to the State. Now do you see what I mean?'

'Yes,' I replied. 'You have made it very clear. But what do *you* get out of this?'

'Two things. First, I have an old score to pay off against Rasul Baksh. Secondly, the Khan, if you so advise him, will certainly reward me by giving me half the Zarakzai lands.'

I had been slow to recognise the import of Zahri Khan's proposal. Now, when its full infamy was borne in upon me, I lost my temper. I was shocked and angry, and felt insulted that he should think me capable of being his accomplice in such a despicable plot. My spectacles were in my hand, and I flung them at him, bidding him leave my house and never darken its doors again. He crossed the room to where the spectacles had fallen (fortunately unbroken), picked them up and presented them to me as though he were giving me a prize – for cricket, perhaps! Without another word he left the 'daftar' and went out to the verandah to put on his sandals again. There, a few minutes later, I saw my three-year-old daughter Xanthe playing 'This little pig went to market' with the toes of his bare feet. Happily absorbed in this innocent game he appeared quite oblivious of the storm that had just broken over his guileful, guilty head.

In the spring of 1936 I went home on ten months' leave and never subsequently returned to Kalat. I believed at the time that I had been a successful Chief Minister and had laid the foundations of a sound administration. The press was complimentary. 'The most important achievement of Mr Wakefield's administration,' wrote *The Times of India*, 'was the restoration of Kachhi province to its ancient position as the granary of Kalat State, through the co-operation of State officials and Zamindars.'

Alas, my 'most important achievement' was short-lived. By reducing taxation I had attracted cultivators back to the land and, having got them there, I had protected them from harassment by greedy officials. I had, indeed, fulfilled my ambition of re-populating Kachhi. But I had failed to associate the Khan with my plans for developing the economy of the State. I had worked alone, or with my official colleagues, and had not taken him into my confidence as I should have done. Moreover, the pledges I had given to cultivators ploughing new land in Kachhi, though given on behalf of the State, were associated with me personally rather than with the Khan. And so, within a year or two of my departure, when confronted by an intractable Budget deficit, the Khan allowed taxation to be raised to its former exorbitant level. Predictably, the inward flow of immigrants ceased. Soon the flow was reversed and became an exodus. Kachhi again sank to the derelict condition from which my measures had rescued it.

I see too, in retrospect, that I had failed to appreciate at a sufficiently early stage the delicate constitutional and political problem posed by the equivocal relationship subsisting between the Khan and his Sirdars. With greater political experience I might well have found a solution which would have consolidated the State under the Khan without giving offence to the Sirdars. Fifteen years later I would have avoided many of the mistakes I made during the first eighteen months of my period as Wazir-i-Azam. On the other hand, fifteen years later I would not have had the physical energy to carry out those strenuous tours by means of which I had gained personal knowledge of every locality in the far-flung State. Si jeunesse savait, si vieillesse pouvait!

On various occasions during the next decade when the fortunes of the State reached a low ebb, Ahmad Yar asked that I should return to the State as his Wazir-i-Azam. But I had moved on by then to pastures new and could not readily be spared from other duties.

CHAPTER 13

The Thakurs of Gujarat

ONE of the greatest pleasures incidental to service abroad is returning home on leave. It is a pleasure comparable to those enumerated by Spenser in 'The Faerie Queen':

> *Sleep after toil, port after stormy seas,*
> *Ease after war, death after life does greatly please.*

Our delight in returning to England in the spring of 1936 was tempered by sadness at the loss of Imogen. But another baby was on the way, and in July Lalage gave birth to our elder son, Humphry. The months of leisure raced by and, when 1937 arrived, I began to wonder what my next appointment would be.

The Under-Secretary in the Political Department at Delhi was responsible for initiating proposals for what were known as 'postings', and was thus in a position to do a friend a good turn. A friend, he would ingenuously suggest, might best be employed to the public advantage in Baluchistan or Kashmir, where the climate was agreeable and facilities for sport abounded. A less favoured colleague might be consigned to Western India or the Persian Gulf, where the climate was unhealthy and amenities scarce or non-existent. In the Persian Gulf, indeed, there was the financial attraction of liberal local allowances, but the posts in Western India lacked even this compensation. As the Under-Secretary at Delhi in 1937 was a friend of Lalage's as well as of mine I was disappointed when I heard, early in that year, that I was to be posted to Western India as Political Agent, Sabarkantha Agency. However, protests would have been unavailing and so, at the end of January, leaving behind the children (Xanthe and the six-month-old Humphry), Lalage and I dutifully set sail for Bombay.

From Bombay we travelled by train 300 miles northwards to Ahmedabad. There we had to transfer ourselves and our luggage to another train. This would bring us in half an hour to Dabhoda, whence it was only fifteen miles by road to Sadra, my new headquarters.

We arrived at Ahmedabad in the late afternoon. On the platform to greet us was an unprepossessing gentleman, about fifty years of age, who introduced himself as Kesarisinhji, Thakur (ruling chief) of Ambaliara, one of the States in the Sabarkantha Agency. We had an hour or so to wait before our train left. During the interval the Thakur entertained us, in a station waiting-room which he had specially reserved for the purpose, to a large unappetising meal of coarsely-flavoured tea, tired fruit and crumbling fly-ridden confectionery. I suspected his motives for proffering this unwanted hospitality but had, perforce, to accept it with as good a grace as possible.

We arrived at our new home at dusk. It was a fifteenth-century fortress built along the top of a cliff 100 feet above the broad bed of the Sabarmati river. It had been built by Sultan Mahmud Bigarha, a contemporary of the English king, Henry VII. The fame of this Sultan had spread far beyond the bounds of his kingdom of Gujarat. History narrates* that his beard came down to his waist and that his moustaches were so long that he used to tie them over his head. His appetite was prodigious and he was reputed to eat more than 20 lb. weight of food every day of his life. Like Mithridates he had been dosed with poison from his earliest childhood in order to give him immunity from its effects. The story was told that his blood became so tainted with venom that a fly rash enough to bite him would instantly drop dead. Samuel Butler, in *Hudibras*, has given him a place in literature:

The Prince of Cambay's daily food
Is asp, and basilisk, and toad.

* *The Oxford History of India* by Vincent A. Smith, 2nd Edition, p. 270

The principality of Gujarat, ruled by Sultan Mahmud from 1459 to 1511, was conquered by Akbar in 1573 and remained under Moghul control for nearly two centuries. Thereafter the Marathas held sway until, in the first quarter of the nineteenth century, the Maratha power was broken and British supremacy established. Something remarkable then occurred. The conquering British incorporated into their growing dominion only a small part of the territory they had wrested from the Marathas. The greater part was left in the hands of the former rulers, to whom guarantees were given that their existing rights and privileges would be respected. Before the final collapse of the Maratha Empire much of the territory comprising it had fallen into the hands of freebooting chiefs, captains of robber bands who maintained themselves and their followers by plunder and pillage. It was to these connoisseurs of rapine and murder that guarantees of protection were then given, as well as to established rulers of more extensive and orderly tracts. Thus a single fleeting moment in the long and varied history of Gujarat was caught, as it were, by the British – was caught, and stabilised, and perpetuated. The stream of history was suddenly arrested, the current of change and development ceased to flow.

When I arrived in Gujarat in 1937 the structure of society had been embalmed for more than a century. In the Sabarkantha Agency there were forty-six so-called States, each with its own ruling chief, or Thakur, exercising jurisdiction, albeit limited, over his own subjects. These States varied greatly in size. Some of them were relatively large. Tharad was more than 1,200 square miles in area. Its ruler, in the words of one of my predecessors in the Agency, 'combined the appearance of a buffalo with the mentality of a mule'. He grossly misruled his subjects, some of whom were Chauhan Rajputs who had been in continuous occupation of their lands since before the Muslim conquest at the end of the fourteenth century. Other States were small, ludicrously small. Sudasna, for instance, had an area of only two square miles. Yet its chief, Thakur Prithisinhji, with an ancestry going back 2,000 years to Vikram the Great of Ujjain, was a model ruler of his 7,000 subjects. In Anglo-Saxon England he would have ranked as a minor thane. In modern England he would have been a respected village squire and chairman of the local bench of magistrates. In Gujarat, in 1937, he was the ruler of a State enjoying the protection of the Paramount Power.

Nationalist politicians in British India argued that the States were an anachronism and ought therefore to be abolished. The argument was valid in respect of the petty States of Western India. But the British were bound by engagements entered into more than a century ago with the ancestors of the present ruling Thakurs. They could find no honourable means of terminating these engagements; and the Thakurs, understandably, clung tenaciously to the rights and privileges they had inherited from their forefathers. Individual Thakurs intrigued endlessly against each other but combined powerfully whenever the existence of their order as a whole was threatened.

The task of a Political Agent in Western India was to exercise general supervision and control over the rag-bag of diminutive States committed to his political charge. Some of my immediate predecessors had been less diligent in performing their official duties than in organising their escape from 'tedious work among uncongenial people in a lonely place with an unhealthy climate' (the quotation is from a letter I wrote at the time). Thus I found myself confronted with a massive accumulation of semi-legal, semi-political cases, the arrears of years rather than of months. One of these cases, I was interested to see, related to a long-standing dispute about land between the Thakur of Ambaliara, my host at Ahmedabad railway station, and his neighbour, the Thakur of Ramas. Ambaliara was the bigger of the two States. Its Thakur had 10,000 subjects and a police force more than forty strong to keep them in order. The Thakur of Ramas, on the other hand, had only 1,600 subjects and a proportionately smaller police force – an inspector and four constables. The quarrel about land had been going on for many years and was likely, so far as I could see, to continue indefinitely into the future.

While the weather was still cool I spent some weeks visiting the States in my political charge, and Lalage accompanied me.

In Sudasna the Thakur wanted to tether a live kid to a stake as bait for a leopard which he had promised me the chance of shooting. Lalage asked whether the leopard, if it came, would maul or kill the kid. The Thakur replied that it would. As Lalage was unhappy about this the Thakur gave the kid the protection of a specially constructed cage with strong bars. When the leopard came, the thudding of the frightened kid's feet against the wooden floor of its cage made it suspicious and it delayed its near approach for an hour or more. In the end, however, its caution yielded to the temptation of a succulent meal, and it came close enough to the cage for me to kill it with a single shot from my Rigby rifle.

In Tharad and Warahi we had the delight of watching the wild asses that still roamed the salt flats bordering the Little Rann of Cutch. In Wao, a State adjacent to Tharad, Lalage was presented by the Rana with a valuable diamond and emerald necklace set in platinum which, of course, she refused to accept. The Rana of Wao had a dispute with the Thakur of Tharad which he hoped I would settle in his favour.

Among these rulers of petty States there were two or three men of energy and vision who were respected, even revered, by their subjects. For the most part, however, like the Istimrardars of Ajmer, they were degenerate and irresponsible. Such energy as they possessed was devoted to the fabrication of plots designed to injure neighbouring rivals and adversaries. It was largely these antagonisms, rooted in the distant past but still flowering vigorously, that gave the Political Agent so much work to do.

Lalage and I had not long returned from our tour when Sir Courtenay Latimer, Resident for the States of Western India, invited us to visit him at his headquarters in Rajkot. The Resident maintained political relations directly with the rulers of eighteen large States and indirectly, through three Political Agents (of whom I was one), with the rulers of more than 100 smaller States. When we arrived at Rajkot Sir Courtenay Latimer did not ask me whether I was enjoying my work at Sadra. He must have known what the answer would be. Instead, he told me that he was very glad to have me at Sadra and hoped that I would stay there for the full term of my appointment, the usual three years. Seeing my glum looks, he explained (what I already knew) that the last two Political Agents in Sadra had only been there for six months before being transferred elsewhere. As a result of this, he said, the Thakurs in the Sabarkantha Agency were becoming restless and had complained that there was no one with experience of their affairs to whom they could turn with confidence for advice and guidance. 'In the whole of India,' he continued, 'there is no better training ground for a young political officer than the three Agencies in Western India. As I said, I am very glad to have you as one of my Political Agents and I am quite sure that you will profit by three years in Sadra as you will gain most valuable experience.'

What Sir Courtenay Latimer said was certainly true. The Political Agencies in Western India did provide admirable training in political work. There was unlimited scope for initiative in mediation and peace-making, and the consequences of mistakes, though they might be serious for those directly concerned, were not far-reaching. But I was still not attracted to the prospect of three years in Sadra.

The weather during the weeks preceding the arrival of the monsoon was hot and humid and oppressive. From a window in our fortress overlooking the Sabarmati river Lalage and I would watch water-birds fishing. Their techniques differed. Indian skimmers, not unlike terns in appearance, would fly up and down the placid river in flocks, cleaving the surface of the water with their lower beaks. Parties of pelicans, clumsy on land but buoyant in the water, would form themselves into a line and, beating the water with a flurry and scurry of wings, would drive the fish into shallow water where they became vulnerable to the birds' capacious beaks and pouches. Pied kingfishers would hover 15 to 20 feet above the surface of the river and then, with a sudden downward dart, stoop on their prey like hawks.

But human beings also forced themselves on my attention. Early one morning I was lying in bed when a nauseating stench drifted in through the open windows. I wondered idly what it could be. Soon it became overpowering, so I looked out of the window. Gathered in the courtyard below was a group of men, half a dozen perhaps, who had deposited on the ground, slung between poles, the burden they had been carrying. I thought I knew what it was – the carcass of a leopard they had killed for which they now wanted the standard 10-rupee reward. I told the men to take the body out of the courtyard, out of sight and smell, and I would see them later. They seemed agitated, and shouted up to me in a Gujarati dialect which I could not understand. I told them firmly that I would not listen to them until they had removed the stinking carcass. This they then did, but soon returned to the courtyard and continued to chatter and gesticulate excitedly.

When I went downstairs to hear what they had to say I received a shock. What they had brought to show me was not, as I had supposed, the carcass of a leopard; it was the bodies of two men butchered, I was told, by followers of the Thakur of Ambaliara in the course of an attack on Ramas. The affray had taken place forty-eight hours earlier. Lacking other means of transport, the men had travelled on foot twenty-four miles across country carrying the rapidly rotting corpses of their comrades. The Political Agent was the highest authority they knew of, and they doubtless hoped that, if they confronted him with this impressive evidence of their enemies' crime, redress would quickly follow. While I was sceptical about the truth of the story they told me, I was impressed by their feat of physical endurance. I arranged for the two corpses to be sent to the local mortuary so that a post-mortem could be carried out. I had the men's statements recorded by one of my assistants, and I sent a police inspector to Ramas to carry out an investigation on the spot. But I never learned the true story of what had happened.

At the end of June, or early in July, the monsoon arrived. For two months or more, rainfall was almost incessant. From bank to distant bank the broad Sabarmati river became a turgid muddy torrent. Fields were flooded, roads awash. For eight weeks Lalage and I did not leave Sultan Mahmud's fort except to take walks in the immediately surrounding countryside. On such occasions we felt like prisoners taking their quota of permitted exercise.

In those days there was no television. Even a wireless set was useless during the monsoon. We soon exhausted the resources of the Sadra Victoria Memorial Library. But the library had one unusual feature from which, lacking other forms of diversion, we extracted a measure of amusement. Many of the volumes in the library had been used as textbooks by local students of English. Boys and girls the world over, when they are studying a foreign language, underline those words in their textbooks that they do not understand and, having looked them up in a dictionary, make a note of their meaning in the margin. Sadra students of English must have found their subject particularly puzzling. One student, annotating R. L. Stevenson's 'The Wrong Box', had marked the word 'Box' and entered against it in the margin, 'slap on the ears'. A character in the book is described as 'a man of parts'. The same student, underlining the last of these words, had noted against it 'genitals'. Queen Victoria, in memory of whom the library had been erected, would not have been amused. I reflected that countless English schoolboys, studying French or Latin, must have been guilty of comparable deviations from orthodox translation.

The humid heat was utterly depressing. Perhaps we could have found recreation in fishing. But the fish from the river were unpalatable if not quite uneatable. They were large enough, up to 10 or 12 lb. in weight, but were full of bones and tasted of mud. Moreover, we did not relish using live frogs as bait. We saw little of the actual fishing as this was done at night. But we used to watch the bait being collected. A man would go to some small mud-fringed pool or pond. Having threaded two or three worms on to the end of a string of worsted he would crouch behind a bush and cast his worsted line on to the mud at the margin of the pool, a few inches from the water. At once a frog would emerge from the water and seize the bait. As it was swallowing it, the man would jerk his worsted line towards him – and the frog would come with it. In this way a man would collect a dozen live frogs in less than half an hour.

While the monsoon lasted it was not possible to play outdoor games of any kind or to engage in any form of sport such as riding or shooting. Studying the habits and behaviour of birds and animals was our only outdoor occupation. Brown monkeys with red bottoms abounded and were a scourge to the countryside. Being sacred they could not be killed, but the local Thakur spent a large sum of money every year trapping them. When they had been trapped they were put into spacious cages and sent away to be released in the countryside twenty or thirty miles away. But their numbers never seemed to grow less.

Even more entertaining than the brown monkeys were the larger, grey coated, langurs. They went about in troops, leaping from tree-top to tree-top, a single male being accompanied by nine or ten females. On one occasion we watched a female langur submitting to the embraces of her lord and master. As soon as she was released her female companions, chattering with rage (or was it jealousy?), jumped on her and thumped and pummelled her so savagely that we wondered if she would survive the chastisement. The lord and master looked on quite unconcerned.

In the evenings, lacking anything better to do, we would sit indoors watching lizards stalking their prey. The four walls of our drawing-room were their hunting ground, and moths or mosquitoes (moths for preference) were their quarry. There were also numerous blister-flies (cantharides) on the walls and windows of the drawing-room, but these the lizards wisely avoided. A fat moth would settle on the wall, 10 feet away from a lurking lizard. The lizard would stiffen and eye it for awhile. Then it would make a sudden dart in the direction of the moth, stopping 2 or 3 feet away. After a pause it would advance, slowly and stealthily, until it was only a few inches away. Finally, it would make a sudden rapid rush at the unfortunate moth and envelop it in the clasp of its lightning tongue. Often, of course, the moth would see its danger in time and make its escape. But the odds, we calculated, were about six to four against the moth.

Lack of exercise, the enervating climate and the absence of any social life had a depressing effect on both of us. Letters from England telling us about the children's doings brought occasional gleams of sunshine into the drab monotony of our lives. But even these letters had their sting because they reminded us that as long as we were stationed at Sadra there could be no hope of having the children out to join us. I wrote to my friend the Under-Secretary at Delhi. I did not in so many words ask for a transfer but gave him an account of our circumstances that would, I hoped, engage his sympathy and bear fruit when the time came for him to make proposals for the autumn postings.

Shortly after I had sent off my letter I had a remarkable experience. The time was before breakfast, and I was sitting at my dressing-table in front of a large mirror, shaving. My face covered with lather, I was repeating to myself some lines from Housman that matched my prevailing mood:

If here to-day the cloud of thunder lowers,
To-morrow it will hie on far behests.
The flesh will grieve on other bones than ours
Soon, and the soul will mourn in other breasts.

This melancholy recital was interrupted by a flutter of wings. A blue-rock pigeon, flying in through an open window, alighted on the crown of my head and began to preen itself in the mirror. Ignoring the slight scratching of its claws I remained motionless, watching it in the looking-glass. It was there only for a few seconds. Looking at its own reflection in the mirror it suddenly caught sight of the human head on which it was perched. It flew off, alarmed, with a beating of wings that fanned my lathery face.

It happened that the Thakur of Varsoda came to see me later that morning. He was greatly interested when I told him about the incident. It was, he assured me, a most auspicious omen, and he prophesied that luck would come my way.

It did. Three weeks later I heard that I was to leave Sadra at the end of September and go to Secunderabad as Secretary to the Resident for Hyderabad, the premier State in India.

CHAPTER 14

The Punjab States

I DID not, in fact, go to Secunderabad. I was sent instead to Lahore as Secretary to the Resident for the Punjab States.

At the top of the ladder in the Indian Political Service were nine posts of Resident, First Class. To qualify for one of these appointments it was necessary for a member of the Service, at some period of his career, to have spent two years as Secretary to a Resident. I was glad to be given the opportunity to acquire that qualification at such an early stage of my career. I was also glad to be back again in my old Province, the Punjab.

My predecessor, Ambrose Dundas, had not enjoyed being Secretary to the Resident for the Punjab States and had wanted a transfer from his post as much as I had from mine. He had not found the Resident, Sir Harold Wilberforce-Bell, a congenial person to work for. Short in stature, with scanty grey hair that was always neatly brushed back over an almost-bald cranium, Sir Harold gave the impression of being a discontented man. He possessed a clear mind and forceful personality but, like many small men who would like to have been born big, was over-much concerned with his own dignity. In Lahore, where the Resident ranked below the Governor of the Punjab, Sir Harold would avoid attending receptions at which the Governor was present as he did not like to be number two. His preoccupation with questions of status and precedence irked and irritated a succession of able Secretaries – Cecil Griffin, George Gillan, Ambrose Dundas. In Simla, the summer headquarters of the Resident, Dundas felt that the extreme limits of absurdity had been passed when he was asked to arrange for Sir Harold's dhobi (washerman) to have the use of a stone at the dhobi-ghat above rather than below the stone used by the Commissioner of Lahore's dhobi. Truly this was descending to the level of the servants' quarters, where quarrelling could take place about who should serve the 'senior' vegetable at a dinner party.

Sir Harold's father had been a Military Knight of Windsor. Sir Harold felt, in some strange way, that this gave him a special connection with the Court and invested him with personal responsibility for ensuring that privileges or prerogatives of the British Royal family suffered no encroachment. In India, Sir Harold insisted, the epithet Royal was properly applicable only to the British Sovereign and members of his family. A similar restriction (with three authorised exceptions) applied to the title of Prince. When these words, Royal or Prince, were used in connection with members of the ruling families of Indian States Sir Harold would snort with indignation. And if they occurred in letters from Durbars (State Governments), I would be instructed to send a scalding reply. On one occasion we were attending a gun-dog trial in one of the Sikh States as guests of the Maharaja. As we approached the luncheon tents I saw a notice 'For Royalty only'. I hoped Sir Harold would not see it, but he did. He stopped the car in which we were travelling and had the notice taken down.

All the rulers of Indian States displayed a crown above their coats of arms. Some of them used an arched crown. This latter practice, Sir Harold averred, was improper. In his view it amounted almost to high treason since it 'impinged upon the Royal prerogative'. How often did I use these words when writing to offending Durbars! On this issue Sir Harold engaged in direct combat with the influential Maharaja of Patiala, a former Chancellor of the Chamber of Princes and A.D.C. to the King-Emperor. Here was David challenging Goliath, indeed. The battle raged for weeks, but Sir Harold was technically correct and eventually the Maharaja gave in. Other rulers compromised by using a crown that was semi-arched, or even three-quarters arched. Sir Harold would study such coats of arms with a magnifying glass to see whether they transgressed his strictly enforced rule. Only the Maharaja of Kapurthala got the better of him. Acknowledging a stern letter from Sir Harold on this prickly topic he sent a courteous reply from the George V Hotel in Paris. At the top of the hotel notepaper was a gigantic arched crown. . . .

In matters of dress Sir Harold was punctilious himself and demanding of others. Those who worked under him had to conform to his standards. Brook Neal, his Personal Assistant, got so tired of being told that he was not suitably dressed that he had a number of suits made for himself exactly matching those in Sir Harold's wardrobe; and he would find out before breakfast every morning what suit Master was going to wear. When it was hot I would work in my office, 100 yards away from the Residency, in shorts and an open shirt. But I always had a suit and tie ready to put on in case Sir Harold sent for me or (which he rarely did) came across to see me. Once, when we were staying at Chamba and were having breakfast preparatory to a day's shooting, Brook Neal came into the room wearing khaki shorts. He was sent out to put on a pair of long trousers. On that occasion, I remember, Sir Harold was dressed formally, indeed, but not appropriately. He was wearing a starched collar and black elastic-sided boots!

Sir Harold's insistence that his staff and entourage should always be impeccably dressed reflected his concern that his own dignity should not be injured even at second-hand, as it were. He conceded that I must put on shorts in order to play my favourite game of squash but thought it undignified that his Secretary should ride to the squash courts half a mile away on a bicycle. I continued to do this in spite of his disapproval but, like a schoolboy fearful of being caught out-of-bounds, I would jump off my bicycle and hide behind a road-side tree if I saw a Residency car approaching.

Sir Harold was also – there is no other word for it – a snob. He had not been educated at one of the major public schools and felt that this constituted a chink in his social armour. To compensate for this deprivation he would keep a copy of the Eton College Chronicle lying about the house. If a caller wrote his name in the Residency Visitors Book and described himself as

'Landowner', Sir Harold's eye would light up, he would look up his caller in Burke or Kelly and, if he turned out to be 'one of us', he would at once be invited to luncheon or dinner.

If my account of Sir Harold's idiosyncrasies makes him appear a figure of fun it is misleading. He was, in fact, a most formidable person. It is true that he was a bully but, unlike most bullies, he was quite fearless and, the bigger the opponent, the better he enjoyed the tussle. The Punjab States were not petty estates like the majority of so-called States in Western India. They were powerful, autonomous States, with their own civil administration and military forces, and were subject only to the overriding authority of the British Crown, to which their rulers owed allegiance. They were ruled, moreover, by men of character and, in some cases, of great distinction. To establish his personal authority over these Durbars, as Sir Harold did, was a considerable feat. Sir Bertrand Glancy, the Political Secretary, had great respect for him. He once said to me that, while one could laugh at 'Wilbur's' oddities, he could be relied upon more than any other Resident to enforce on Durbars compliance with the policy of the Paramount Power however distasteful it might be to them.

This was a high compliment, but well deserved. Sir Harold had great political experience and found an answer to every problem, however intricate or teasing. Often he used the bludgeon when a more delicate weapon (as I thought) would have been equally effective. But always he got results, the results that were wanted. His family motto was *Gratia gratiam parit* (Courtesy begets courtesy). It should have been *Oderint dum metuant* (Let them hate provided they fear).

The Resident for the Punjab States maintained political relations directly with fourteen major States and indirectly, through a Political Agent, with twenty-two minor ones. These minor States varied greatly in size and importance. The largest, Tehri Garwal, had an area of 4,500 square miles, the smallest,

Darkoti, an area of five square miles. They were controlled, with an admirable blend of kindliness and firmness, by the Political Agent for the Punjab Hill States, Major Burnett. He seldom troubled the Resident with the problems of his Rajput-ruled Hill States but, when he did have to refer a case, his proposals for dealing with it were always sensible and always accepted.

Of the States in the Resident's direct political charge Khairpur was the most troublesome. When Southern and Central Sind were annexed by Sir Charles Napier in 1842 Mir Ali Murad Khan, the ruler of Northern Sind, supported the British and was therefore allowed to retain his territory, which later became known as Khairpur State. His great-grandson, Mir Ali Nawaz Khan, succeeded to the 'masnad' in 1921. (Sir Harold would not permit Indian rulers to sit on a throne. If they were Muslims they sat on a 'masnad', if Hindus or Sikhs, on a 'gaddi'.) During the fourteen years of his rule (again, Sir Harold would not allow Indian rulers to 'reign') Mir Ali Nawaz Khan had squandered the resources of his State on private extravagance and left it burdened with heavy debts.

Mir Ali Nawaz Khan was a man of massive proportions, bulkier even than the 24-stone Nawab of Mamdot. I saw him at the Quetta races in 1934 being helped out of a Rolls Royce whose body and doors had been specially constructed to accommodate his mammoth frame. He had just returned, I remember, from a pilgrimage to Meshed, the expense of which had plunged the State even more deeply into debt. Many of the Punjab rulers were extravagant but none matched Mir Ali Nawaz Khan in sheer irresponsibility. At a time when he was already over head and ears in debt he would go shopping in Delhi or Karachi and order, for one or other of his Begums, tens of thousands of pounds' worth of jewelry. His British Finance Minister, Mr Sladen, used to follow in a car, one shop behind, cancelling his orders.

When Mir Ali Nawaz Khan died, in December 1935, he was succeeded by his twenty-two year-old son, Mir Faiz Mohammed Khan. This young man presented a problem. His mind was not so deranged as to justify his formal exclusion from the succession yet he was manifestly incapable of exercising ruling powers. The policy adopted was to place the administration of the State in the hands of a minister responsible to the Resident, to establish Mir Faiz Mohammed Khan, with his wife and four-year-old son, in a private house in a locality far removed from Khairpur, and to arrange, as far as possible, for the child to be properly looked after.

The policy was Sir Harold's but he left it to me, as his Secretary to carry it out. I will not dwell on the difficulties I encountered in controlling the Mir's private household. It is enough to say that every month, if not every week, there was a domestic crisis of one kind or another. Equally difficult and much more important was the task of restoring the State to some semblance of solvency. Fortunately there was in Khairpur State service at the time an exceptionally gifted accountant and to him I entrusted the duty of settling the late Mir's debts amounting to many lakhs of rupees. All claims against the late Mir, including bills which had remained unpaid for ten years or more, had to be examined and their validity assessed. The accountant, Mangharam Wadhwani, used to come to Lahore or Simla every few weeks to see me. He had a harsh, metallic voice and discharged words at me, in a sequence of volleys, as if he were a machine-gun. At the end of the final volley, without giving me a chance to make any observation, he would gather together his papers, thank me for listening to him, and withdraw.

I trusted Mangharam completely. I had to. There was no alternative. He classified the many hundreds of bills into various categories. Those for jewelry were the largest. He recovered some of the jewelry from the Begums and handed it back to the shopkeepers from whom it had been bought. This produced protests from the Begums. He rejected many claims altogether. This produced protests from the shopkeepers. In most cases he negotiated a compromise settlement with the creditors. They were in a weak bargaining position as the Mir and his successor, enjoying quasi-sovereign rights and privileges, could not be sued in a court of law either in the State or in British India. On the other hand it was most desirable, for the good name of the State and its ruling family, that honest shopkeepers should not be deprived of what was justly due to them.

Aggrieved merchants and shopkeepers from Karachi and other towns in Sind petitioned the Sind Government. The Sind Government forwarded the petitions to the Political Secretary. The Political Secretary, in turn, sent them to the Resident, and Sir Harold passed them on to me. I would discuss them with Mangharam, who generally managed to satisfy me that the complaints made were groundless.

I believe, but cannot be sure, that justice was done in the great majority of cases. Most of the shopkeepers in Sind realised full well the danger of giving credit to the spendthrift Mir and, doubling or trebling their prices, took the risk with their eyes open. They were under no compulsion to sell anything to him otherwise than for cash. But shopkeepers living in Khairpur State had been in a different position. They could not refuse credit to their own ruler and for them I had much greater sympathy. For more than two years I watched Mangharam struggling to clear the State of the late Mir's debts. At the end of that period there were not more than two or three particularly controversial claims still unsettled.

If dead rulers presented the Resident with problems arising from the conduct of their private lives, so too did some of those who were still living. One day the Private Secretary of one of the rulers came to see the Resident. 'His Highness is being blackmailed,' he said, 'and hopes that you will help him.' Sir Harold listened to what the Private Secretary had to say and told him to come and see me. While the Private Secretary was on his way over to me Sir Harold rang me up on the telephone and told me that a certain ruler had got himself into a scrape and that I was to do my best to get him out of it. 'I leave the whole affair in your hands,' he said, 'but try, if you can, to avoid any scandal.'

The Private Secretary arrived in my office. 'I will be quite frank with you,' he said. 'You know what His Highness is like. Unfortunately he had an "affair" with an English girl who is married to an Anglo-Indian. The husband found out and is now threatening to expose His Highness. He cannot be bought off. What are we to do?'

'How much can His Highness afford to pay?'

'He cannot afford to pay anything. He still hasn't paid for his last two motor cars. In any case, the man won't accept money.'

'But supposing the man could somehow be persuaded to accept a sum of money to keep his mouth shut, how much would His Highness be prepared to pay?'

'Rs 5,000 or Rs 10,000 perhaps. Rs 20,000 (£1,500) at the very most.'

'Give me the man's name and address,' I said, 'and I will see what can be done.'

This was a sordid affair, I thought to myself, and not at all dignified. No wonder Sir Harold had left it to me to deal with. Yet it was our duty to do our best for rulers who got into trouble of any kind. I must do what I could to help.

I drafted a letter to the aggrieved husband asking him to come and see me. But I was not satisfied with the letter. The truth was that I could not make up my mind what, tactically, was the best approach to make. I decided to sleep over it.

I did not have to send any letter as the man himself turned up next day asking for an interview with the Resident.

Rulers were normally at pains to conceal disreputable escapades from their Resident or Political Agent and I had been a little surprised that this ruler should have asked the Resident for advice in a matter which was so little to his credit. I now realised (what I should have realised before) that the injured husband, as part of his campaign of blackmail, must have threatened the ruler that he would take his grievance to the Resident; and that the ruler had shrewdly got to the Resident first with his own story and enlisted his sympathy and support.

Sir Harold sent the man to me. He was a small man, fair-skinned for an Anglo-Indian, and he appeared to be very angry.

I let him tell his story, the details of which do not now matter. As he talked I tried to size up his character and assess his real feelings and motives. I gained the impression that he looked on his wife as a possession rather than a partner, and that what he most valued in her was the contribution she made, by her English birth, to raising his own social status. He was angry and indignant at what had happened but not, I thought, genuinely distressed in the way a true husband should have been. I guessed that he was suffering more from injured vanity and hurt pride than from a broken heart. I disliked the man and felt sorry for the woman who was married to him.

He had come to the Resident, he said, to ask for redress. If he did not get satisfaction he would tell his story to every newspaper in Northern India and show up the ruler for the blackguard he was.

I said that I fully understood his feelings. Every honourable man would feel exactly as he did (may I be forgiven for the lie). But honourable men, in his circumstances, were faced with a cruel dilemma. If he denounced the ruler would he not necessarily involve his wife in the scandal?

I then asked him whether he proposed to divorce his wife. He said, no, he was a Roman Catholic. That, I said, made the difficulty even greater. If he were not going to divorce his wife, publicity would entail grievous social consequences for him as well as for his wife.

I then asked him to tell me exactly what he wanted the Resident to do. He replied that he wanted the ruler to be punished. I agreed that the ruler should be made to suffer for his disgraceful behaviour but pointed out that we could not send him to prison, or exile him from his State. What could we do? Fine him?

He agreed that this was the only punishment the Resident could inflict. With some show of reluctance he also acquiesced in my suggestion that, as he was the injured party, the fine should go to him. He insisted that he was not being bought off. Certainly not, I said, there was no question of buying his silence.

It was only from the most honourable motives, and out of consideration for his wife, that he was refraining from taking his story to the Press. On this exalted note our talk ended, with Rs 10,000 agreed upon as a suitable figure for the fine.

Our two children, accompanied by their nurse, had come out from England to join us in Lahore in October 1937. In the late spring of 1938 we all went up to the Simla hills and spent the summer there. Sir Harold was ill in hospital for many weeks, and I did his work under the supervision of the Political Secretary, Sir Bertrand Glancy. In September our second son and fourth child, Hady, was born. We moved down to Lahore again in October and spent the winter there.

In the spring of 1939 Sir Harold went home on leave preparatory to retirement. He had been tolerant of my mistakes and generous in his appreciation of anything I had done well. I was glad, therefore, to be able to render him one final personal service. He had been worrying, characteristically, about his departure from Lahore by train. As Resident for the Punjab States he had always travelled in his own saloon. But now, when he was making his last railway journey in India, he would have handed over charge of his appointment and would not be entitled to the use of a saloon. He did not at all relish the thought of being seen by everyone, divested of all his glory, entering an ordinary first-class carriage. Acting on my own initiative I approached the railway authorities and found them co-operative. They duly provided a saloon, and Sir Harold, on his departure, was spared the indignity of descending in public to the lowly level of a private citizen.

Sir Harold's successor, Mr Skrine, went to the railway station to see him off. As the train drew out of the platform he said cheerfully 'Let's have a party.' We went back to the Residency and had a party. The atmosphere of the Residency, in less than an hour, completely changed in character. From then on it was gay, informal, almost Bohemian.

We spent the summer of 1939 at Mashobra, near Simla. When war broke out, on September 3rd, we had been enjoying a spell of perfect weather. The distant Himalayas, capped with snow, conveyed an impression of eternity. They had a quiet splendour and a quality of timelessness that made the activities of mere man seem irrelevant and trivial. The wooded slopes about our house were like Persian carpets, bright with flowers. Anemones and lilies of the valley were beginning to fade, but mallows and potentillas were blooming, and orchids and balsam and grass of Parnassus. At a time when others were experiencing all the horrors of war I felt a sense almost of guilt to be living in tranquillity in such a Paradise.

I salved my conscience by applying myself with redoubled energy to the novel tasks that the outbreak of war thrust upon us. Emergency regulations had to be promulgated in each separate State in our political charge. Aliens had to be screened, censorship established, detention camps set up. The Government of India were doubtless right to insist, as they did, that all enemy aliens, without exception, should be arrested and sent to detention camps. But there were a number of hard cases. For example, Dr Politzer, the Chief Medical Officer in Patiala State, was an Austrian Jew who had fled to India to escape from Nazi persecution. Hitler could hardly have had a more bitter enemy. Yet he and his wife, because they were technically enemy aliens, had both to be sent under arrest to an internment camp, and some weeks elapsed before I was able to secure their release. It was fortunate for me, as future events were to show, that I did succeed in obtaining Dr Politzer's release.

On October 9th we returned to Lahore, and a week later, accompanying Mr Skrine, I set off on a tour of some of the States. We visited Mandi first and from there went on to Sundernagar, the capital of Suket State. Thence we travelled by a narrow mountainous road to Dahar, on the Sutlej, where the river forms the boundary between the States of Suket and

Bilaspur. From Dahar we made our way downstream to Bilaspur, the capital town of the State, ten or twelve miles away. Our journey was by 'Khatnao' and was described in a letter I wrote home at the time.

> A Khatnao [I wrote] is a craft composed of two seats facing each other, set on a wooden platform lashed to four inflated cow-skins. These inflated hides support the platform from below, and one is tied to each corner of the platform. The whole craft is launched on the stream and is propelled where the current is sluggish, or guided where the current is fast, by a number of men, each of whom lies over an inflated cow-hide of his own. The men propel their individual cow-skins by means of a paddle, which they hold in one hand and use in conjunction with their legs. They lie along the cow-skins on their bellies, with faces turned downwards towards the water. . . . There were several rapids on the way down. We did a 'porterage' past one of them but 'shot' the others. At one place we got into a whirlpool and our whole craft went spinning round and round. . . . We had lunch on the river bank and arrived at Bilaspur, where the Raja met us at some steps leading down to the river, exactly on time – 5.30 p.m.

Sir Harold would not have thought such a method of progression dignified but Mr Skrine enjoyed it as much as I did.

It was almost exactly nine years since I had last visited Bilaspur. Then I had gone to quell a rebellion. This time I came as the guest of a popular young Raja who was actively engaged in modernising and democratising his State. On all sides were new buildings – a girls' school, a hospital for women, a men's club, a public library, a cinema. The progress made in a few years was astonishing. We arrived back in Lahore on October 27th having visited en route yet another State, Nalagarh.

I had now been Secretary to the Resident for my full term of two years. A change was due, and the change came. I was appointed President of the Council of Regency of Nabha State. Humphry, our elder son, aged three and a half years, had been clamouring for a pony. He would now ride, not a pony, but an elephant.

CHAPTER 15

The Maharaja of Nabha

NABHA was one of three Sikh States, known as the Phulkian States, which were situated in the S.E. Punjab. The rulers of these three States, Patiala, Jind and Nabha, had a common ancestor in Chaudhri Phul, a Revenue Collector under the Moghul Emperor Shah Jahan. All three States had been carved out of the decaying Moghul Empire in the last quarter of the eighteenth century.

Nabha State, with a population of 340,000, was the size of an average English county but did not, like an English county, form a compact geographical unit. Portions of Nabha territory were interspersed, like pieces in a jig-saw puzzle, between tracts of British India and the much larger Patiala State. The district of Bawal, on the borders of Rajputana, was as much as 200 miles away from Nabha, the capital town of the State.

Nabha State was totally different in character from Kalat State. Kalat had been vast in size, sparsely populated, poverty-stricken and mediaeval. Nabha was small, populous, wealthy and modern. The Khan of Kalat, a Muslim, had held dubious sway over a loosely-knit confederation of primitive tribes. The Maharaja of Nabha, a Sikh, was the head of a well-administered, orderly and progressive State.

As Secretary to the Resident for the Punjab States I had handled Nabha affairs for two years and had visited the State more than once. I was therefore well acquainted with its past history and present circumstances.

For forty years, from 1871 to 1911, Nabha had been beneficently and wisely ruled by Maharaja Sir Hira Singh. That was Nabha's Golden Age. He was succeeded by his son, Maharaja Ripudaman Singh. The son did not inherit his father's virtues. His rule was, indeed, so oppressive that in 1923 he was compelled to sever his connection with the State. He went to live with his family in Dehra Dun, while the State was administered by a British officer appointed by the Government of India. But the Maharaja continued to engage in intrigue and in 1928 he had to be deposed. His eight-year-old son, Pratap Singh, succeeded to the 'gaddi', and a Council of Regency was appointed to administer the State until such time as the Maharaja was old enough to be invested with ruling powers. When I went to Nabha in November 1939 Maharaja Pratap Singh, who had been in England with his mother since 1934, had recently had his twentieth birthday, and plans were being made for him to return to India and undergo a course of administrative training before assuming control of his State.

My predecessor as President of the Council of Regency had been that same Gyan Nath who, nine years earlier, had been sent to Bilaspur to deal with civil disturbances there and had subsequently made such a hurried return to Lahore. He was an extremely able administrator and, in addition to building up an efficient civil service, had given the State new High Court and Secretariat buildings, new hospitals and schools, new roads, a new gaol, new barracks for the State forces, a new guest house and modern drainage. In spite of all this capital expenditure he had been able to increase the State's Reserve Fund to a total of nearly 50 lakhs of rupees.

On the surface Nabha seemed to be a model State. But when I penetrated beneath the surface I found much to disturb me. In the gaol, for example, there were too many 'political' prisoners. They had been properly tried and sentenced, it is true, but their offences had not been clear-cut – they had been found guilty of 'bringing the Government into hatred and contempt', i.e. criticising the administration. Gyan Nath was a vain man and sensitive to any form of criticism. I wondered whether it was his vanity that had been hurt or whether, after his unfortunate experience in Bilaspur, he had resolved to forestall possible trouble by suppressing agitation the moment the least sign of it appeared. I consulted my three colleagues on the Council of Regency. I wished to release the political prisoners without more ado. Did they agree? They would not express a definite opinion one way or the other. And so, as they did not oppose my design, I had the prisoners brought before me. Having lectured them on the limitations that the State must, in the public interest, impose on the exercise of the right of free speech, I ordered their release. Only one of them subsequently made himself troublesome – but, fortunately for my peace of mind, outside the State.

A graver defect in the administration was its neglect of the interests of the sturdy Jat peasantry who formed the backbone of the State. There was a particular emergency that had to be dealt with at once and a more general problem requiring careful study and deliberation.

The nature of the general problem can be succinctly stated. With the extension of canal irrigation the Jat agriculturists found their land becoming more and more valuable. As the value of their land increased, so did their credit with the banias (money-lenders) to whom they pledged their land as security for loans. As Jats normally borrow to the limit of their credit, their debts multiplied, they were unable to pay the excessive rates of interest commonly charged (5 per cent per month, or 60 per cent per annum), unpaid interest would be added to the capital sum originally borrowed, and eventually the bania took over the land in discharge of the swollen debt. The Jat ceased to be a peasant proprietor and became little more than the bania's serf. This process was going on apace and, in my view, had to be stopped if an independent peasantry was to be preserved.

The particular emergency requiring immediate attention had occurred in distant, neglected Bawal. There the harvest had been a total failure for the second year in succession. I toured the district before Christmas and visited nearly fifty villages. Conditions were appalling. On all sides cattle were dying of starvation. Most of the men-folk had left their homes in order to find work in Delhi or the Northern Punjab, leaving their wives and children behind to carry on as best they could. Even the trees were leafless – they had been stripped of their foliage to provide minimal sustenance for starving flocks and herds. Meanwhile these wretched people were being pressed by State officials to pay their Land Revenue which, understandably, had fallen heavily into arrears.

I had had experience of somewhat similar conditions in January 1929, when I was at Palwal, so I knew what action to take. Fodder was purchased from the United Provinces and distributed to each village according to its need. Payment of Land Revenue was either suspended or remitted (it had never before been remitted in Nabha). State loans were advanced, free of interest, for the purchase of plough-cattle and seed grain. The Revenue Member of the Council, Chaudhri Nasarullah Khan, though a Muslim, was also a Jat. He accompanied me on my tour, encouraged me to be liberal in making concessions, and subsequently saw to it that the arrangements we planned were carried out with honesty and expedition.

In those early days in Nabha I leaned heavily on Chaudhri Nasarullah Khan. He was neither a native of Nabha nor a Sikh. This gave him an independent outlook and made him objective in his judgments. And since he came of Jat stock he knew instictively everything that was to be known about the manner of life of Jats, their habits, their ways of thinking, their probable reactions to any given situation. Over and over again I would test his knowledge and never found it wanting. Perhaps we would see, two or three miles away from any village, an old man leading a small girl by the hand. 'What on earth are those two doing so far away from home?' I would ask. Chaudri Sahib might give an answer that seemed to me improbable, even fanciful; so I would go up to the old man, pass the time of day with him, ask about the weather and crops and finally inquire where he and the child were going and on what errand they were bound. The answer invariably confirmed Chaudri Sahib's conjecture.

While I was in Nabha I learned a great deal about the Jats

and I learned most of it from Chaudri Nasarullah Khan. If he had a weakness it lay in his deep-seated hatred of the usurious money-lending classes – the Brahmin mahajans and banias. This prejudice clouded his judgment in cases where members of these communities were concerned – but even this failing of his taught me something about the Jat outlook. Generous and open-handed themselves, Jats, whether Hindu, Sikh or Muslim, had a whole-hearted contempt for meanness in others.

I was tired when I returned to Nabha for Christmas but glad that I had reached Bawal in time to save the district from utter desolation.

In February 1940 the Maharaja of Nabha returned to India accompanied by his mother. While in England he had been to school at Badingham College, Leatherhead, and had then gone on to the R.M.C. Sandhurst for a year's military training. Schoolboys do not like to be different from their fellows and Pratap Singh had conformed to English practice by having his hair cut and keeping it short. Nor, later, had he allowed his beard to grow. This was contrary to the tenets of the Sikh religion which forbids its followers to shave or cut their hair. The Resident, Mr Skrine, had written to the Maharaja's mother urging her to persuade her son to let his hair grow. It was essential, he wrote, that a Sikh ruler should abide by the precepts of his religion; and he advised most strongly that Pratap Singh should let his hair grow before returning to India. The Maharani wrote back saying that there were medical reasons which prevented her son from growing a beard or wearing his hair long, and she enclosed with her letter a certificate from a Harley Street skin specialist.

And so, when Pratap Singh arrived in India, he was still clean-shaven. This was not a matter of small moment. At the time there was disaffection and uneasiness in all the Sikh units of the Indian Army. A specific grievance of the Sikh troops was that they were required to wear a battle helmet which, being of one piece, offended against the rules of their religion. But Sikhs generally, whether soldiers or civilians, were also enraged that the British, as they were led to believe, had forced a young Sikh ruler, the Maharaja of Nabha, to cut his hair. And Sikhs, especially in the Punjab, were bombarding the Government with protests and threats, demanding that the Maharaja of Nabha should not be invested with ruling powers until he conformed to Sikh religious practice and grew a beard. There were even demands that he should be forced to abdicate.

In Nabha itself there was no such agitation. The people of Nabha were traditionally loyal and were far too glad to have their Maharaja among them again to worry about his orthodoxy. When he arrived in Nabha, in the first week of March, he was given a wildly enthusiastic reception, and thereafter, wherever he went in the State, he was welcomed as though he were a god.

At this time the Council of Regency had decided to double the strength of the State forces, the Nabha Akal Infantry, who were later to render distinguished service in North Africa and Italy. It was easy to find recruits with the necessary physique to fill the ranks. The difficulty was to find suitable officers. Those whom I interviewed seemed to fall into one of two categories. Either they were Jat Sikhs, well built and active, natural leaders of men, but lacking the educational qualifications required; or they were Sikhs of non-agricultural castes, well educated and intelligent, but incapable of leadership. Hard though I tried, I failed to find the necessary quota of officers with the right combination of qualities.

Many Nationalist politicians in British India were opposed to their country's participation in a war between European powers and sought, by every means open to them, to obstruct and hamper India's so-called 'War effort'. One of the weapons they employed to achieve their object was the dissemination of false information and damaging rumours. These rumours were seeping into the State from outside and I was at a loss to know how to counter them. However, Sirdar Shivdev Singh came to the rescue. Shivdev Singh was a respected and influential Sikh Sirdar who in his younger days had been cast into prison by Maharaja Ripudaman Singh and had been fortunate to escape with his life. For some years he had lived in comfortable retirement, training gun-dogs, shooting, looking after his large estates. He had not been associated in any way with the administration. On the contrary, he was known to have been critical of many of Gyan Nath's activities. Now he came forward with the suggestion that a weekly newspaper should be started with the object of scotching false rumours and giving an impetus to local activities connected with the war. We both realised that an obviously State-controlled newspaper would carry little weight with the public as it would inevitably be regarded as a mere vehicle for official propaganda. So we decided that, while the newspaper should give unqualified support to the prosecution of the war, it should also, to give it the appearance of independence, publish articles and correspondence critical of the State administration. Such was the genesis of Nabha Akhbar (*The Nabha News*).

The newspaper was a success from the very start. The first few issues contained articles severely criticising the Council of Regency for its neglect of the interests of the agricultural classes. These articles served three purposes. They demonstrated the apparent independence of the newspaper; they made it popular and won it a wide circulation; and they paved the way for the agrarian reforms that I was planning. They also had a consequence that I had not foreseen. Believing the newspaper to be independent, people who were hostile to the administration sought to use it as a medium for expressing their views and ventilating their grievances. Their letters enlightened me about a sector of public opinion of which I would otherwise have been ignorant and, at the same time, provided me with a useful clue to potential sources of disaffection.

At the beginning of the hot weather the Maharaja went to Srinagar, in Kashmir, to pursue a course of administrative studies under the tutelage of a senior I.C.S. officer, Mr Wace. Lalage and I and the children spent the summer in Simla, where we stayed at Stirling Castle, a house belonging to the Nabha Durbar. It was a comfortable commodious house which, being built on top of a rocky eminence, commanded a panoramic view of the distant Himalayas. Only once during the summer did I have to descend to the heat of the Punjab plains. The occasion was a critical situation at the Nabha gaol, where a group of fanatical Akalis (militant Sikhs) had gone on hunger-strike and were strenuously resisting all attempts to apply methods of forcible feeding. I went to see them and listened to what they had to say.

Their complaint was against the Head Gaoler who, they alleged, was prejudiced against them and was withholding from them privileges that were freely accorded to other prisoners. When I asked them whether their grievance related only to the Head Gaoler, they confirmed that this was so. I told them that I would find an appropriate remedy. They hoped, no doubt, that I would dismiss the Head Gaoler or transfer him elsewhere. Instead, I transferred them to the gaol at Bawal where the heat was greater than at Nabha and the amenities of the gaol far inferior. When I saw them at Bawal some months later they begged to be allowed to return to Nabha. I said that the same Head Gaoler was still there. They replied that, even so, they would much prefer to be at Nabha. So back to Nabha they went and made no further complaint about the Head Gaoler.

At the beginning of September Mr Wace was recalled by the Punjab Government. His official designation had been 'Administrative Tutor and Guardian to H.H. the Maharaja of Nabha.' As nobody suitable could be found to take his place I agreed, at Mr Skrine's suggestion, to take on this additional responsibility myself. Mr Skrine pressed me to accept a substantial honorarium for the extra work but this I declined. The addition to my pay would, of course, have been very welcome, but I was disinclined to receive payment for services to the Maharaja which I felt I could render equally well, and perhaps better, as a friend.

The agitation about the Maharaja's 'sacred' hair, so far from subsiding, had become more clamorous. Army Headquarters and the Punjab Government were both worried. To invest with ruling powers a beardless Sikh Maharaja would intensify existing unrest both among Sikh units in the Army and throughout the Punjab with its large Sikh population. To refuse to invest him would result – I was sure of it – in disorder, and possibly rebellion, in the State.

When I visited the Maharaja in Srinagar at the beginning of September I had little expectation that I could persuade him to change his mind about growing his hair and beard. I could hardly hope to succeed where Mr Skrine, and even the Viceroy himself, had failed. Nevertheless I had to try. But first I had to get to know him better and, if possible, win his confidence.

Pratap Singh gave me a friendly welcome when I arrived. He told me that Mr Wace had given him a 'holiday' for September. I did not know whether this was strictly true but I was perfectly prepared to accept his word for it and share the holiday with him. He had several guests staying with him, including my friend Shivdev Singh, and had arranged a full programme of sporting activities – a day in the hills after black bear, fishing in the Maharaja of Kashmir's strictly preserved trout streams, snipe shooting over paddy fields, duck shooting from the banks of jheels. We enjoyed a strenuous fortnight of sport, active during the day, relaxed in the evenings over cards and gossip.

At the end of this period of close companionship I found that I had become genuinely attached to Pratap Singh. This made it all the more difficult for me to broach with him the distressing subject of his hair. However, I had to leave Srinagar in the early morning of September 20th (the day before the Maharaja's twenty-first birthday) and on September 19th I asked if I could have a word with him in private. He knew at once what I wanted to talk to him about. He must have been dreading the interview quite as much as I had. But he did not try to put me off. He came over to my houseboat, where we would not be disturbed, and listened attentively to all I had to say. I made no threats. I simply appealed to him, for his own sake and in his own interests, to conform to the rules of his religion; and I added that, in view of the unrest among Sikh troops, he could make no bigger contribution to the successful prosecution of the war.

'I wish I could help you,' he replied. 'But I can't do it. I just can't.' And he went on to say that, if it would help the Government, he was prepared to renounce his title to the 'gaddi' and see his younger brother installed in his place.

I was astonished that he should be willing to abdicate rather than grow a beard. But his offer showed the depth of his feeling on the subject and I realised that I was confronted by a psychological barrier of repugnance that was virtually insurmountable. I did not attempt to argue. I saw that he could not do what I asked and I accepted defeat. But I was filled with pity for him; and with admiration, too, for his readiness to make so great a personal sacrifice in order to relieve the Government of its embarrassment in relation to the Sikh troops.

So it was that, when the Maharaja said that he was prepared to abdicate in favour of his younger brother, I exclaimed, 'Oh, no. Don't do that. I'm sure we can make things all right. I will see the Viceroy and explain everything to him. . . .'

Pratap Singh interrupted me. 'You mean that you are on my side in this?'

'Of course I am,' I replied. 'I will do everything I can to help you.'

'Then I will grow my hair,' he said. 'But it is only because you ask me, not for any other reason.'

I was dumbfounded. But I knew that, having given his word, he would keep it.

He did not want to start growing his hair at once. He had a soldier's regard for the smartness of his personal appearance and dreaded appearing unshaven before his friends. So I suggested that he should accompany me on a tour of the Bawal district in November and there, among people who did not know him, he could begin to make the change. To this suggestion he readily agreed.

Throughout the summer I had been working intermittently on a draft of legislation to prevent agriculturists' land from falling into the hands of the money-lending classes. The final draft, based on a Punjab Government precedent, was approved by the Council of Regency on September 29th and became law (The Nabha State Alienation of Land Act) on October 1st. This was my major contribution to the well-being of the State and its subjects and I had hopes that the new law would prove to be a kind of Magna Carta for the Nabha peasantry.

In November I accompanied the Maharaja on a fortnight's tour of the Bawal district. We went from village to village on horseback and everywhere he received a rapturous welcome. Rejoicing was all the greater in that this was the first visit that a Maharaja had paid to Bawal for more than twenty years. I, too, received a share of the plaudits as there had been a bumper harvest, the best in living memory, and the villagers well knew that without the help of the State they could not have reaped the benefit of the good monsoon for they would have had neither bullocks to plough with nor seed to sow. The contrast with conditions a year earlier was astounding.

One of our party was Hardev Singh Palta, an intelligent and friendly young Sikh, town-bred and clean-shaven, whom Mr Wace had employed as his Personal Assistant. The Maharaja had taken him on to his staff and was trying to make a courtier of him. Following his master's example Hardev Singh now began to grow a beard, but he never learned to shoot or to sit a horse properly. One day, on one of our rural rides, Hardev Singh had a fall. 'Well, Hardev, what happened?' asked the Maharaja. 'Sir,' replied Hardev, with a querulous note in his voice, 'the horse ran off without giving adequate notice....'

Hardev Singh's career must have had a parallel in many courts throughout the ages. Having risen high in the Maharaja's favour he had a correspondingly heavy fall. One day he had an accident when driving the Maharaja's favourite car and damaged it. Jealous tongues made the most of the opportunity and poor Hardev Singh was cast out in disgrace. He had never abused the confidence placed in him by the Maharaja and I was glad to help him in finding less hazardous employment outside the State.

Where there is a carcass there will be vultures. Where there is a court there will be intrigue. In Nabha, competition for the Maharaja's favours grew apace. In particular, there was jealousy of anyone from outside Nabha who held a position of authority in the State. My own position seemed secure enough but Chaudhri Nasurullah Khan was vulnerable. He was a 'foreigner' and, as Revenue Member of the Council of Regency, he had been associated with the unpopular Gyan Nath. Many mean attempts were made to discredit him. At a tea party he would be handed a ham sandwich which he would innocently take and eat, thus rendering himself 'unclean' in Muslim eyes. At partridge shoots there was always keen rivalry over the number of birds shot by each gun. Birds which Chaudhri Sahib had shot would be seized and added to the Maharaja's bag in order to provoke him into protest and set him at odds with the Maharaja. Chaudhri Nasarullah Khan was too outspoken to be a courtier and would not stoop to intrigue. He wisely left the State before his temper was tried too far.

Lalage and I and the family spent the Christmas of 1940 in a house belonging to the Nabha Durbar at Dehra Dun, but I was back in Nabha early in the New Year, and in January and February I toured the northern parts of the State collecting money for the Nabha War Fund, stimulating recruitment to the State Forces and training the Maharaja, now long-haired and bearded, in the duties of a ruler. In particular, I tried to teach him, by example as well as by precept, the most valuable lesson that anyone invested with authority can learn – never to give orders on a petition without hearing both sides of the case.

On March 5th, 1941, at a magnificent and colourful ceremony in the Durbar Hall at Nabha, Mr Skrine formally invested the Maharaja with ruling powers. He announced at the same time that the Viceroy had accepted the Maharaja's request that I should stay on in the State for at least a year as his Diwan (Chief Minister).

The State was peaceful, recruitment was going well and the people of Nabha were happy to be ruled again by their own

Maharaja. Encouraged by the confidence that Pratap Singh continued to show in me I applied myself busily to my new duties.

In the second half of April I had an attack of sand-fly fever. I was treated by one of the State doctors but did not recover as I should have done. I began to have bouts of nausea and my face took on a dull, yellowish hue. Lalage suspected jaundice and thought that I should be treated for that ailment. By chance Dr Politzer, the doctor whom I had rescued from an internment camp and who was now back again in Patiala, came over to Nabha on official business. Hearing that I was ill, he called to ask after me. Lalage told him she suspected that I was suffering from jaundice and asked his advice. Dr Politzer was dissatisfied with my appearance and took away with him, for analysis in Patiala, what is politely termed a 'specimen'. The next day he returned and advised me to leave for the hills at once. It was now mid-May and the temperature was 115 degrees in the shade. Dr Politzer was confident, he told Lalage, that the change to a cool climate would soon put me to rights. I took his advice, had myself driven to our house at Mashobra, near Simla (we had relinquished Stirling Castle to the Army), and within a fortnight had fully recovered my health.

In July the Maharaja was asked to relieve me of my duties in the State as my services were required in the Persian Gulf. And so, early in August, after only five months as Diwan, I handed over charge of my office to my trusted friend and counsellor, Sirdar Shivdev Singh. I may note here that I still have a right to the style and title of Diwan since the title, for one who has held the office of Diwan in a Sikh State, is both permanent and hereditary. Once a Diwan, always a Diwan. My sons Humphry and Hady can also, if they choose to do so, call themselves Diwans.

I was deeply moved by the circumstances attending my final departure from Nabha. From Amloh, from Phul, from distant Bawal, people came in their hundreds to bid me farewell and wish me God speed. I was touched most of all by the presence of the political prisoners whom I had released from gaol and of a large representative delegation from the dreaded Akalis.

I felt, when I left Nabha at 5.30 a.m. on the morning of August 12th, that I had not a single enemy in the State. I was mistaken. Five years later I met Dr Politzer in Delhi. He told me that the 'specimen' he had taken to Patiala for analysis contained antimonium, a poison which, if I had continued to take it in large doses, would have ended my life. The poison, he said, was being administered to me in the medicine which was being sent to me daily from the dispensary at the State Hospital.

'But who would do such a thing?' I asked. 'And why should anyone have wanted to get rid of me?'

Dr Politzer explained that Sirdar Shivdev Singh's advancement, for which I had been mainly responsible, had frustrated the ambitions of a jealous rival who sought, by getting rid of me, to destroy the influence that favoured Shivdev Singh. Dr Politzer had thought it wiser to say nothing to me at the time about the cause of my prolonged illness as he did not want to alarm me; nor did he want to become involved, even indirectly, in Nabha plots and conspiracies. Moreover he believed, quite rightly, that I would be in no danger in the Simla hills, and he felt that, if a warning were necessary, it would be time enough to give it when I returned to Nabha in the autumn.

I shall never know the full story of the plot to poison me by antimonium. I only know that I was being deliberately poisoned and that I probably owe my life to Dr Politzer's timely intervention.

CHAPTER 16

Arab Interlude

I WAS informed, when I was summarily removed from Nabha, that I would in due course be appointed Political Agent, Bahrain; but that, before going to Bahrain, I must learn Arabic. I was to begin my course of instruction in Arabic at Basra, in Iraq, and continue it at Kuwait. Only when I was reasonably proficient in the language was I to assume charge of my new post at Bahrain.

I arrived at Basra on August 14th, 1941, and was given a comfortable room in the Airport Hotel. As most of the hotel had been requisitioned for use by British Army officers, and the remaining rooms were required for passengers in transit, I was told that I could not occupy my room for more than three days. In the end I succeeded in keeping it for seven weeks although, in the course of that period, I had several awkward encounters with the management and on one occasion narrowly escaped eviction by physical force.

The British Army officers at the hotel seemed to be very busy and were continually holding conferences. They were also unusually secretive. The reason became apparent when, less than a fortnight after my arrival, British forces invaded Persia. From the roof of the hotel I watched a constant stream of aircraft passing overhead.

My Arabic teacher was a Jewish student, twenty years of age. He was intelligent, and patient with me, but could never understand my amusement at some of the words and phrases he taught me. 'Leg-leg', I thought, was an enchanting name for a stork. And it delighted me to find that in Arabic a lobster was called 'mother of prawns' and a crab 'father of scissors'. The Jewish youth himself lived in the grip of constant fear. He would start guiltily if there was a knock at the door. Should he hear footsteps behind him he would look round apprehensively. He was never at ease or relaxed. During Abdul Rashid's rebellion three months earlier many Jews in Iraq had lost their lives or property and this young Jew felt, no doubt, that every man's hand was against him. I hope that he, and others like him, have long since found asylum in some other country less unfriendly to their race.

My concentrated study of Arabic was interrupted at the end of September by eye-headaches which came on every morning with the severity of a bad migraine, lasted for two or three hours, and left me exhausted for the rest of the day. I consulted a number of doctors. One of them diagnosed the source of the trouble as the 'frontal sinus' and alarmed me by saying that, if the source of infection were not removed, my eyes, and possibly, my brain, would be affected. He advised me to undergo an immediate operation, but added that the dust and dirt of Basra would make it dangerous to have this particular operation done there.

The pain in my eyes every morning had become almost unbearable when I learned that there was an ear, nose and throat specialist, Colonel Drummond, at the Military Hospital at Shaibah, twenty miles away. I decided to go and see him. I engaged a taxi and on the journey out practised my six-week-old Arabic on the driver. He readily understood what I said to him but I could make little of his replies. This was unfortunate as, on our way out to Shaibah, we passed the ruins of the ancient city and port of Basra, where Sinbad the Sailor had been born and from where he had set sail on his fabulous voyages; and the taxi-driver entertained me with humorous – and I suspect bawdy – stories of Sinbad's adventures in London and Paris.

We arrived at the Military Hospital and I asked to see Colonel Drummond. With Colonel Drummond in his room was a senior R.A.M.C. officer, a full colonel, who was carrying out an inspection of the hospital. When I explained who I was the R.A.M.C. colonel said that, as I held no military rank, I could not be treated at a Military Hospital, and that Colonel

Drummond must confine himself exclusively to military medical duties. Grievously disappointed, I began to plead the severity of the pain I was suffering. But the Colonel cut me short. I must go elsewhere for relief, he told me brusquely, and had me shown to the door. Colonel Drummond came after me.

'Where are you staying?'

'At the Airport Hotel at Basra.'

'I'll see you there at six o'clock this evening.'

Colonel Drummond was as good as his word. He came to the hotel that evening, examined me, and made his diagnosis – an infection behind and below the frontal bone. He said that the normal course was to operate but there was also a less drastic method of treatment which in his experience had invariably proved successful. I had to be something of an acrobat to carry out this treatment for myself, as it involved nasal gargling with liquid paraffin with my head upside-down. However, I did exactly what I was told to do and within three days the pain had disappeared. Meanwhile, in far-away Simla, a General's wife was meeting Lalage for the first time and, hearing her surname, carelessly inquired, 'Any relation of the poor man in Basra who thinks he is going blind?'

When I motored from Basra to Kuwait in the second week of October I entered the real Arab world for the first time. In this world I was to live and move and have my being for a full two years. I was most fortunate, therefore, to be initiated into its mysteries by an expert as knowledgeable as Tom Hickinbotham. I was his guest at the Kuwait Political Agency for more than three months. In the course of my education during that period I was continually being surprised.

I was surprised, in the first place, by the desert itself. It was difficult to believe that any part of Mother Earth could be so barren, so negative, so utterly desolate. I wondered what the desert larks lived on, or the occasional large lizards that the Bedouin ate and found so succulent. I had to revise, too, my ideas about desert wells. There were no oases near Kuwait; there were only water-holes yielding a meagre supply of brackish water and marked, not by palm trees or any patch of green, but by a few empty kerosene-oil tins or perhaps a couple of black Bedouin tents. The mirages belonged to a world of fantasy not of fact. Even Hickinbotham, who found his way about the trackless, featureless desert as though there were signposts every few miles, was sometimes puzzled. On one occasion, fifty miles from anywhere, we saw what appeared to be a large solidly-built house about a mile away. After travelling towards it at thirty miles an hour for ten minutes, during which period it became sometimes smaller, sometimes larger, we eventually found the supposed mansion to be a small bush, 18 inches high, which, because of the low sun behind it, cast a greatly exaggerated shadow.

Hickinbotham himself sometimes surprised me. One day at the end of November I was working at my Arabic (I was to take an examination shortly) when he came into my room. 'I've brought a visitor to see you,' he said. He had just returned from a visit to Basra and I wondered who he could have brought with him. He wouldn't tell me who it was but said I was to come and see for myself. I went to the front door and there I saw, in the back of his capacious saloon car – a donkey! He had come across it in the desert. Its owner had abandoned it, and it was dying of thirst and starvation. As it was only a young one, and small, he brought it along with him. It soon recovered condition and I heard it braying lustily on Christmas Day.

At this period of the war the German armies had advanced deep into the heart of Russia. Should they succeed in breaking through the Caucasus there was only the 10th Army in Iraq to oppose their further advance to the shores of the Persian Gulf, where half the world's oil supplies would lie at their mercy. The 10th Army had only a single line of retreat southward. This was by the Shatt-al-Arab, the river which carries the combined waters of the Tigris and Euphrates past Basra, through groves of date palms, to the head of the Persian Gulf. For long stretches the Shatt-al-Arab is only a narrow river, and a single transport sunk in one of these reaches would block indefinitely a military evacuation. As an insurance against this contingency it was thought desirable to provide a second line of retreat, and surveyors had established the feasibility of building a port at Umm Qasr, a long-abandoned cluster of mud huts situated at the extreme north-west tip of the Persian Gulf. But a difficulty now arose. It was not known whether Umm Qasr was in Iraq or Kuwait territory. No boundary had ever been demarcated, and each of the two countries claimed that Umm Qasr was on its own side of the border. The Foreign Office in London supported Iraq, the Government of India in Delhi supported Kuwait. Hickinbotham was instructed to submit a detailed report, and this he asked me to prepare for him.

At the north-west extremity of the Persian Gulf lies an uninhabited island called Bubiyan. It is quite a large island, nearly three times the size of the Isle of Wight, and is of no interest to anyone except falconers who raid it annually to replenish their stock of young hawks. Two arms of the Gulf embrace Bubiyan Island and separate it from the mainland. At the point where these two arms meet is a desolate area of semi-submerged sandbanks which local Arabs dignify by the name of Warbah Island.

Hickinbotham and I discovered Warbah Island when we visited Umm Qasr in connection with the Kuwait-Iraq boundary dispute. The tide was high, the area of island temporarily unsubmerged was small, and we took advantage of these conditions to sail round the island in our launch. At that time neither of us had his name included in *Who's Who*. As we sat in the launch we had a friendly argument about which of us would achieve this distinction first. We settled the argument, as arguments between friends should always be settled, by compromise. We made a pact that the one of us who first had his name included in *Who's Who* would ensure simultaneous inclusion of the other's name by recording our joint circumnavigation of Warbah Island. Hickinbotham reached *Who's Who* status before I did. For twenty years now the names of

Hickinbotham, Wakefield and Warbah Island have been linked together in its pages.

In preparing my report about Umm Qasr I had to examine a mass of old records. The research involved took up a great deal of time which I could ill spare from my study of Arabic. Nevertheless, before Christmas I had managed to pass my examination in Arabic and thus qualify for appointment to Bahrain as Political Agent; and I had also completed my report on Umm Qasr. My report proved to the satisfaction of the Government of India that Umm Qasr was situated in Kuwait territory. But the Foreign Office were not convinced of this – they did not want to be. However, the issue soon lost its importance as the plan to build the port was shelved when Russian resistance to the German onslaught proved tougher than had been expected.

When I reached Bahrain on January 16th, 1942, I found that Lalage and the children had already arrived there, having travelled by sea from Karachi. It was more than five months since I had seen them, and the time had seemed to pass very slowly.

Kuwait in the war years was relatively unimportant since oil, though it had been found there, was not yet being produced. It was Bahrain, with its oilfield and refinery, which was the centre and hub of activity in the Persian Gulf. And the Political Agent there, in addition to his duties in Bahrain itself, was responsible for the Sheikhdoms of Qatar and the Trucial Coast. The Resident for the Persian Gulf, with headquarters at Bushire in Persia, was remote from the main current of events on the Arab side of the Gulf. In any case, means of communication with him, otherwise than by cable, were irregular and unreliable. Throughout the year and three-quarters that I spent at Bahrain I had to act and take decisions almost entirely on my own responsibility. I was in direct telegraphic communication with London, Cairo, Jeddah, Teheran, Baghdad and Delhi. It was my good fortune that Hugh Weightman, who knew Bahrain and knew me, was in the External Affairs Department at Delhi and invariably gave me support when I most needed it.

Arabs in Bahrain followed with intense interest any and every development in the war between what they termed 'The Axis' and 'The Democracies'. They hated the Japanese, as the Japanese, with their cultured pearls, had ruined the trade in natural pearls which, until oil was discovered, had been the Bahrainis' principal source of livelihood. They also hated the Italians, mainly because of their treatment of Moslems in North Africa. On the other hand, they had considerable regard for Mussolini, simply because he was a Successful Dictator. Arabs respect success and power, and admire those who become successful and powerful. For this reason they greatly admired Hitler also. Their respect for Churchill increased as the tide of war turned in our favour in the winter of 1942. By the autumn of 1943 he was their universally acknowledged hero.

In the spring and summer of 1942, when the fortunes of the Allies were at their lowest ebb, I could never tell from my talks with the Sheikhs what they really thought of the British. They were always courteous and correct in what they said to me. But I was able to divine their real feelings from the behaviour of the slaves in attendance on them. The slaves heard all that their masters said, knew what they were thinking, and did not trouble to conceal from me their contempt and hostility if they had gained from their masters the impression that the British were losing the war.

Slaves in Bahrain were neither more nor less than privileged household servants receiving food and clothing and shelter but not wages. If they wanted to be free men they only had to come to the Political Agent and say so. Then they would be granted certificates of manumission whose validity was never challenged. But there was another type of slavery outside Bahrain which was intolerably harsh. Children would be brought across from the Persian coast and sold on the mainland of Arabia, like sheep or goats, to the highest bidder. Sometimes the captain of a dhow would visit a Persian coastal village, tell its destitute inhabitants plausible stories of prosperity on the Arab side of the Gulf, and persuade parents to send their children in his charge to the illusory land of plenty across the seas. More often children would be forcibly abducted. For a time I had a slave of my own, a boy of fifteen or sixteen, called Mohammed bin Ali. I kept him at the Agency while I tried, in vain, to trace his parents. This is the story he told me early one morning in the spring of 1943:

> I belong to (Persian) Mekran. I lived in a stone house there. My father used to be a pearl-diver. I was his only son. About ten years ago I was with ten other children, nine boys and a girl, bathing on the shore some distance from the town. It was in the afternoon, at the end of the summer. There was a dhow at anchor near where we were bathing. Arabs came from the dhow in a small boat and caught us. They took us to the dhow and tied us up. The Arabs in the dhow took us to Qatar – we were about a month in the boat. We arrived at Dohah and for two days we were left in the boat. Then we were taken to the house of Sheikh Abdullah bin Jasim, who bought all of us. I heard later that I had been bought for Rs 300/– (£22 10*s*.). I think that from Rs 300 to Rs 1,000 (£75) was paid for the others as some of the boys were older, about the age I am now. Abdullah bin Jasim gave me to his brother Thani and I was his slave until I escaped from him ten days ago. I was sent out to the desert in the south of Qatar and I did not see the others again. I heard that some had been given away and sent to Nejd.
>
> I became a camel boy in the house of Sheikh Thani, brother of Abdullah bin Jasim. I was badly treated, and beaten, and I asked to be sold to someone else but they would not sell me. I was often hungry.
>
> I did not see the other boys from Mekran because I was a long way off in the desert. The girl is still in the house of Abdullah bin Jasim and her brother is there too. Both are younger than I am.
>
> Sheikh Thani has about twenty slaves, men and women. Some of them are fair, some dark. He has no others from Mekran. About a year ago he bought three new slaves, dark ones; they were sold to him by some Houlis from Persia. Their names are Sa'idan, Ferraj and Suleiman. They are all grown up and they prefer being slaves in Thani's house to belonging to the Persian Houlis. These three slaves were put in the hands of the auctioneer in Dohah and

when they had reached their price the auctioneer informed the Sheikh and he bought them.

We used to be given dates and curds to eat at midday, and rice without fat for dinner. Twenty slaves would be given one dish so the big ones ate all the food and I used to be left hungry. The men who have always been slaves do not mind because they become used to being beaten, but I was not a slave and have never become accustomed to this. Bin Thani himself beats the slaves with a stick, and if he has not got a stick by him he uses a stone.

Last year I ran away and arrived at Dohah. I wanted to find a boat. The Amir was told that I had escaped and had the boats watched, so they caught me. I was taken back and kept many months – six months – in a tent. Then I was let out.

About ten days ago I ran away from Sheikh Thani's place, Om Maslan, and came to Dohah. I heard that the Sheikh was deporting all the foreign poor people to Bahrain, Kuwait and elsewhere. I joined the people who were being sent away. Several boats were sent off with destitute people and the fares and food were provided by Sheikh Abdullah. I went on board the boat as it was leaving and nobody prevented me. I arrived at Bahrain and we were caught by the police.

I would like to go back to my home in Mekran.

In fiction the story of Mohammed bin Ali would have had a happy ending and he would have found his way back to his home in Mekran. The truth, alas, was different. For some months he lived in our household happily enough. Lalage was kind to him and he became completely devoted to her, following her about the house like a faithful dog. King Ibn Saud sent me a present of a hundred 4-gallon kerosene-oil tins packed with dates. I gave one of these to the boy and he wolfed its contents, never letting the tin out of his sight until, in an incredibly short space of time, he had emptied it. When I gave him some money, the first he had ever had, he spent all of it hospitably regaling the Agency staff at the nearest coffee-house. When Lalage left for India in the summer he attached himself to me, and I was hard put to it to find useful things for him to do. But in August he had a severe attack of malaria and died in the hospital at

Manama. It would take a poet, such as Simonides, to write his epitaph and convey in words the pathos of his life and death.

I was interested to learn that the Sheikh of Qatar was deporting what Mohammed bin Ali called 'foreign poor people'. This meant, of course, that there was not enough food in Qatar to feed everyone and the Sheikh was reserving for his family and his Arab subjects the limited stocks that still remained. If conditions were bad in Qatar, on the Persian side of the Gulf they were appalling. Boatloads of starving men, women and children crossed to the Arab side of the Gulf in the hope of finding relief. But they were not allowed to land. The Sheikhs of Abu Dhabi, of Sharjah, Dubai and Ras al Khaimeh could hardly feed their own subjects. They could not be expected to admit foreigners. Whole boatloads of Persians, in despair at not being allowed to land, threw themselves into the sea and were drowned. Others landed at night, at unguarded parts of the coast, but found no food and died. In Dubai I saw people dying in the streets with stretchers laid beside them on which the Sheikh's men would carry them away when they had drawn their last breath. Near the Sharjah aerodrome I saw an elderly Persian woman, without a stitch of clothing on, gaunt and emaciated, crying for food. Others near her were on their knees cropping grass like animals.

In Bahrain the problem of food supplies gave constant anxiety. Bahrainis lived mainly on fish, dates and rice. Only a few of them ate bread. By May 1942 there was no flour left and stocks of rice were dwindling fast. It was only due to constant and successful improvisation, with the co-operation of the oil company, that Bahrain escaped the privations that beset the Sheikhdoms of Qatar and the Trucial Coast. Blow followed blow. Iraq banned the export of dates – and Bahrain could only grow half its requirements of dates. India banned the export of rice – and Bahrain was entirely dependent on India for rice. By the beginning of 1943 Sheikh Salman, the ruler of Bahrain, was in despair. There seemed to be no means by which he could ensure that his people were fed. I told him, bravely, that I would accept responsibility for seeing that his people did not starve. A few hazardous weeks followed and then, in March 1943, the Middle East Supply Centre, based on Cairo, formally assumed responsibility for feeding Bahrain and the Sheikhdoms of the Trucial Coast. Thereafter Bahrain had adequate supplies of flour though rice remained scarce. In April the monthly ration of cereals was still 20 lb. per head but only 4 lb. of this was rice. The rest of it was wheat or flour. Apart from myself only Sheikh Salman and his Adviser, Belgrave, realised how narrowly Bahrain escaped starvation during the early months of 1943. It was a harrowing time for all three of us.

Sheikh Hamad bin Isa al Khalifah was the ruler of Bahrain when I first went there. He died in February 1942, shortly after the fall of Singapore, and was succeeded by his son, Sheikh Salman. Succession in the Sheikhdoms of the Persian Gulf is often a delicate matter and the Political Agent plays an important but unobtrusive part in seeing that the most suitable choice is made. Advised by Belgrave and Bertram Thomas, my Public Relations Officer, I made the right gestures at the right time and Sheikh Salman was grateful to me for the quiet support I gave him. This was fortunate because, soon after his accession, I was given a difficult diplomatic task to perform. I had to explain to him that, while the Allies would certainly win the war, there was a danger that the Germans might break through the Caucasus and sweep down into the Persian Gulf to secure possession of the oilfields there; and that, with this contingency in view, many of the wells in Bahrain were to be plugged with cement in order to deny them to the enemy. This was hard tidings, indeed, for the new ruler, but neither then, nor at any subsequent time, did he waver in his loyalty to the British cause. When H.R.H. the Duke of Gloucester visited Bahrain in the summer of 1942 he found in Sheikh Salman a true friend.

While I was at Bahrain I did a great deal of travelling. I toured the Gulf in a cruiser, H.M.S. *Capetown*. I travelled by car over extensive tracts of Saudi Arabia, and I frequently flew in R.A.F. aircraft to and from the Trucial Coast or Karachi. I had two aeroplane crashes, one at Bahrain and one at Sharjah. Most alarming of all, I had a forced landing in a rough sea off Karachi in a Catalina seaplane. I also had the exciting experience of spotting a Japanese submarine off the Mekran coast and pointing it out to the pilot of the Wellington bomber in which I was flying at the time. He sent a signal to Karachi, and the submarine, caught in shallow waters, was forced to the surface by depth charges and captured.

Incidents such as these punctuated an existence that was rendered generally depressing and disagreeable by the climate. In the Political Agency only one room, a bedroom, was air-conditioned, and that was almost always occupied by a guest. Heat and humidity combined to make the atmosphere insufferable. In such climatic conditions, and against the depressing background of the war, the introduction of some element of light relief was essential. Bertram Thomas was a keen amateur ornithologist and I and my staff amused ourselves, and puzzled him, by dipping a sparrow into a bottle of red ink and then releasing it. He studied his books for many hours in an attempt to identify its species. And my fortnightly reports to the Government of India were not always concerned with grave matters. Here are some extracts:

> 15th May, 1942. The Qadis have protested to H.H. the Sheikh against the increase of immorality in Bahrain, which they attribute largely to the presence here of so many foreigners from the West. They mentioned particularly the blatant behaviour of the prostitutes who parade along the Manama-Awali road, and the growth of liquor drinking among the Moslem community. Steps are being taken by the Bahrain Government which will, it is hoped, result in confining immoral practices to certain specified quarters which the Qadis will not, or certainly should not, visit.
>
> 31st May, 1942. The prostitutes of Manama resent Government interference with their trade and have threatened that, if the restrictions recently enforced are not removed, they will either (a) emigrate to Kuwait or (b) go on strike. The junior members of the Al Khalifah are greatly worried by the situation which has now developed.

15th June, 1942. It was reported that the prostitutes of Manama had threatened either to emigrate to Kuwait or to go on strike. In the end they adopted the latter alternative. But idleness is irksome to people who love their work, and already the ranks of blacklegs are nightly receiving fresh recruits.

30th June, 1942. The prostitutes' strike is over and Bahrainis have resumed their normal social activities.

In April 1943 I had a severe attack of amoebic dysentery. This was reported under the customary heading 'Movements of Officials' as follows: 'The Political Agent had intended to visit the Trucial Coast during the period under report but succumbed to an attack of amoebic dysentery. His movements were therefore only local.'

By the summer of 1943 the Persian Gulf had been freed from any danger of invasion from the north and food supplies were assured. I was glad when, in the autumn, I received a summons to duty in a very different sphere.

CHAPTER 17

Duel with a Maharaja

'THE purpose of this letter is to ask you if you are willing to do what is likely to be the dirtiest job undertaken by a Political Officer since I myself – greatly daring – went to Alwar as Prime Minister.'

Sir Francis Wylie, who wrote to me thus, was Political Adviser to the Crown Representative and head of the Political Department in Delhi; and he was inviting me to go to Rewa to set up a new administration there.

Rewa was a State in Central India to the south of the United Provinces, and was about the size of Holland, with a population of nearly two million. To make intelligible the situation that had developed there I must give a brief sketch of the background.

As I have explained in the Preface, the rulers of Indian States were required, by usage if not by treaty, to accept the advice of the British Government in certain matters. This advice was tendered to them by the Viceroy in his capacity as Crown Representative. But the Crown Representative could not intervene in the internal affairs of a State unless misrule had become so gross as to be intolerable.

In the case of Rewa the limits of what was tolerable had been reached, and surpassed, early in 1942. The Maharaja's powers were then suspended and he was made to leave the State while a specially constituted Commission of Inquiry conducted an investigation into his alleged misdemeanours. The two principal charges against him concerned his complicity in the murder of one Shanker Prasad; a lesser charge was that he had deputed an agent 'to obtain confidential information from the office of the Resident for Central India by bribing persons employed therein.' It was believed in Rewa that the Maharaja had committed at least twelve murders, and there was little doubt about his guilt in three of them; but only in the case of Shanker Prasad was it possible to produce convincing evidence. In the other cases the witnesses concerned were either too loyal or too frightened to give evidence against their ruler.

The Commission of Inquiry was not unanimous in its verdict and, at the end of January 1943, produced two reports. The majority report, signed by the three Indian members of the Commission, absolved the Maharaja of guilt. The minority report, signed by the two British members, found that all three charges had been proved.

The Crown Representative, after long deliberation, reached the conclusion that the two graver charges had not been 'judicially proved' but that the third charge, that of bribery, had been fully established. He decided that the Maharaja could not be permitted to return to the State with ruling powers 'until certain important new appointments had been made there and until he [the Crown Representative] was fully satisfied that the administration as thus reconstituted had been firmly established.'

I had handed over charge of my duties in Bahrain to Hickinbotham in the first week of October, but it was not until December 2nd, 1943, that I actually arrived in Rewa. During the intervening period I suffered a severe attack of dengue fever. I also had leisure to ponder over the dangers and difficulties of my new assignment. When the Maharaja returned to Rewa in six or eight months' time I would be his Diwan, or Chief Minister. It was inconceivable that our relationship could be one of mutual trust and confidence such as that which had grown up between myself and Pratap Singh in Nabha. On the contrary, he was bound to resent most bitterly the imposition on him of a British Political Officer, a member of what he was pleased to term contemptuously 'the discoloured races'.

So far from being the Diwan of his choice, to his eyes I would present myself as a jackal of the Crown Representative, the Viceroy's spy and policeman. My position would be, to say the least of it, uncomfortable – the unwanted Minister of a Maharaja reputed to be a multiple murderer!

I went to Lahore to consult Sir Conrad Corfield, who had succeeded Mr Skrine as Resident for the Punjab States. Corfield had been Adviser to the Maharaja of Rewa for two years in the early 1930's and must, I was sure, know him intimately. Corfield proved to be familiar with every facet of the Maharaja's many-sided personality. He warned me that Maharaja Sir Gulab Singh would try to provoke or entice me into indiscreet words or conduct and would seek every possible means of discrediting me. He would probe for my weaknesses, exploit them, and try to compromise me in order to establish some kind of hold over me. He would use his wealth and influence to undermine my position in the State and, finally, he would employ against me all the resources of his elaborate system of espionage. Corfield advised me always to treat the Maharaja with the courtesy due to a person of his rank and to be helpful and accommodating in minor matters or in matters touching his comfort or convenience, but to be absolutely unyielding – to make no concessions at all – in important matters where questions of principle were involved. 'If you give him an inch,' said Corfield, 'he will take an ell.'

Corfield also enlightened me about the social structure of the State. Rewa in the twentieth century, it seemed, had much in common with the England of Henry III. At the Court, jealousy and intrigue among the ruler's favourites, all of them seeking influence and grants of land; among the nobles, determination to cling to their privileges, and resentment at the way in which they were treated by their Sovereign. 'Servants do not judge their master,' said Henry III. 'Vassals do not judge their prince or bind him by conditions. They should put themselves at his disposal and be submissive to his will.' This was exactly the attitude of the Maharaja of Rewa. He had ignored the rights of his nobles, guaranteed to them in a settlement negotiated by Corfield in 1934, and they were angry and resentful. But they had their champion, their Simon de Montfort. This was the

Rao of Chorhat, an able, ruthless and most competent man, implacable enemy of the Maharaja. Corfield advised me to come to an understanding with the Rao Sahib as soon as I could manage to do so. He would be an invaluable ally, he said, in my duel with the Maharaja.

I spent my first seven months in Rewa building up an administration which would, I hoped, be loyal to me and proof against either bribes or threats from the Maharaja. At the head of the Army, with the grandiose title of C.G.S., I had a redoubtable Sikh, Brigadier Jai Singh, who entertained a hearty contempt for anyone who did not come from Northern India. Sir Francis Wylie sent me a reliable police officer from the United Provinces to be Inspector General of Police. As Home Minister I had an experienced administrator who had served in the State for a number of years and was anathema to the Maharaja as he had helped to collect evidence to go before the Commission of Inquiry. I imported from Bombay, to be Minister of Commerce and Industry, a man of great ability and unimpeachable integrity. And finally, to ensure that the Maharaja did not stir up 'loyalist' agitation among teachers and students, I made the Rao of Chorhat Minister of Education.

For the most part the Rewa administration was corrupt, or inefficient, or both. The police had only one method of detecting crime. They lodged all possible suspects in a cell and beat them until one or other confessed. If no confession was forthcoming, beating was followed by torture. Most of the beds in the few hospitals were occupied by patients with venereal disease. The disease was spread by itinerant Sadhus, Hindu 'holy men', who, with naked bodies smeared with ash, travelled from hamlet to hamlet blessing the ignorant inhabitants and taking payment for the blessings in food and pleasure. The schools were generally over-crowded, classes of seventy or eighty illiterate children being taught by a single semi-literate teacher. All these abuses occupied my attention but my energies were mainly directed to reorganising the State's shellac factory at Umaria and to devising a workable rice-procurement plan.

The story of the shellac factory is quickly told. Shellac was needed for the war. Lac, a kind of resin, was available in unlimited quantity in the State's 6,000 square miles of forest, but the forest-dwellers were inadequately remunerated for bringing it to the factory, and the factory itself was incompetently managed. I reorganised the system of work at the factory, put it under new management and doubled the price paid for lac. Within a year the factory's output had trebled with consequential benefit both to the prosecution of the war and to the State's exchequer.

The difficulties connected with rice were less tractable. In Bahrain there had been no local production of rice and the problem had been one of import. In Rewa there were many thousands of tons of rice surplus to local requirements and the problem was one of export. Famine was raging in Bengal, whole communities were dying there of starvation, and rice was desperately needed. But Rewa grain merchants, however generously they bribed the railway officials, were unable to obtain more than an occasional wagon. Though I exerted pressure, locally at Jubbalpur and centrally at Delhi, all my attempts to secure railway wagons failed. In the end I adopted a drastic solution. I purchased, on behalf of the State, the whole of the Rewa rice crop surplus to local requirements. I engaged contractors to carry it to three named railway stations where there was adequate storage; and I sold it, at the railway stations, to the Bengal Government. This sounds simple; but the detailed organisation of a novel scheme of this kind presented endless complications. There were half a dozen varieties of rice, each with its own price tag; many of the rice-producing villages were inaccessible to wheeled vehicles; and the contractors wanted far more petrol than could possibly be spared to them. However, the scheme worked and my toil had its reward as the rice did reach Bengal in time to save many lives.

Early in the summer of 1944 I was informed that the Maharaja was pressing hard to be allowed to return to his State, and the Crown Representative could not withhold permission much longer. I reviewed my security arrangements and found them reasonably adequate. My household servants I had brought with me and I was satisfied that all of them, and particularly the cook, were trustworthy. I was doubtful about my steno-typist, a meek little Indian Christian; but he did not belong to the State and I calculated that the Maharaja would not dare to try and bribe him so soon after the disclosures made before the Commission of Inquiry. From the first day of my arrival in Rewa, however, I had been dubious about the trustworthiness of my head orderly, Jemadar Chhotu Ram. Large, fat and unpleasantly obsequious, he was also extremely efficient. He told me that he knew no English; but one day, through the half-open door of my study, I saw him reading a type-written note in English that I had left on my desk. I decided not to interrupt him but to leave him with the impression that I still believed him to be ignorant of English. Confidential telegrams to and from Delhi were sent in a code to which I alone had the key. Letters were normally posted in the local post-office but, if a letter contained anything that I particularly wished to keep secret, I had it posted on the mail-train at Satna thirty miles away.

At the beginning of July I told Sir Francis Wylie that we in Rewa were ready for the Maharaja's return but that I was apprehensive about the reception he would be accorded on his arrival. Shopkeepers intended to decorate the streets, and villagers in their thousands would flock into Rewa from the surrounding countryside to welcome – or at least to get a glimpse of – their returning ruler. The last thing I wanted to see was the Maharaja enjoying a triumphal entry into Rewa. Whatever action the police took to control the crowds would invite his hostile criticism. Moreover, I did not want the Maharaja to have the opportunity of haranguing an excited crowd. He was a notable orator and could with very few words, if he so wished, arouse dangerous passions. My difficulty was that I could not myself forbid the shopkeepers to put up flags nor restrain the villagers from welcoming back their ruler. I suggested that it should be conveyed to the Maharaja that, if he were willing to make his return to Rewa private, without public ceremony of any kind, the Crown Representative would be prepared to allow him to return to his State forthwith. My suggestion was adopted. In order to secure his early return the Maharaja, albeit grudgingly, agreed that it should be of a private character; and I was able to inform everyone in or near Rewa, first, that it was His Highness's express wish that his return should be unaccompanied by demonstrations or ceremonies of any kind, and, secondly, that I was determined to see that his wishes were respected.

It was characteristic of the Maharaja that he should choose for the day of his return a Hindu holiday, Nag Panchami, when the Rewa populace would be thronging the streets in festive mood indulging in an orgy of snake-worship. At 4.30 p.m. on Tuesday, July 25th, 1944, his train drew in at the platform of Satna station. It was shunted backwards and forwards until his saloon was exactly opposite the red carpet that had been laid down for him. When he emerged I stepped forward to greet him. Completely ignoring me, he acknowledged the salutations of a few friends and made his way directly to the station exit where his car was waiting for him.

I had arranged for the Ministers to receive the Maharaja at a point on the Satna road two miles outside the town of Rewa where there could be no danger of a crowd collecting. Here the Maharaja's car was signalled to a stop. I had followed in my own car, and now I approached the Maharaja and told him that his Ministers wished to pay their respects to him. He hesitated for a moment but then got out of his car and I presented his Ministers to him. No one would have suspected, when the Maharaja and the Rao of Chorhat greeted each other, that they were inveterate enemies. Both of them behaved with the utmost propriety. The Maharaja then continued his journey to his residence at the Fort, preceded by a police escort which took a route avoiding the festival-thronged bazaars, So far, I thought, so good.

Beyond sending a note to say that I was at his service whenever he wished to see me, I took no steps to force myself on the Maharaja. Five days after his arrival he invited me to tea. He complained of the unjust treatment he had received at the hands of the Viceroy and his advisers; he warned me to beware of the Rao of Chorhat who, he said, was a snake (he smiled sourly when I reminded him that his subjects worshipped snakes); and he asked for my help in arranging for his son to pay a visit to Rewa. The son, Maharajkumar Martand Singh, was twenty-one years of age, was the Maharaja's only son, and was at the time undergoing a course of administrative training in Mysore. I replied that I would consider the request sympathetically but made no promise to comply with it.

The Maharaja of Rewa had two wives. The Senior Maharani, a sister of the Maharaja of Jodhpur and mother of Martand Singh, had arrived in Rewa a week before her husband. She had come with a close relative from Jodhpur, Sir Ajit Singh, who told me that the Maharani was not on good terms with her husband and asked me to give her my protection. I promised to befriend her as best I could but I did not anticipate, when I gave my promise, the kind of situation that arose shortly after the Maharaja's return. At one o'clock in the morning I was aroused from sleep and given a frenzied message from the Maharani begging me to come to the Palace without delay as she had been poisoned by the Maharaja and was dying. As I hurriedly dressed, intending to go to the Palace at once, it occurred to me that the Maharaja would have a good deal to say if it were reported to him, as it certainly would be, that I had been visiting his Maharani in the early hours of the morning. I decided to be cautious. I rang up Colonel Makand, the Chief Medical Officer, told him that the Maharani was very ill and believed that she had been poisoned (I did not say by whom) and asked him to go to the Palace immediately. He went there, administered the necessary treatment, and all was well. I said nothing to the Maharaja about the incident nor did the Maharani when we next met, say anything about it to me.

Whenever I saw the Maharaja during the first three weeks of

August he pressed on me his request that his son might be allowed to interrupt his course of training at Mysore to pay a visit to Rewa. For some time I delayed giving a definite reply as I thought it advantageous to have it in my power to refuse the Maharaja something that he wanted. But as his conduct in official matters continued to be in every way correct, and as he made no obvious attempt to subvert the administration, I felt that it would be unreasonable to deny him this favour. So I made arrangements for the Maharajkumar to have a holiday in Rewa; and he duly arrived in September with his tutor, Mr Owens.

Having got what he wanted out of me, the Maharaja at once changed his attitude and became aggressive and dictatorial. Annually, at the Dussehra festival, the Maharaja held a grand review at which his feudatory nobles paraded with the elephants, camels, horses and armed followers that they were obliged to maintain to comply with the terms of the grants under which they held their estates. At the parade on September 27th, 1944, the Maharaja found fault with many of his nobles. Some failed to produce the quota of men and animals stipulated in their grants; others were not present in person but were represented only by sons or nephews; yet others he accused of being disrespectful in that they did not make full obeisance when saluting him as he sat in state on his gorgeously caparisoned elephant. The Maharaja sent me a list of the offending nobles and ordered me to inform them that, in default of a satisfactory explanation of their shortcomings, their estates would be forfeited.

This was bad enough; but worse was to follow. The Maharaja informed me that Brigadier Jai Singh, the C.G.S., had passed him in the street without saluting him. The Maharaja demanded a full apology in writing. Failing an apology, he wished Jai Singh to be dismissed. I spoke to Jai Singh. He denied any knowledge of having passed the Maharaja in the street and said that in no circumstances would he tender any kind of apology. I explained to the Maharaja that Jai Singh had not seen him in the street and had certainly not intended any discourtesy. But the Maharaja was adamant; an apology or dismissal.

All this was tantamount to a declaration of war by the Maharaja. I remembered Corfield's advice, not to yield an inch where important questions of principle were involved; and it was certainly important that I should show myself capable of protecting the nobles, and Jai Singh, and any others on whom I could rely for support against the Maharaja. On the other hand, I was reluctant to accept the Maharaja's declaration of war and enter into open conflict with him. In the end, of course, having the backing of the Crown Representative, I was bound to win the contest; but there would be many casualties in the course of the encounter and innocent people would suffer. I reflected that the Maharaja had shown himself conciliatory, even friendly, during the period when he was dependent on me for granting him a favour – the visit to Rewa of the Maharajkumar – and I decided to make an attempt to re-create comparable conditions.

The Maharaja's greatest weakness was his love of money. During the twenty-two years that he had ruled Rewa he had annually allotted to the Privy Purse large sums – tens of thousands of pounds – and had placed this money in deposit in his own name with the Bank of England in London. By 1944 there was a sum of more than two million pounds standing to the credit of his account there. The Political Department in Delhi took the view that this money, or the greater part of it, belonged to Rewa State rather than to the Maharaja personally, and had asked me for a detailed report on the matter.

It occurred to me that if the Maharaja knew, or had reason to believe, that the disposal of his two million pounds depended on my recommendation, he would be chary of making an enemy of me. Accordingly, confronted with the Maharaja's demands in respect of Brigadier Jai Singh and the nobles, I dictated a note to the Under-Secretary at Delhi saying that I was making good progress with my examination of the State's accounts but was not yet in a position to say what part, if any, of the funds held by the Bank of England on behalf of the

Maharaja of Rewa should properly be restored to the State. I marked the note Secret, put it in an envelope which I asked Jemadar Chhotu Ram to seal for me, and told him that I was going to Satna to post it. I left a copy of the note folded up on my desk, feeling fairly confident that, as soon as I left for Satna, the Jemadar would read it and report its contents to the Maharaja.

My confidence in the Jemadar's loyalty to the Maharaja was not misplaced. He must have passed on to the Maharaja everything that I said in my note because, within twenty-four hours, the Maharaja's attitude completely altered. He modified his orders about the offending nobles; he said nothing further about Jai Singh; he invited Lalage and the children to tea with him at the Fort, and he asked me to go tiger-shooting with him. At our first tiger-shoot I noticed his rifle, from a neighbouring machan, pointing straight at me. Thereafter, being frightened of an 'accident', I always saw to it that there was someone sitting in my machan between myself and the Maharaja. However, fears for my personal safety did not prevent me from enjoying several exciting and successful tiger-shoots in the Maharaja's company.

The honeymoon atmosphere continued. On Christmas Eve two cars arrived at our house loaded with toys for the children. I sent them all back, but not before the children had caught sight of them. 'Can't we keep just *one*?' pleaded Humphry. But I was inexorable. I could not afford to place myself under any obligation, however slight, to the Maharaja.

On Christmas Day Lalage and I went to the Fort to give His Highness our Christmas greetings. After a few minutes of polite conversation, the Maharaja asked if he could have a private word with me. Lalage withdrew, and His Highness, reminding me that Christmas was the season of goodwill, said that he would like to show his friendly feelings for me by giving me a present. As he spoke he held out to me a thin envelope containing, as I could see from the colour showing through it, a cheque. I reacted exactly as he ought to have known I would react. Putting my hands behind my back to avoid so much as touching the bribe, I took a step backwards, in recoilment. He was not at all abashed. 'I quite understand your difficulty,' he said. 'But your father is alive, isn't he? I could make it out in his name, or in the name of anyone else you care to mention.' He advanced many arguments to justify my acceptance of his 'Christmas present', and for a long time refused to accept my rejection of his gift as final.

I was glad that I had not opened the envelope. If I had done so, and seen the amount of the cheque, he would always have believed that my refusal to accept it was due to greed, to my desire to be given more than he offered. Believing that two million pounds was at stake, he should have made the cheque a large one. Ten lakhs of rupees (£75,000) would have been a nice round sum. But, being the miser that he was, he may have thought that he could win me over, and at the same time compromise me, at much smaller expense to himself. Alas, my curiosity on this point will never now be satisfied.

It was a few weeks later, in January 1945, that I had my most dramatic meeting with the Maharaja. He had had an attack of measles followed by pneumonia. His condition rapidly deteriorated and the doctors said that his life was in danger. I sent for the Maharajkumar from Mysore but he had not yet arrived in Rewa when, at three o'clock one morning, I was summoned to the bedside of the supposedly dying Maharaja. He had a high temperature but was not delirious. He believed that he would not survive the night and wanted me to record his last will and testament. His face was a ghastly colour, and sweat poured down his cheeks as he dictated, and I recorded, his dying wishes. He bequeathed the money in the Bank of England to his son. He excluded the Senior Maharani from any share in his estate but made bequests to several of his favourites. His son was enjoined to refuse absolutely to employ any British Officer in the State. The Maharaja asked me to read out what I had written. I did so. 'Make it clear to my son,' he said, 'that it is his sacred duty to abide by my wishes in this respect. He must not, in any circumstances, employ a British Officer in the State.' He spoke partly in Hindi, partly in English, and exhausted himself by his efforts to make himself clearly understood. When he finished I took my departure, expecting to hear later in the day that he had died. However, the crisis passed and he gradually recovered.

Meanwhile, my own health had been giving cause for concern. I was suffering, said the doctors, from 'tropical neurosis brought on by prolonged residence in the tropics and associated with hard and anxious work. The nervous mechanism of the alimentary system appears to have been deranged....' The important thing, from my point of view, was that a Medical Board certified that a period of twelve months' leave was 'absolutely necessary', and that an early passage home was also necessary if 'serious and permanent impairment of health' was to be avoided.

I left Rewa in the first week of February 1945. In the course of my final interview with the Maharaja I remarked that I could well understand his aversion to British officers interfering in the administration of his State (he himself was the thirty-fourth ruler of his line) but I was puzzled to know why he should have chosen me to convey to his son his dying wishes in this respect. He replied, simply and straightforwardly, 'because I could not trust anyone but a British Officer to pass on the message.'

I have told the story of my fourteen months in Rewa from my own viewpoint. I would like to have heard the story from the Maharaja's angle, but that is now impossible. He was deposed the year after I left and died in exile some years later as a result of what the newspapers called an accident. Perhaps it was an accident; but he had made many enemies for himself.

CHAPTER 18

The End of the Indian States

FOR Britain, 1945 was a momentous year. In May the war in Europe ended; in July the electorate rejected Churchill and put a Labour Government in office; in August the Japanese surrendered. Being on sick leave I was only a passive spectator of these historic events. But in December I was given a clean bill of health, and early in January 1946 I flew to Delhi to fill a new post in the Political Department which had been created to help the Political Adviser to the Crown Representative in dealing with constitutional questions arising out of the changing relationship between the States and the rest of India.

The British Government had promised India Dominion Status, i.e. Independence within the framework of the British Commonwealth of Nations. In relation to British India the Government's main problem was how to deal with Mr Jinnah's demand, passionately resisted by the Congress Party, for the partition of India and the establishment of a separate State for Moslems. The problem in relation to the States was different. Successive British sovereigns, from Queen Victoria onwards, had given the Indian Princes firm pledges that they would be maintained in possession of their territories and in enjoyment of their dignities and prerogatives. It was impossible to see how, when British India became independent, the British Government could carry out its obligation to protect the States. Where would our troops be stationed? Or how could they be reinforced without infringing the sovereignty of the new Dominion? The political leaders of British India were certainly in no mood to agree to any limitations on the sovereignty of the new Dominion. Moreover, if the ruler of a State were to ask for British protection, the request would almost certainly be for protection against aggression on the part of the new Dominion itself. The truth was that the two pledges, the new one of independence for British India and the old one of protection for the States, were mutually incompatible. It was not possible to honour both.

In 1946 Lord Wavell was Viceroy and Sir Conrad Corfield was his Political Adviser. They saw that, if the British were in a dilemma, so too were the rulers of the Indian States. The rulers certainly did not want to dispense with the British shield behind which, for a century or more, they had sheltered in confident security. On the other hand, if they insisted on British forces remaining in India to protect them, they would incur the implacable hostility of the whole of Nationalist India, they would be branded as traitors to the Indian cause and might even alienate the loyalty of many of their own subjects.

I attended the meeting of the Chamber of Princes which took place in Delhi in the third week of January 1946, and heard Lord Wavell address the assembled rulers. Speaking of their relationship with the Crown and the rights guaranteed by their treaties and engagements, he gave a solemn assurance in carefully chosen words. 'I can assure you,' he said, 'that there is no intention on our part to initiate any change in this relationship or these rights without your consent.' This amounted to a pledge that there would be no unilateral repudiation of our treaties with the Princes. However, Lord Wavell also expressed at the same time his confidence that the rulers would not wish to withhold their consent to necessary changes if by so doing they obstructed the growth of India to its full stature, i.e. Independence.

On the following day the Chamber of Princes passed unanimously a Resolution affirming the desire of the Indian States for the immediate attainment by India of her full stature, and undertaking to make every possible contribution towards the settlement of the Indian constitutional problem.

This was a triumph for the diplomacy of Lord Wavell and his Political Adviser. The position was now established that the

Indian Princes desired India to achieve her freedom; and thus, by implication, they waived their rights to British protection since maintenance of those rights would have been incompatible with the independence of India as a whole.

The sombre political scene was illumined, at the beginning of March, by a superb and deeply impressive victory parade to which all branches of the Indian armed forces contributed. This was the final exhibition of the might of the British Raj. Only Kipling could have expressed the feelings with which I, and many like me, viewed this splendour of the setting sun. It was symbolic, perhaps, that the R.A.F. Hurricanes, dipping in salute as they passed over the Viceroy, disappeared from view to the west.

India was on the brink of communal civil war when, in an attempt to break the deadlock between the Congress Party and the Muslim League, the British Prime Minister, Mr Attlee, despatched a Cabinet Mission to Delhi. The Mission's task was, in their own words, 'to assist the two main political parties to reach agreement upon the fundamental issue of the unity or division of India.' The three members of the Mission, Lord Pethick-Lawrence, Sir Stafford Cripps and Mr A. V. Alexander, all knew my elder brother in the House of Commons and this gave me an agreeable personal link with them. They arrived in Delhi on Sunday, March 24th, and I met them the following morning in their private conference room at the Viceroy's house.

At this first meeting I observed with amazement the importance which these eminent statesmen attached to articles in the Indian press about the Mission. The general tone of these articles had been cautious but not unfriendly, and the absence of hostility afforded them much satisfaction. But the influence of most of these newspapers was negligible and I thought at the time that the Ministers were mistaken if, as they appeared to do, they equated editorial comment with public opinion. However, if the Ministers surprised me, I also surprised them. Sir Conrad Corfield had arranged for a large map of India to be hung in the conference room on which the territory of the Indian States was clearly distinguished from British India. I drew their attention to this map. Lord Pethick-Lawrence and Mr Alexander were astonished, and even Sir Stafford Cripps was surprised, by the sheer magnitude of the territorial possessions of the Indian Princes – two-fifths of the whole sub-continent. Before coming out to India they had been fully briefed about British India and the conflict between the Congress Party and the Muslim League. About the Indian States, until I enlightened them, only Sir Stafford Cripps appeared to have anything but the most elementary knowledge.

The Cabinet Mission stayed in India for more than three months and I saw a great deal of them during this period. Mr Alexander was not interested in the Indian States and made no contribution to our discussions. Lord Pethick-Lawrence, mentally vigorous in spite of his seventy-four years, used his exceptional reasoning powers to dissect and analyse the complex problem presented by the States but could discover no solution. It was left to Sir Stafford Cripps, with his inexhaustibly flexible and creative mind, to devise an All India constitutional structure in which the States could find an honourable place.

Although the Cabinet Mission's scheme for a Union of India embracing both British India and the States was eventually abandoned in favour of partition, their declaration of the British Government's attitude towards its treaties with the States was unequivocal and final. The Congress Party argued that, in the same way as the new Government of independent India would succeed to the powers and authority formerly exercised by the British Government in British India, so it should step into the shoes of the British Government in its relationship with the States, and should inherit, together with the British Government's treaty obligations to the States, all those overriding powers of the Crown comprised in the term Paramountcy. This argument was strongly opposed by the Indian Princes. Their treaties, they urged, had been concluded with the British Government, not with the Government of India. Their allegiance was to the Crown and the Crown could not, without their assent, transfer that allegiance elsewhere.

The Cabinet Mission rejected the Congress Party's argument and stated clearly that the British Government could not, and would not in any circumstances, transfer paramountcy to an Indian Government. They went on to say that, since the British Government would be unable to carry out the obligations of paramountcy, they would also cease to exercise its powers.

> This means [said the Cabinet Mission] that the rights of the States which flow from their relationship to the Crown will no longer exist and that all the rights surrendered by the States to the paramount power will return to the States. Political arrangements between the States on the one side and the British Crown and British India on the other will thus be brought to an end. The void will have to be filled either by the States entering into a federal relationship with the successor Government or Governments in British India or, failing this, entering into particular political arrangements with it or them.

The Cabinet Mission's energies, through the enervating heat of an Indian hot weather, had been mainly devoted to prolonged and earnestly sustained endeavours to effect a compromise between the conflicting views of the Hindu and Moslem leaders. In this they failed; but their efforts left their mark on at least two members of the Mission. I attended a small party which the visiting Ministers gave at The Viceroy's House on the eve of their departure from Delhi at the end of June. Lord Pethick-Lawrence, in the course of little more than three months, seemed to have aged ten years. He had become a disappointed old man, tottering and tremulous. Sir Stafford Cripps, broken in health if not in spirit, was so emaciated that his clothes hung loosely on him as though they were draping a skeleton. Only Mr Alexander had survived the ordeal without obvious ill effects. He was clearly delighted to be going home again, to surroundings and pursuits which were familiar to him, and away from people and problems outside the range of his experience and understanding.

If the Cabinet Mission had failed in their attempt to win acceptance of their plan for a Union of India, at least they had clarified the constitutional position of the States when India became independent. The States, too, would then become independent, at least in theory; and it was now up to the States, with the help of the Crown Representative, to negotiate their relationship with the new India.

There were some 565 States in India. It was clearly impracticable for them to enter individually into negotiation with the leaders of British India, and the Political Adviser's first task was to arrange for a States Negotiating Committee to be set up. This Committee would have two principal functions. The first would be to negotiate for the States as a whole an acceptable place in the new constitutional structure of India. The second function would be to conduct negotiations with representatives of British India in regard to the future regulation of matters of common concern, especially in the economic and financial field. The Political Adviser also had to put pressure on the smaller States to form composite administrative units large enough to fit into the new constitutional framework. But the most important and exacting of all his tasks, as it seemed to him, was to help the States to preserve a united front vis-à-vis British India since, if the Princes started quarrelling among themselves, their bargaining power would be destroyed, they would be absorbed, willy-nilly, into British India, and the new India would be deprived of powerful stabilising elements in its future social and political development.

The British Government had declared that, when India became independent, all the rights surrendered by the States to the paramount power would return to the States. This declaration, as a statement of principle, was unexceptionable; but it was not always easy to give effect to it. There was, for instance, the question of the Hyderabad province of Berar which, though it had been under British administration for nearly a century, was indubitably part and parcel of the Nizam's dominions. With the lapse of paramountcy and the determination of all treaties and agreements between the Crown and rulers of the Indian States, Berar ought legally to revert to Hyderabad. The Nizam, 'Faithful Ally of the British Government', whose sovereignty over Berar had been confirmed as recently as 1936, had every justification for demanding that his territory in Berar should be restored to his possession by the British before they left India. But the people of Berar, though technically subjects of the Nizam, had no wish to be governed by him; and the British Government, for practical and political reasons, elected to ignore the obligations both of honour and of law.

I spent many weeks during 1946 studying the Berar case. My researches carried me back nearly 200 years, to the first association of Nizam Ali Khan with the East India Company. The fruits of my labours were incorporated in a lengthy Memorandum which now, I suppose, rests in peace in the archives of the India Office library. Perhaps some university student of Anglo-Indian history, looking for a theme for a fellowship thesis, may one day disinter it.

A similar problem arose in relation to the strategically important military cantonment of Quetta. This was occupied by the British but belonged to my friend the Khan of Kalat. It should have been, but was not, restored to him when the British left India.

I had a happier experience in dealing with the north-east border States of Sikkim and Bhutan, and was able to help them in coming to a satisfactory accommodation with the new leaders of British India. The Maharaja of Sikkim wanted to reward me for my services but I could not, of course, accept a present in the usual sense of the word. However, I did tell him that, if he could obtain for me from Tibet a Gyakhi (Tibetan spaniel) bitch, my wife, who wanted to re-introduce the breed to England, would be delighted. Gyakhis are the treasured pets and watchdogs of Tibetan monasteries, and the monks are no more ready to part with a Gyakhi than is a desert Arab to part with his mare. I did not know it at the time but the Maharaja was patron of a monastery at Phari Dzong in the Chumbi valley of South Tibet (well known to successive Everest expeditions) and had no difficulty in obtaining a young Gyakhi bitch for me. I had forgotten all about my suggestion to the Maharaja when, some months later, his emissary, clothed in a long broad-sleeved robe, arrived at my house in New Delhi. He held in both hands a purple silk cushion, and on the cushion, fast asleep, lay a small golden-haired Gyakhi. Her name was Dolma and she was about four months old. Her children and grand-children and great-grandchildren have won countless awards at Crufts; and she herself ruled our Derbyshire household until, in 1962, old age led (she was a Buddhist) to her translation.

During the latter half of 1946 there were communal disturbances in many parts of India, and Delhi too had its share of rioting. On the morning of October 25th, a Hindu holiday, my Muslim bearer, Zain-ud-Din, was on his way to the bazaar to do some shopping for me when he was knocked off his bicycle by a gang of Hindu hooligans and given a savage beating. The police intervened and arrested his assailants. They also took Zain-ud-Din to hospital, where I visited him the same evening. He presented a pitiful spectacle. His eyes were closed and his whole head was a shapeless lump of bruised and lacerated flesh. I was horrified to see that he was chained to his bed by handcuffs. The doctor who was treating him told me that he would probably recover but might lose the sight of one eye. Zain-ud-Din could not see me but recognised my voice when I spoke to him. He thought he was going to die. 'Sahib,' he said, 'please tell my wife that my brother will look after her and the children. She will find Rs 40 (£3) in a shoe in the tin trunk below my bed. I would like the elder boy to be sent to school. The dhobi (washerman) has three pairs of socks and two shirts of yours. Your Honour must make sure that he returns them to you....'

The dying wishes of this humble loyal servant were in marked contrast to those of the Maharaja of Rewa which I had recorded the previous year. But Zain-ud-Din, like the Maharaja, recovered in the fullness of time, though he never regained the use of his left eye.

After visiting the hospital I hurried off to the local police station and asked the Inspector there to have Zain-ud-Din's handcuffs removed. 'I am sorry,' he replied, 'but we have orders to be strictly impartial where Hindus and Moslems are concerned. The members of the gang of Hindus who assaulted your servant are being kept in handcuffs and until the case has gone before a magistrate I cannot treat your servant differently from them.'

I protested that Zain-ud-Din had been the innocent victim of an unprovoked assault and ought not to be treated as a criminal. The Inspector consulted the police report of the incident. 'It certainly appears,' he said, 'that your servant was the one to be attacked. But until the case goes to Court I must treat him in the same way as the others. There must be no discrimination between Hindu and Muslim.' The Inspector was polite but firm, and I had to go over his head, to the Senior Superintendent of Police, before I was able to secure the removal of Zain-ud-Din's fetters.

On February 20th, 1947, Mr Attlee announced in the House of Commons that Lord Wavell was being recalled and that Lord Mountbatten was to be appointed Viceroy 'with the task of transferring to Indian hands responsibility for the government of British India in a manner that will best ensure the future happiness and prosperity of India.' Mr Attlee announced at the same time the British Government's definite intention to transfer power to Indian hands by June 1948 at the latest.

Lord Mountbatten arrived in Delhi on March 22nd, 1947, almost exactly one year after the Cabinet Mission's arrival. During the intervening twelve months communal strife had intensified and Hindu-Moslem animosity had grown more bitter. It was clear that a culminating crisis could not long be delayed. June 1948, the date by which power was to be transferred to Indian hands, seemed a long way off.

In spite of all his efforts Lord Mountbatten was unable to persuade Mr Jinnah and the Muslim League to join in the work of the Constituent Assembly, which was engaged in framing a constitution for the Union of India envisaged by the Cabinet Mission. Partition became the only alternative to total chaos and civil war involving tens of millions of innocent, helpless people. Accordingly, on June 3rd, the British Government published their plan for the partition of India and announced at the same time their intention to legislate in the current session of Parliament for the transfer of power, not by June 1948, but during 1947. Indian political leaders had scarcely recovered from the shock of this announcement when they were informed that August 15th had been fixed for the transfer of power. '38 days left to prepare for transfer of power' were the words inscribed on the first page of a tear-off calendar covering the period July 8th to August 14th which Lord Mountbatten distributed to all Government offices. '1 day left to prepare for transfer of power' were the words appearing against August 14th, the last day of the British Raj.

Influenced no doubt by his Political Adviser, Lord Wavell's policy in relation to the Indian States had been clear and simple. He believed that we should carry out our obligations to protect and help their rulers as long as we were in a position to do so. In his view (and it was also my own strongly-held view) this was not only the path of duty, it was also the path of wisdom. Admittedly, many of the States, particularly the smaller ones, were indifferently administered, but they did stand as bastions of sanity and tolerance in a country that was seething with communal hatred. Moreover, the traditional loyalty of State subjects to their rulers was an asset of incalculable value capable of making a substantial contribution to the stability of India as a whole if only the rulers themselves could be responsibly associated with the new All India Government.

It was possible, however, to take a different view of the part the States might play in the new India. More than once in India's long history strong central governments had ruled from

Delhi. Invariably, when their authority declined, local governors or chiefs had seized power and established their own independent régimes. India had suffered sorely in the past from fragmentation of this kind. To students of Indian history it must seem dangerous folly to permit the survival of powerful States capable of challenging the supremacy of the central authority.

I do not know whether Lord Mountbatten shared this latter view. I certainly did not, nor did Sir Conrad Corfield, his Political Adviser. I only know that from the date of Lord Mountbatten's arrival in India as Viceroy policy towards the States underwent a remarkable change. Ignoring all the ties that had grown up between the Crown and the Indian Princes, he applied the whole force of his immense prestige and his unique powers of persuasion to securing the assent of the rulers to new agreements that would permanently subordinate them to the successor Governments of India and Pakistan. Except in the case of two or three States, the pressure that he exercised proved effective. The Princes of India signed their own death warrants and their States disappeared from the face of the map. Once allies of the Crown, they are now pensioners of a Republic.

Early in August, under Lord Mountbatten's instructions, I visited Alwar, ninety miles south-west of Delhi, to inquire into the truth of reports that the Meos, Muslim subjects of the Maharaja, were victims of a campaign of wholesale slaughter. My journey took me through a part of the Punjab where communal atrocities were at their worst. Because I was travelling in a Viceregal car, flying a Union Jack, I was not molested. But I was shocked and sickened by the sights I saw; charred corpses by the roadside, children with arms and legs chopped off, mutilated women with gaping wounds. I saw houses being set alight, with armed men waiting outside to cut down any who sought escape from the flames. I will not dwell on my experiences that day though they are still fresh in my memory. The people of India paid a high price for their freedom.

My career in India came to an end at midnight on August 14,

1947. The new Government of India invited me to stay on as Joint Secretary in their States Department, and the new Government of Pakistan pressed me to accept appointment as their first Governor of Baluchistan. These were flattering offers and I felt honoured by them. But I did not accept either of them. I had spent my life in the service of the Crown and did not feel disposed to serve a different master. Moreover, I was weary from over-work and yearned to be at home again with Lalage and the children. And so, sadly, on August 19th, 1947, twenty years older and twenty years wiser than when I first greeted her, I bade farewell to India.

Index